JAILBIRD
THE DREADLOCK RECOLLECTIONS

KERRY WENDELL THORNLEY

The SubGenius Foundation
GLENN ROSE
2023

Cover Design by Kevin I. Slaughter.

Thornley, Kerry Wendell
[English]
Jailbird: The Dreadlock Recollections
ISBN 978-1-946529-04-6
1. U. S. History
2. Crime
Kerry Thornley (1938–1998); Rev. Ivan Stang (b. 1953); Rev. Onan Canobite (b. 1966)

Are we controlled by secret forces?
Are alien space monsters bringing a startling new world?
Do people think you're strange?
Do you??

...Then you may be on the right track!

JOIN... The Church of the SubGenius

subgenius.com

Contents

Jailbird: The Dreadlock Recollections

Diced and Other Essays

Illustrations

Introduction

by Rev. Ivan Stang

"At the risk of sounding paranoid, I don't think it is a coincidence that I am famous only among conspiracies." — Kerry W. Thornley

SOME know Kerry Thornley as the witty co-author of *The Principia Discordia*, the "Bible" of the Discordian faith, a noble predecessor of The Church of the SubGenius — to which Thornley was also a contributor. He is known as well for more serious endeavors, such as his novel *The Idle Warriors* and for having to defend himself against accusations of involvement in the assassination of President John F. Kennedy.

This book is a compilation of his somewhat piecemeal written memoirs concerning his many conversations over the course of many years with two men that he was later convinced were in fact directly involved in the murder of JFK: "Slim" Brooks and Gary Kirstein (also known as Brother-In-Law).

The whole memoir is a fascinating mixture of events that probably did happen, roughly as Thornley recounts them, and some events that he himself was not so sure really happened. I have to wonder what he decided to leave out.

The conversations are confusing to the reader, and they were to Thornley. Thornley describes constantly trying to figure out when Gary was being serious, testing him, humoring him, or brainwashing him. I share his confusion.

Indeed, Gary mentioned how behavioral scientists could induce nervous breakdowns in lab mice by regularly changing the outcomes of tests on them. The conversations certainly make for a choppy read as Gary jumped from subject to subject. At one point Kerry comments that "This man's attention span didn't seem very impressive." The reader is led to suspect that Gary was doing this deliberately. Was he a con man hiding informal brainwashing in plain sight and pretending to have a short attention span, to disrupt the thinking or self-confidence of his victim?

Why would anyone go to so much trouble to drive an unknown New Orleans beatnik crazy? Maybe because the beatnik happened to be a one-time friend of Lee Harvey Oswald?

Then came the events of November, 1963.

Kerry's peculiar Ayn Rand-influenced philosophy made him gleeful that someone had killed JFK — a mere two weeks after the aforementioned discussions.

The sinister rabbit hole got deeper and deeper until poor Kerry Thornley, toward the end of his life, finally became what he most feared he might become — a true paranoid.

Horribly, none of this sounds unfamiliar to anyone familiar with how (for example) the Q-Anon cult works. Nothing is ever quite spelled out; the potential recruit is led by one transparent "clue" after another to "come to his or her own conclusions." Of course these conclusions appear blatantly steered, to anyone familiar with extremist propaganda techniques — or with role-playing games, for that matter. Was Kerry being steered? Why? To be a spare Oswald? Gary talking about the rich and powerful publisher Henry Luce sounds very much like Q believers talking about Bill Gates, with the mind-control brain implants to turn everybody into obedient human robots. I'm afraid the obedient human robots are the ones who don't question all these impossible things. As my friend Orton Nenslo put it, "Once you believe one impossible thing, it becomes much easier to believe the next impossible thing, and the next." Eventually it gets to the point that you can no longer believe any possible things, because they all contradict your new secret supernatural knowledge.

In distant 1957, Gary gleefully described controlling important people by giving them opportunities to participate in snuff films... thus building "a network of blackmailed murderers." Q-Anon's "baby-eating elite Satanic globalists," anyone?

As nutty as this all got, modern news headlines have become even nuttier. So... was Kerry Thornley really the crazy one? And if he was, did he start out that way? That's not the impression I get. A telling line: "I was determined to oppose Communism; nevertheless, I found vociferous nationalism and enthusiastic militarism to be nothing less than frightening — not because I feared war — I didn't — but because I feared anything that I could identify as systematic mindlessness."

What Kerry was so afraid to believe, in case it was all just crazy paranoia, is today looking not just familiar but almost normal. I can't begin to guess what's real and what's not in this morass, but Kerry Thornley, for better or worse, was way ahead of his time.

This memoir is no easy read unless you're into 1950s and 1960s political history and deep philosophical arguments. I personally find all the detailed conversations involving absolutes, -isms and what-ifs too much like a dog chasing its own tail, an overly complicated form of oversimplification. Like Rush Limbaugh "making the complex simple" — the problem is, the complex is complex, and when you simplify it, you're lying about it, even if only to yourself. The endless search for universal truths is just that. Humans just refuse to fit into categories so neatly.

On the other hand, the collection of random, disconnected essays at the back of this book exemplify the kinds of funny but perplexing handwritten rants Thornley used to send me for SubGenius publications. And, uncannily, the specific subject matter of many of those rants just happens to repeatedly intersect with a just-published SubGenius fictional spy thriller set in the 1960s, *The Agent and Mister Dobbs* by Rev. Teeters LeVerge. COINCIDENCE?

No. Cross-fertilization.

The first chapters sadden me because Kerry wrote so clearly and sanely about his desire not to end up insanely paranoid. But by the time we met in person in Atlanta in the 1990s, he was, well, a wreck, and almost homeless, dependent on old friends. He seemed inexplicably nervous, and the friend accompanying him later told me Kerry had somehow become scared of me.

He sure was a funny writer, though! And what a consummate weirdo!

Kerry once sent us a photo of himself, nude, fucking a chair. Seriously. I published it — it's in an old *Stark Fist* zine, albeit with the Thornley boner blacked out. (It required a rather large black bar!) As does "Bob" Dobbs, Kerry had love in his heart for all things, even chairs.

The SubGenius Tarot Card Set was one of Kerry's uncompleted SubGenius projects. He got about six cards into it over the years. One "card" was a crushed cigarette pack. Maybe someday another great Discordian can complete it.

Eris Discordia Herself, Goddess of Chaos, must have set up the scheduling the week Kerry Thonley died. I was in Austin to open for a Fringeware event featuring Robert Anton Wilson, who popularized Discordianism and is the main reason many of us ever heard of Kerry. While there I also started work on a project with Steve Jackson of Steve Jackson Games, whose game company was at that time perhaps the closest thing to a Discordian headquarters — a contradiction in terms, of course. If only Greg Hill, William Barker, and the ghosts of Thornley and Jimi Hendrix, had been there, it would have been the perfect signal to the Greys to cue UPLIFT SEQUENCE 23, the Conjunction of the Whatever.

Well... no doubt we'll all eventually meet Kerry Thornley on the Other Side... that is, if "Bob" or Eris or somebody equally important remembers to flip the tape to Side Two!

The Weather Conspiracy

by Rev. Onan Canobite

Jailbird: The Dreadlock Recollections by Kerry Wendell Thornley is an autobiographical account of his grooming for the assassination of John F. Kennedy by two men he called "Brother-in-Law" (Gary Kirstein) and "Slim Brooks." This is the first publication of the complete text, under the author's preferred title, with related unpublished essays, annotations and an index. The history of earlier, fragmentary editions of Jailbird is as complex as the life of its author himself.

Kerry Wendell Thornley was born in 1938 in Los Angeles, California. In the late 1950s he and his friend Greg Hill invented The Discordian Society, a religion that credited Eris Discordia, goddess of chaos, as a better explanation for the world than any deity of order. In the 1960s, Kerry was the first to recognize the early hippy movement as modern paganism, a return to the Dionysian mysteries of sex, intoxication and frenzy. In the 1970s, Kerry was an editor and contributor to "right anarchist" (individualist, as opposed to collectivist left anarchist) periodicals such as The Innovator. In the 1980s Kerry's background allowed him to be woven throughout the self-published zine world, appearing in as many weirdo religion zines as individualist politics zines as humor zines as conspiracy zines. I had read about Kerry in the Illuminatus! trilogy by Robert Anton Wilson and Robert Shea, and I had read Principia Discordia. The Principia Discordia, It was through zines that I made contact with Kerry himself. But long before that...

Kerry was in the United States Marines with Lee Harvey Oswald, later found guilty of assassinating President John F. Kennedy. Kerry used Oswald as a character in his book The Idle Warriors, which led the Warren Commission investigation into the assassination of Kennedy to ask why Kerry had written a book about Oswald years before Oswald shot the President. Kerry was also questioned by Jim Garrison regarding his role in the assassination of Kennedy. These queries brought back memories of Brother-in-Law and Slim, as recounted in *Jailbird*. Kerry spent the remainder of his days writing, questioning his own mental health, alienating friends and through it all retaining some measure of a sense of humor. He died in Atlanta, Georgia in 1998.

Author Adam Gorightly writes in *Caught in the Crossfire*[1] that in 1975, "Kerry composed a series of memos detailing his long-ago conversations with Kirstein and Brooks, then began distributing them to friends, law enforcement officials, and politicians (including the House Select Committee on Assassinations) to ensure there'd be evidence left behind if he were suddenly 'silenced.'" One version of these memos is dated 1976 and titled "Affidavit to Jim Garrison." These "JFK assassination-related memos" are the earliest form of *Jailbird*.

Jailbird was subtitled "A Serialized Book" in a 1983-1984 self-published edition. This edition was copyright by Thornley "solely to prevent copyright and subsequent monopolization by authoritarians: reprint anything you like, providing proper credit is given." Each chapter was a single page, and each page was sold four for a dollar while Thornley was living in Florida. The first two chapters of the "Serialized Book" edition ("Brother-in-Law" and "Slim") correspond to the passage from "... another subject... " to "... talk show... " (pp. 126 to 127) in this edition. That same passage appears on page 87 of a 1989 manuscript edition of *Jailbird*.

Caught in the Crossfire states[2] that circa 1988, editor Ron Bonds of IllumiNet Press considered publishing *Dreadlock Recollections*, "the origins of which dated back to the series of affidavits [Thornley] composed in the mid-seventies detailing his memories of Brother-in-Law and Slim Brooks." [...] "According to Kerry — and others I have talked to — Ron was afraid to publish *Dreadlock Recollections* for fear that it

[1] Gorightly, Adam: *Caught in the Crossfire: Kerry Thornley, Lee Oswald and the Garrison Investigation*. Port Townsend: Feral House, 2014, pp. 101-102.

[2] *Crossfire*, p. 165.

would be hazardous to his health[1]." IllumiNet published *The Idle Warriors* in 1991. Ron Bonds died of food poisoning in 2001. The IllumiNet manuscript for *Jailbird* was preserved in a single copy by a source who wishes to remain anonymous. That manuscript was kindly shared with me in 2021, adding lengthy content not found in any other source. Significantly, "Aftermath" (p. 227) is an antidote to the madness found throughout the rest of *Jailbird*.

Crossfire also states[2] that Thornley and author Sondra London collaborated on *Confession to a Conspiracy*, "which was a work based primarily on Kerry's self-published tome *Dreadlock Recollections*." *Confession to a Conspiracy* was published online in 1992. Sondra allowed me to make a small edition of the book after she temporarily removed it from her site. That small edition is long out of print. This is the first publication of the complete, restored text of *Jailbird*; the first publication under the author's preferred title; the first publication of the supplementary material in full; the first edition to be annotated and indexed.

My connection to Sondra began two years before *Confession to a Conspiracy*, in 1990. She asked me for a back cover blurb for her book *Killer Fiction*, an anthology of stories by G. J. Schaeffer. London and Schaeffer had dated in high school. Schaeffer went on to become a police officer and a multiple murderer. London contacted Schaeffer to help her understand how someone she had cared about at one time had become a murderer. Schaeffer sent her his stories, which London self-published with my back-cover blurb. *Killer Fiction* was later published through Feral House Books. London later ended her contact with Schaeffer, who was stabbed to death in prison in 1995.

I also have a connection to Feral House. In 1994 they published the anthology *Kooks*, edited by Donna Kossy. *Kooks* includes an essay by myself and an essay by Adam Gorightly. Feral House also published books by Gorightly about Kerry Thornley. Gorightly founded the Discordian Archive, which

---

[1] *The Prankster and the Conspiracy* by Adam Gorightly (New York: Paraview Press 2003) p. 266.
[2] *Crossfire*, p. 140.

has published significant works by Thornley.

In addition to *Jailbird*, I have published another book by Kerry Thornley: *The Absolute Elsewhere*[1]. In the late 1980s, Kerry gave an interview to Allen Greenfield of the Eulis Lodge of the Ordo Templi Orientalis in Atlanta, Georgia. The recordings of that interview were transcribed by Andrew Stephens. Andrew moved to Portland, where we met and became friends. After several years of encouragement Andrew wrote an introduction and allowed me to publish the book-length interview. *The Absolute Elsewhere* came out in an edition of thirty-three copies. Andrew received eleven copies, the distributor Underworld Amusements received eleven copies, and I kept eleven copies. I hope that *Jailbird* will receive a wider circulation.

Kerry wrote constantly. He wrote notebooks for himself, he wrote letters, he wrote for the underground press, and he wrote for mainstream publishers. I learned about Kerry by reading the *Illuminatus!* trilogy by Robert Anton Wilson and Robert Shea in the late 1970s, near the time I began self-publishing. Kerry was a constant contributor to many of the works I was reading in the early 1980s. I saw Kerry in the Loompanics book catalog, in the magazine *Factsheet Five*, in *Anarchy* magazine and elsewhere. He mailed out handbills and the recipients would mail them out again, some of them coming my way. I wrote Kerry and we corresponded for several years.

In the late 1980s I met Kerry Thornley. I was in Atlanta, Georgia, visiting some friends. I did not have Kerry's telephone number or home address, but I knew Kerry was living in Atlanta and I knew that he spent time in the Little Five Points district. I went to Little Five Points hoping to meet him, and there he was. I saw him sitting on the sidewalk, talking to himself and writing in a small notebook. I walked up and said "Kerry?" He looked up in fear. I introduced myself. "Oh, hey man, good to meet you! What are you doing here?" he said, his face lighting up. I said I was in

---

[1]Portland: OVO 2018

Atlanta visiting friends, and he said that was great. Then his face darkened and he resumed talking to himself while facing me. He talked about his guilt in not being able to control his stray thoughts, and that his stray thoughts were causing changes in the weather, and those changes in the weather were causing famines and floods. He talked about his frustration in not being able to be left alone by a conspiracy that wanted him to rule others. He talked about the cameras in his eyes and the microphones in his ears that transmitted information to that conspiracy. The tone and content of what he was saying to himself (and to the voices only he could hear) is of a kind with what he wrote in his notebooks, three of which are published for the first time here beginning on page 237. I listened and did not speak for perhaps an hour. Then I said: "Kerry, I have to go." His face lit up again with a smile, we shook hands and he said it was good to meet. As I walked away, his darkness returned.

I received a letter from Kerry a short time later. In the letter Kerry said that he was very sorry but once he met a person that person became part of his conspiracy, and that he could never speak to me again. I wrote back that I was sorry about that too, and that if he ever changed his mind I'd be happy to stay in touch. I continued to write him, but he never wrote back. I kept Kerry's letters, his notebooks, and the manuscript pages to *Jailbird*. Through research and good fortune I found more works related to *Jailbird*. I now conspire to publish *Jailbird* in its final form.

Claims made in other books by other authors against the conspirators named in this book have resulted in defamation lawsuits, each of which were rightly lost by those who made the claims. Everybody knows that Lee Harvey Oswald, acting alone, assassinated John F. Kennedy. There is no such thing as mind control, be it through social pressure or electro-chemical. All conspiracies are the delusions of the mentally ill. None of the people mentioned in this book have ever existed, and none of them did or said what is described in this book. There are no secret messages hidden in this book.

As to my own opinion about the claims made by Kerry Wendell Thornley in *Jailbird*, I will close with a quote from someone who knew him better than I knew him:

All phenomena are real in some sense, unreal in some sense, meaningless in some sense, real and meaningless in some sense, unreal and meaningless in some sense, and real and unreal and meaningless in some sense[1].

---

[1]Robert Anton Wilson: *Nature's God* (New York: New American Library 1991).

Jailbird:
The Dreadlock
Recollections

Foreword

L ET the reader understand I possess nothing resembling a photographic memory. How unreliable my recollections sometimes are is driven home to me whenever I attend the same movie a second time. On the other hand I seem to have a very good memory for things most people are inclined to forget until, many years later, I remind them of this or that incident.

I am using quotations to convey a sense of the conversational dialogue that took place in New Orleans in the early sixties. That way I am able to capture the mood of each personality and situation much more accurately than would be possible simply describing, in a general way, what happened. Yet by no means am I at this late date able to present anything like a word-for-word transcript of what was said.

Most of my memories of these talks were repressed completely for many years. In 1975 I recalled only that Slim Brooks had a weird brother-in-law who seemed obsessed with Nazism and who spoke once or twice of killing John Kennedy, and that I had decided he was just putting me on.

Lee Harvey Oswald

IN the spring of 1959 I was stationed at an annex of El Toro Marine Base in California. Another Marine in that unit was Lee Harvey Oswald. We became acquainted.

Then in June of that year I shipped out for a tour of duty at the Navel Air Station in Atsugi, Japan, where Oswald served previous to our time together at El Toro.

My ambition all along was to become a novelist, and I had decided to write a book based upon my overseas experience in the military. That autumn I read in the newspaper that Lee Oswald had, upon being discharged, gone to Moscow and applied for Soviet citizenship. By then I'd decided to call my novel about peace-time Marines in the Far East *The Idle Warriors* and Oswald's dramatic act inspired me to center the plot around a character based on him.

Convinced that I understood his reasons for becoming disillusioned with the United States and turning to Marxism, feeling they were similar to my own, I at first intended to write "a poor man's *Ugly American*" sharply critical of US imperialism characterized by the bungling of the Eisenhower era.

Unfortunately for the clarity of my novel's political theme, my own ideology shifted – as a result of reading Ayn Rand's polemical novel *Atlas Shrugged* aboard ship on my way back to the States. Discharged from the Marines immediately thereafter, I entered civilian life convinced of the efficacy of *laissez-faire* capitalism.

My young friend, Greg Hill, and I then traveled from our home town of Whittier, California, to the New Orleans French Quarter, where I continued work on the first draft of *The Idle Warriors*.

There I met the principal character of this work of nonfiction I call *The Dreadlock Recollections*–a man I am belatedly but firmly persuaded played a central role in organizing the assassination of President John F. Kennedy, for which I am equally certain Lee Harvey Oswald was framed.

During most of my life I have been inclined to reject conspiracy theories of history. Notwithstanding my willingness to admit that conspiracies exist, I felt that a grasp of political events depended upon an understanding of the power of ideas. In my view, conspiracies were insignificant. My tendency was to challenge the motives of conspiracy buffs when I did not, as was more often the case, question their mental health.

Balancing my occasional doubts was a fear of becoming paranoid. When Oswald was accused of assassinating Kennedy, my first hunch was that he was innocent and had been blamed in a misunderstanding that would soon be cleared up. When the media continued to insist there was ample evidence that Oswald, and Oswald alone, shot the President, I quickly changed my mind.

Two years later, when a *Warren Report* critic confronted me with the many discrepancies between the conclusions of the Warren Commission and the testimony and exhibits contained in the twenty-six Volumes, I could no longer hide from myself the probability that either Oswald was innocent or he had not acted alone.

Yet even then I did not want to think an elaborate conspiracy was involved. Maybe Lyndon Johnson or some of his Texas friends had arranged to kill Kennedy and perhaps it had not occurred to the Warren Commission to probe that possibility. A more complicated theory would seem paranoid.

Above all else, I did not want to seem paranoid.

One year elapsed between the time I began doubting the lone-assassin theory and the beginning of tribulations in my own life suffered at the hands of a man most journalists insinuated was a paranoid. First, District Attorney Jim Garrison made a bizarre attempt to recruit me as a witness for the prosecution in his probe of a New Orleans-based conspiracy to assassinate John Kennedy. When I expressed my unwillingness to cooperate, he accused me of working for the CIA and summoned me to appear before the grand jury.

After asking me what seemed like a lot of irrelevant questions, he charged me with perjury for denying, truthfully, that I had met with Lee Harvey Oswald in New Orleans during the months previous to the assassination. I had not seen Oswald in person, nor had I communicated with him in any other way, since June of 1959–at the latest.

Yet Garrison struck me as sincere. Moreover, his assistants showered me with any number of disturbing coincidences linking me to his assassination theory. I was at a loss to explain them, except in light of the notion that Jim Garrison's conspiracy theory was an elaborate paranoid construction.

This experience forced me to examine the evidence surrounding the events in Dallas more carefully than ever before. As a result, I became convinced not only that Lee Harvey Oswald had not acted alone but, moreover, that he was not even on the sixth floor of the Texas School Book Depository when the shots that killed Kennedy were fired. Yet, because I also had to cope with Jim Garrison's wild and irresponsible charges, I also became more certain than ever that paranoia was by far more dangerous than any actual conspiracy that might, from time to time, sabotage the normal functioning of history.

In other words, if conspiracies were significantly dangerous, it was because they tended to spawn paranoia.

When Jim Garrison ultimately neglected to bring me to trial, I took it as a tacit admission he had at last perceived the error of his ways.

Charles Manson

MEANWHILE, in the realm of public affairs I busied myself with other concerns. Of all newsworthy events, the John Kennedy murder seemed to me the most boring.

For reasons I could not clearly identify at the time, I was to find the murder of Hollywood actress Sharon Tate far more disturbing, When I read *The Family* by Ed Sanders (E. P. Dutton, 1971) my uneasiness increased. Charles Manson was not typical of the hip counter-culture I had gradually come to consider my own, after the appeal of Ayn Rand's philosophy diminished in my eyes. Nevertheless, something about him and his followers seemed far more menacing and important than I could justify in terms of a few sensationally gory killings. As if warned in a forgotten nightmare, I felt that I had expected someone like Manson to appear on the scene. All that I read about him confirmed this eerie, elusive anxiety.

Besides that, much like Jim Garrison, Charles Manson was a paranoid. Nowhere is this more evident than on page 129 of *The Family*, where he is quoted as saying: "Christ on the cross, the coyote in the desert–it's the same thing, man. The coyote is beautiful. He moves through the desert delicately, aware of everything, looking around. He hears every sound, smells every smell, sees everything that moves. He's always in a state of total paranoia and total paranoia is total awareness. You can learn from the coyote just like you learn from a child. A baby is born into the world in a state of fear. Total paranoia and awareness... " Once again I was grappling with the riddle of a man who appeared to act on the basis of a supreme confidence in the validity of his own delusions.

Escalation of the Vietnam war had radicalized me, once again, politically, so Charlie Manson's affinity for right-wing organizations was something else that alarmed me. Most particularly I was spooked by allegations about links between Manson's people and the Process Church, for when I had returned to New Orleans in order to clear myself, unsuccessfully, of Jim Garrison's suspicions, I encountered the Process Church there–in circumstances giving me ample reason to suspect they were at least partially involved in framing me.

So as to avoid the mistakes of people like Garrison and Manson, it seemed essential to study psychology. That was another subject I found more fascinating than conspiracy theories about the John F. Kennedy assassination. Already acquainted with Freud and other pioneers of psychoanalysis, I began devoting my attention to more recent trends. That the older theories were unconsciously tainted with reactionary ideology was frequently mentioned in my political readings.

In 1972 I discovered a psychology book that dovetailed beautifully with my political opinions, by then both anarchist and left of center. A collection of readings compiled by Jerome Agel and the *Radical Therapist* newspaper staff, *The Radical Therapist Anthology* found the roots of nearly all neurosis and psychosis outside the individual, lodged firmly and visibly in the authoritarian class structure of society. As a sociology major at Georgia State University, I had already begun to suspect as much.

There was only one hitch, best summed up in "The Radical Psychiatry Manifesto" by Claude Steiner: "Paranoia is a state of heightened awareness. Most people are persecuted beyond their wildest delusions."

I wondered if that could be true. Certainly it was not without personal relevance, in terms of my own very unsatisfactory adjustment to the John F. Kennedy murder mystery. Perpetually fearing that my radical friends would think I was a CIA agent because of what Garrison had said, and yet afraid that I would become paranoid if I delved into the unanswered questions about Oswald too deeply, I walked an uncomfortably narrow line.

Fear of Paranoia

"THERE is still another psychological process that I have run across in my explorations of failure to actualize the self. This evasion of growth can also be set in motion by a fear of paranoia."

Although I was not to read those particular words in *The Farther Reaches of Human Nature* by Abraham Maslow until many years later, I was versed enough in the modern literature of psychology to realize that traditional Freudian notions of paranoid schizophrenia and classical paranoia were under attack by more than just wild-eyed radicals.

One of my textbooks in school contained a sociological study of a man who was committed for symptoms of paranoia; it demonstrated that, due to his rather unpleasant personality, he was actually being secretly harassed by his co-workers who, upon being interviewed, admitted to as much.

At that point I took a long second look at the origins of my own fears of paranoia.

What popularized that brand of psychosis for my generation was the film, *The Caine Mutiny*, with Humphrey Bogart clicking his steel marbles compulsively, saying "I kid you not," and making a fool of himself over a few stolen scoops of ice cream.

Another French Quarter writer who worked in a record store next to the Bourbon House, where I ate and drank and socialized when I lived in New Orleans, possessed a book about color psychology that said brown was the favorite color of most paranoids. He added that most novelists tended toward paranoia, something about which we both laughed a little nervously.

Another Quarterite, a painter named Loy Ann Camp who was among my closest friends, had a textbook from her days in nursing school that said paranoia was related to fear of latent homosexuality. Since my reason for joining the Marines earlier had been to prove to myself that I was a man in every sense I didn't find that information comforting either.

From additional sources I gathered that paranoids were quite undesirable cranks who took to sitting in corners stroking their chins and observing those around them with sidelong glances. Senator Joseph McCarthy was said to have been a paranoid, as was Robert Welch, founder of the John Birch Society.

In fact, all the really famous paranoids seemed to be anti-Communist — a consideration that did not sit well with my own rational capitalist philosophy of those days. Paranoids, in addition to all the other problems they were causing, were giving my politics a bad name with outlandish notions like Welch's charge that grandfatherly old Ike was "a conscious agent of the Communist conspiracy" and his grandiose ambition to impeach Earl Warren from the Supreme Court.

Intellectual respectability required mental health, and it was becoming evident to me by then that mental health consisted of trusting everyone about everything as much as possible — and, for good measure, poking fun at anyone who didn't. Especially to be trusted were the mass media, whose owners and personnel were not to be regarded as minions of the Establishment because, as they themselves used to attest with confidence, there was no Establishment in the United States of America. Only foreigners and paranoids believed that there was.

Intellectualizing and joking about paranoia was a favorite pastime of post-Beatnik, pre-Hippie Bohemian America — for reasons that were undoubtedly the result of coincidence, at least among individuals who did not want their sanity called into question.

An habitué of the Bourbon House, Chris Lanham, once entertained us with the diabolical theory that the psychological classification of paranoia had been developed by conspirators for the purpose of discrediting anyone bent on exposing them.

When his friend, Jack Burnside, suggested sharing this hilariously evil notion with a wandering conspiracy buff we called Crazy David — because he thought people like the Rockefellers and DuPont controlled the government — we told Jack the joke had gone far enough. Crazy David might actually believe him. And, as everybody knew, paranoids who received reinforcement for their delusions could become very dangerous.

In retrospect, I realized that Crazy David's views about who rules America did not seem especially insane. By 1972, my own analysis resembled it in many essential respects.

Then came Watergate.

Watergate

A GAIN my attention was absorbed by a public event that did not seem related to the John Kennedy assassination. That a reactionary warmonger like Nixon might be unceremoniously ejected from the White House for crimes that even conservatives would find shocking seemed almost too good to be true.

Eagerly, I followed the scandal, becoming more and more aware at the same time that conspiracies were a fact of political reality, even in America.

During the summer of 1973 I was in New York City, visiting my old friend Greg Hill, who in years past had accompanied me to New Orleans and lived as my roommate there for a few months. At a folk concert in Washington Square I was approached by a Yippie who wanted to sell me the latest issue of *The Yipster Times* for a quarter. A glance at the headline and cover photos convinced me it was worth the price.

What I found there has since been published in an excellent book by A. J. Weberman and Michael Canfield called *Coup d'état in America*. Convincing photographic evidence tends to establish that Watergate burglars E. Howard Hunt and Frank Sturgis were in the immediate vicinity of Dealy Plaza in Dallas the day John Kennedy was shot. That possibility brought to mind something I had almost managed to happily forget.

A decade earlier in New Orleans I had discussed, among other things, the idea of assassinating President Kennedy with a man who in many unsettling respects bore a resemblance to the members of the Watergate break-in team. As I was to say to Weberman in a letter two years later, this man was "a Plumbers type of guy."

Although he even looked something like pictures of E. Howard Hunt, his bald head diminished any direct physical similarity to that now-famous spy. More a matter of style than anything else seemed pertinent then. Also relevant were links between the CIA and organized crime that were coming to light in the wake of the Watergate revelations. For the man I spoke to used to let on that he was somehow associated with New Orleans mobster Carlos Marcello.

Already I had been suspecting tie-ins between Watergate and the JFK murder because both crimes seemed connected to the Southern Rim or Cowboy faction of the American Establishment — the so-called military-industrial complex. I had, however, been bending over backwards not to jump to conclusions. Something about those photos of that man *The Yipster Times* argued was Edward Howard Hunt made such restraint harder. What, exactly, it might be continued to elude me.

Something else occurred that same summer that wore at my ability to keep believing this is the least conspiratorial of all possible worlds. Again, it was nagging rather than sensational. After I wrote an article published in Atlanta's underground paper, *The Great Speckled Bird*, titled "Did the Plumbers Plug JFK, Too?" — I got two unusual phone calls.

First was a male voice imitating the sounds of a speeded-up tape recorder or a gibberish-talking cartoon character. Ten years earlier a Quarterite named Roger Lovin and I used to address one another in the Bourbon House with noises identical to those I was now hearing on the other end of the line, as an inside joke intended to freak out strangers.

This time I simply replied with a word or two of bewilderment, and the caller hung up.

Within seconds, the phone rang again. Now a male voice — not Roger's — said very clearly, "Kerry, do you know who this is?" When I answered in the negative, he said, "Good!" And hung up.

Enough similarity existed between that voice on the phone and the voice of the man I had talked to all those years earlier about assassinating John F. Kennedy, that I became increasingly uncomfortable with the idea of keeping my suspicions to myself much longer.

I nevertheless persisted in my silence for more than another year. That was more than a little uncharacteristic of me, to consciously nurture something without talking or at least writing of it. But, while I was no longer as worried about going paranoid as in years past, I remained concerned that others would think me paranoid.

Then, too, there was another thing. This suspect of mine more than once had claimed a connection with the Mafia. Even if he was innocent of assassination, were I to accused him in public, he might have what he considered a good motive for getting me killed. Until I was certain of his guilt, I didn't want to open my mouth.

Meanwhile, I continued to think about the phone calls. Was the caller trying to determine indirectly whether or not I'd spoken recently with Roger Lovin? Could Roger have known something that I happened to guess in my *Bird* article?

As a matter of fact it was not so long before that Roger Lovin had called me, making an appointment to come by the house while he was in town for a visit. On the day of his expected arrival, I went out for brief interval with the woman I was living with. We returned to find all her jewelry missing, and Roger never showed up. I recalled that when I had known him in New Orleans, the same year Kennedy was assassinated, his principal reputation was that of a talented con artist.

I shrugged. That wasn't much to go on.

Soon there was enough information in the news about assassination plots involving organized crime to draw my attention in that direction.

In February of 1975, I had begun making cramped, secretive notes about the mysterious bald-headed man I had known in New Orleans. For the first time since the assassination, the Establishment was expressing suspicions of conspiracy, pushing for a Congressional probe of the events in Dallas. Only recently I had been called by CBS. And someone from *Reader's Digest* was even attempting to contact me. Expecting that before long I would be called before a Congressional committee to testify, I didn't want to divulge anything sensational until I could speak under oath.

Instead, I prepared — quietly. As soon as my notes were completed to the point where they told a coherent, if abbreviated, story — I began discreetly searching for a politically radical attorney. Employed part-time as a student assistant and distrustful of the Establishment because of their dishonesty in the past about the assassination issue, I wanted a lawyer who was an idealist because, neither financially nor politically, could I afford any other kind. If my information was relevant, and I believed now that it probably was, doing anything useful with it was still going for a long shot.

On the other hand, I was less worried than ever about seeming paranoid. If one thing had been made perfectly clear, it was that in the United States of America, suspicions of conspiracy were no longer regarded as symptoms of mental illness.

A Serialized Book: THE DREADLOCK RECOLLECTIONS by Kerry Wendell Thornley

Let the reader understand I possess nothing resembling a photographic memory. How unreliable my recollections sometimes are is driven home to me whenever I attend the same movie a second time. On the other hand I seem to have a very good memory for things most people are inclined to forget until, many years later, I remind them of this or that incident.

I am using quotations to convey a sense of the conversational dialogue that took place in New Orleans in the early sixties. That way I am able to capture the mood of each personality and situation much more accurately than would be possible simply describing, in a general way what happened. Yet by no means am I at this late date able to present anything like a word-for-word transcript of what was said.

Most of my memories of these talks were repressed completely for many years; in nineteen seventy-five I recalled only that Slim Brooks had a weird brother-in-law who seemed obsessed with Nazism and who spoke once or twice of killing John Kennedy, and that I had decided he was just putting me on.

CHAPTER ONE: Brother-In-Law

A bald head was his most conspicuous feature. As he was almost certainly in disguise, he may have shaved his pate, wearing a toupee while on less clandestine business.

The name he used was Gary. He must have been in his late thirties or early forties.

Of medium build, I guess he stood about five-foot ten, my height. Although his arms were muscular, he had a pot belly and a slightly sunken chest.

A somewhat protruding lower lip had resulted because of his constant pipe smoking.

An unsavory character by my twenty-three-year-old French Quarter standards, besides being a reputed underworld fringer, he dressed like an off-duty policeman or an engineer.

Slacks, a belt, a little key chain on something that looked like a steel tape measure spool, and a short-sleeve shirt with a plastic pocket guard for pens and pencils comprised his usual attire.

The back of Brother-in-law's head was rounded and protruding as the back of Oswald's head (as I'd noticed two years earlier, serving with Lee in the Marines) had been singularly flat -- a notable feature in both cases that would make convincing impersonation of either man unlikely, since conspirators with any such intention would have to find someone who resembled the subject in skull-structure as well as facially and in build.

A most evident, somewhat nasal, mid-western twang could be discerned in Brother-in-law's voice. Clipped words and abrupt sentences often dominated his speech pattern, sometimes punctuated with short giggles.

Standing very erect and drawing his head back until double chins appeared -- although he was by no means obese -- he would remove his pipe from his mouth and grin, protrude his lower lip belligerently and say cheerfully something something thoroughly obnoxious, as if to assert: "I'm horrible; I know it, and I like myself this way and, what's more, there is absolutely nothing you can do about it -- so there!"

At such times he seemed to me like a species of insect, and his choice of words tended to reinforce that impression. If what he said was not cruel it would be ugly in some other way. "I like smoking a pipe," he once told me, "because it fumigates my mouth."

Among the gently beautiful people of the New Orleans French Quarter he seemed as misplaced as a metalic slam of a car door in a flower patch.

SPARE CHANGE: Box 16441, Tampa, FLA 33679

First page of Chapter One from the serialized edition of
The Dreadlock Recollections (1983).

Martin Luther King

IN July of 1975, I noted in passing headlines in the local Atlanta papers that the City Commissioner of Public Safety, Reginald Eaves, had for some time been quietly investigating anew the assassination of Dr. Martin Luther King, Jr.

Although I had admired King while I held John Kennedy in contempt, I was then so preoccupied with things I was ferreting out here and there about the Presidential assassination that I failed to take much notice. For articles about the John Kennedy murder now seemed to be appearing everywhere.

From time to time I was meeting to compare notes with a staffer on *The Great Speckled Bird* who had written about the Southern Rim. Without mentioning my man in New Orleans with the bald head and links to Carlos Marcello, I sought further evidence that the Cowboys of the military-industrial complex had murdered Kennedy in their war with the Yankees of the Northeastern Establishment. Marcello, as well as Nixon and Howard Hunt, were alleged to belong to this Southern faction. I figured the man I remembered and feared had to be in there somewhere as well.

Then I encountered an article in a scandal tabloid that disturbed me more than anything else, again for largely subjective reasons. For no particular reason, it seems, one of their correspondents who was probing links between Carlos Marcello and the John Kennedy murder had blown his brains out with a .38 caliber pistol. As it happened, this resident of Baton Rouge, Louisiana named Joe Cooper was left-handed and the weapon was found in his right hand.

A woman I knew met with much the same fate in 1964, just before I returned to New Orleans for a visit after a year's absence. She was the former girlfriend of the man with whom I had discussed murdering the President.

Then early one morning the phone rang. On the other end of the line was the American Civil Liberties Union lawyer who was the only person to whom I had confided the conversations summarized in my notes. One afternoon, I had regaled him with a rambling, slightly hysterical account of my worst suspicions.

Now he asked me, "Have you been following this investigation by Eaves of the Martin Luther King assassination?"

I admitted I had not.

"You might want to look into it," he said. "Their witness seems to be talking about some of the same people you mentioned to me in connection with Carlos Marcello."

That afternoon I obtained an Atlanta newspaper and read the article pertaining to what was fast becoming a controversial investigation. A young man who supplied accurate information to the police about a narcotics ring was also insisting that just previous to the murder of Martin Luther King, he had overheard one of its members say of King: "I'm going to shoot that damned nigger in the head and frame a jailbird for it, just like I did with Kennedy."

Had the word "jailbird" been a post-hypnotic trigger planted in my unconscious to release a flood of memories, results could not have been more dramatic. For one of the things my own suspect had discussed with me all those years ago was framing a jailbird for the John Kennedy murder. In fact, I recalled now that I was the one who talked him out of it. Moreover, he had also talked about assassinating Martin Luther King.

No longer in doubt that my man, known to me as Gary Kirstein , possessed advanced knowledge of the John Kennedy murder, I went into action. First I typed up a number of brief memos about our conversations and distributed them almost at random, in order to assure that if I was fatally silenced there would be evidence to indicate why.

Thereafter I endeavored to contact my prospective attorney, only to discover that he was out of town.

Convinced that I should act fast but unsure of what to do next, I wound up taking my information to the office of the Commissioner of Public Safety. That was after I first attended a party where I was given a funny-tasting marijuana cigarette that made me feel uninhibited and talkative, and then questioned intensively by a group of inquisitive individuals. And it was after, within a few days of the first incident, I again met one of the people from that party, who handed me a pipeload of marijuana that blistered the inside of my mouth when I started to inhale the smoke.

Eaves then announced a press conference wherein he stated that he would reveal startling new evidence in the King case. But when the day of the conference arrived, he said he was dropping the probe — because, he said, his chief witness, Robert Byron Watson, refused to take a lie detector test.

I was baffled and frightened.

Then the newspapers announced the disappearance of labor leader Jimmy Hoffa, and I recalled that the man I knew as Gary Kirstein once asked me what I thought about letting Hoffa in on a conspiracy to assassinate Kennedy.

Greg Hill, my former New Orleans roommate, arrived in Atlanta for a visit to find me nearly hysterical. At least once he had met Gary, remembering as I did that we had suspected him of stealing a typewriter from our apartment.

Greg also drew my attention to a magazine article asserting that counter-cultural publisher Paul Krassner had uncovered links between the Kennedy assassination and the Manson family.

Twelve days after I had taken my information to the Atlanta police, ski-masked bandits pulled a stick-up at a party both Greg and I were attending, and stole his identification and mine — taking only money from other guests.

From that day in early August of 1975 until the day of this writing my life has been a constant series of similar misadventures — including poisonings, threats and bribe offers, intense psychological harassments, mysterious interrogations and occasional reminders of those fateful conversations with the unusual man that I call "Brother-in-law."

A bald head was his most conspicuous feature. As he was almost certainly in disguise, he may have shaved his pate, wearing a toupee while on less clandestine business. The name he used was Gary. He must have been in his late thirties or early forties. Of medium build, I guess he stood about five-foot ten, my height. Although his arms were muscular, he had a pot belly and a slightly sunken chest. A somewhat protruding lower lip had resulted because of his constant pipe smoking.

An unsavory character by my twenty-three-year-old French Quarter standards, besides being a reputed underworld fringer he dressed like and off-duty policeman or an engineer. Slacks, a belt, a little key chain on something that looked like a steel tape measure spool, and a short-sleeve shirt with a plastic pocket guard for pens and pencils comprised his usual attire.

The back of Brother-in-Law's head was rounded and protruding as the back of Oswald's head had been singularly flat — a notable feature in both cases that would make convincing impersonations of either man unlikely, since conspirators with any such intention would have to find someone who resembled the subject in skull-structure as well as facially and in build.

A most evident, somewhat nasal, mid-Western twang could be discerned in Brother-in-law's voice. Clipped words and abrupt sentences often dominated his speech pattern, sometimes punctuated with short giggles. Standing very erect and drawing his head back until double chins appeared — although he was by no means obese — he would remove his pipe from his mouth and grin, protrude his lower lip belligerently and say cheerfully something thoroughly obnoxious, as if to assert 'I'm horrible, I know it, I like myself this way, and what's more there is absolutely nothing you can do about it — so there!' At such times he seemed to me like a species of insect, and his choice of words tended to reinforce that impression. If what he said was not cruel it would be ugly in some other way. Among the gently beautiful people of the New Orleans French Quarter he seemed as misplaced as a metallic slam of a car door in a flower patch.

I am not at all certain that his name was really Gary Kirstein. There is every reason to surmise he was not using his own name, and I remember him most as the "brother-in-law" of a French Quarter character named Slim Brooks. And because of Slim's extremely distinctive turn of speech, he himself seldom called Gary "my brother-in-law."

Instead, it was always, "Let's go visit Brother-in-law tomorrow."

I had arrived in New Orleans the day after Mardi Gras in 1961. Except for May, June, July, August and part of September of 1963, I lived there until December 13, 1963.

Beginning in the aftermath of the Bay of Pigs, and continuing up to about the time of the Kennedy assassination, Slim must have uttered those words between fifteen and twenty-five times. Since these invitations were far apart and infrequent, I never turned Slim down.

Sometimes Brother-in-law would come to the French Quarter the next day and get us. More often, Slim would arrange in advance to borrow his car and then would drive us to Brother-in-law's house out in the country.

If it was difficult to take what Brother-in-law said about his plans to murder the President seriously, that is partly because it was difficult to take Slim Brooks seriously. Not that Slim didn't seem honest. On the contrary, he seemed too honest to get himself involved with anyone heavy enough to actually go out and assassinate a President — if Slim would have to lie about it afterwards.

To suspect Slim of being a conspirator seemed too paranoid for words.

Jim Garrison

IN April of 1976, I again had occasion to think about paranoia in relation to the John Kennedy assassination. I attended a lecture in Atlanta by none other than Jim Garrison, for whom by then I felt a lot of sympathy.

In light of what I remembered now, it seemed his suspicions of me were only slightly misplaced. I was not a field agent in the assassination; I was among those who helped plan it!

In the question period after his speech Garrison said something I found both significant and touching: "Of course, I have to lean over backwards not to be paranoid, because I have been accused of paranoia in the past."

One of his diagnosticians had been me; now I was dealing with exactly the same double bind of trying to probe conspiracies without coming on like a paranoid in the eyes of my friends. Through an emissary I let it be known to Garrison that I wanted to meet with him. His reply: "Not only do I not want to meet with Kerry Thornley, I don't even want to hear his name. In fact, I don't even want to think about Kerry Thornley!"

Feeling very much alone, I continued my daily dealings with what were obviously conspiracies — including a correspondence with a man I hoped was a charming crank who was telling me in his letters "why we Fascists assassinated Kennedy." How I got on Stan Jamison's mailing list in the first place was a mystery to me. Since 1970, though, Greg Hill and I both had been receiving from him everything from advice on how to grow organic sprouts to racist newspapers published by White Christians who were armed and quite dangerous.

In reply to one of my memos about Kirstein that had fallen into his hands indirectly, he wrote me to say that the tragedy in Dallas was plotted by the Secret Order of Thule in such a way as to assure that no cover-up could remain convincing forever. Motive: to make the American public paranoid about their government and mass media. For paranoia, he told me, is a big step in the direction of mental health.

People who become paranoid, Stan Jamison wrote, will not rest until they discover every last shred of truth.

Among the devices used to encourage awareness of conspiracy were the many crude Oswald impersonations that occurred just previous to the assassination. Puzzled for more than a decade about exactly that mystery, I had to admit this was the first credible hypothesis to explain it without making the assassins look like idiots. And had they been less than geniuses, there would have been no cover-up at all.

Jamison further informed me that the conspiracy was constructed in concentric circles, like Chinese boxes, with descending levels, so that only the "man at the center" understood afterwards exactly what had happened. Of course, I could not ignore the possibility that man might have been Brother-in-law.

What brought together the many loose ends in the John Kennedy murder mystery for me was this realization that it was a maximum complicity crime. Various factions must have been deliberately implicated on a blind-alliance basis, so that once the event occurred, every group of conspirators was startled at evidence of participation by someone besides themselves.

Like Brother-in-law, Jamison seemed morbidly fascinated with Hitler and Nazi Germany. Both men mentioned particular little-known aspects of the Third Reich — such as the secret pagan rituals of the S.S. and the occult beliefs of Hitler's cohorts. Both repeated a rumor that Nazi rocket scientists discovered energy secrets that oil companies were repressing to this day. Whether either or both were living some kind of macabre hoax or were absolutely fanatical was impossible to determine, since neither man was without humor. For instance, Jamison always signed off with, "Love is alive and well."

As might be anticipated, it struck me that perhaps Stan Jamison and Gary Kirstein were the same person, so in 1977 I dropped in unexpectedly at his address in Sacramento, California. Not only was Jamison not the same man I had conversed with in New Orleans, but it was plain that the spine-chilling ranting in his letters was just a big put-on.

That isn't to say his information about the assassination could not have been valid. A warm, intelligent human being, obviously unsympathetic to Fascism, he nevertheless seemed quite versed in secret society and intelligence community politics.

"I come on all hairy like that in my letters," he told me, "to scare off government agents." Although that statement didn't sound convincing, it seemed a safe bet his motives were not cruel — a consideration that leaves undetermined whether or not they were misguided.

How paranoid is it to fear such an individual? Perhaps that is the wrong question. Maybe we should ask ourselves: Is it rational to dismiss them in the name of popularized notions of sanity? Later on I was to encounter a rumor that Stan Jamison acquired his information from one Michael Stanley, then serving a prison term in California. As Lovable Ol' Doc Stanley, Michael Stanley was known to me personally as one of the heavier, darker characters of the California counter-culture. We met each other in a hip coffee house after I moved to Los Angeles about a year after John Kennedy's assassination. Although I didn't like to admit it for fear of seeming paranoid, I found Michael Stanley terrifying.

Paranoia

PERHAPS if we clearly defined this thing we call paranoia it would not cause us to behave so foolishly. Genuine paranoia actually contains at least three ingredients: fear, suspicion and mystification. Technically, it is heightened awareness, but not yet perfect awareness.

Professional espionage agents are, for example, frequently both suspicious and mystified, but have long since learned to live without much fear. For that reason, we don't call them paranoids.

To be both frightened and confused, without a systematic method of blaming others for those conditions, is to be vulnerable to some other psychiatric classification than paranoia.

Fear and suspicion combined with exact, provable knowledge as to the identity of one's oppressors is generally considered a prerequisite for heroism.

Paranoia, then, only exists in politics where fear and suspicion linger for no external reason and, as is more often true, in cases where the subject is incorrect about who to suspect and what to fear — the condition of mystification.

Unfortunately nearly all oppressors in conspiracy politics strive skillfully to mystify their victims — often with enormous resources to help the work along.

"The arguments he used to justify his use of the alias suggest that Oswald may have come to think that the whole world was becoming involved in an increasingly complex conspiracy against him... Oswald was overbearing and arrogant throughout much of the time between his arrest and his own death. He consistently refused to admit involvement in the assassination or in the killing of Patrolman Tippit." - The Warren Report.

Next I shall provide additional evidence to that uncovered by critics of the Warren Commission that Oswald's perceptions of reality may have been far more accurate even than the words of his accusers.

Slim Brooks

Version I

BY early April of 1961 I had managed to obtain part-time employment as a telephone solicitor for the Foster Awning Company in New Orleans. On that job was where I met Slim Brooks.

After introducing ourselves to each other at work, as I've mentioned, we ambled back to the French Quarter together, comparing interests and opinions in the early spring afternoon weather.

Immediately taking me under his wing, Slim displayed a warm, instructive, though somewhat paternalistic, attitude. "This is a weird town," he said, "much like Japan in that it seems like a wonderful, colorful, magical place at first then the paint begins to chip off."

I didn't want to believe that.

"You'll see what I mean," he insisted. "Yeah, well — you'll see."

In any case, I was more interested in making a new convert to Objectivism than arguing about New Orleans: "Ayn Rand says that all poverty and war and so forth is caused not by selfishness, but by altruism. She actually offers a morality of self interest."

"Hey, I can feature that! Like in the service, where you turn to your buddy and say: 'I got mine; how you doin'?'"

"More or less. Only you'll really have to read *Atlas Shrugged* to understand."

"Maybe somethin' like L. Ron Hubbard's rap. Science fiction writer. Started his own philosophy. Complex, but fascinating."

Slim also mentioned that Hubbard was changing his philosophy to a religion and was now calling it the Church of Scientology.

"T don't blame him," I said. "He won't even have to pay taxes that way. Religion is the only con game in the United States protected by the Constitution."

"Ain't that the truth?"

"That's another thing I like about Ayn Rand," I added. "She's a militant atheist."

"Doesn't like the pork eatin' Christians, eh? That's what the A-rabs call em. I'm not religious, either. If I was, though, I'd be a Moslem. Then every time I elbowed my way through a crowd in front of a church I could say, 'God's curse on all unbelievers!' I like that one so much I say it anyhow, whenever I get the chance."

"Turn this corner with me," I suggested, changing the subject. "I need to get a loaf of French bread at the day-old bakery."

"Is there one in this neighborhood? I'll be damned! You showed me somethin' about this town I didn't know! And here I'm the one that's supposed to be showin' you the ropes."

Then we went to Slim's French Quarter room, where he introduced me to Margaret, "the squaw." Sidekick in drinking, she occupied an adjoining room to his and — as Slim was quick to tell me in advance their relationship was strictly Platonic, since in his opinion Margaret was "twice as ugly as any legendary sea monster spied by any given drunken sailor. In fact, if it came down to it, I couldn't say from personal experience if it's male or female of the species. Furthermore," he said with a laugh, "I'm undesirous of finding out!"

Margaret was chubby and aging, but didn't actually look that bad. Although light eyed and fair skinned, she was part Indian, with characteristic high cheek bones, for which reason Slim called her "squaw."

In the same half-kidding spirit, as I took it, her words for Slim were no kinder. "So how'd this no-good galoot of a landlocked pirate latch onto a nice young man like you?"

Before long I learned that Margaret was famous in the dives along Decatur Street for her singular talent of cussing sailors up one side and down the other for minutes on end without once resorting to nary an officially censorable swear word. That she was hopelessly addicted to alcohol was the worst anyone could say about her.

After we discussed her hangover for awhile, I was taken by Slim back to his room where, alone together, he explained to me in a mood of great seriousness that his real name was

Roderick R. Brooks, that he was in the Navy before entering the merchant marines, and was before that a Midwestern farm boy.

"My mother was in local politics," he remarked, "and that is one dirty, dirty business, I warn you — much worse than anything you suspect from reading books."

Slim was of many definite opinions, most of them quite original. "Now take a young buck your age, Sex and women is most important to him."

True enough. I had been asking Slim where to meet girls.

"An older man becomes interested in success. Making money or, in primitive society, hunting. Providing himself and family with security. Then there are the elders. Old men. They become concerned about tribal welfare, survival of humanity."

(Many weeks later, Slim was to pay me the supreme compliment: "You are actually more like an old man. You identify with the whole nation. I didn't realize that at first.")

"So you're a wordsmith," he said now. "I like that term — because that's what a writer actually is: a wordsmith. I'll have to introduce you to fellow down stairs. 'Nother wordsmith, peckin' and poundin' all day and hours of the night. Contemporary man is his subject matter."

Tom McNair turned out to be a likable young man in glasses and white T-shirt from Mississippi who happened to believe that in writing novels and short stories it was absolutely impossible to improve upon the exact style used by William Faulkner.

One particular short story of his he allowed me to read was about a Mississippi college student who masturbated in socks all the time and wound up committing suicide for obscure reasons. Another was about a man in a Falstaff shirt who killed his dog, again for motives that were unclear to me. Tom's *magnum opus* was entitled *This Small Matter of Dying*, about a draft resister lynched by a mob of patriotic rednecks. Everything was written in paragraph-long sentences linked together with commas.

"I think I messed up a seduction with this one about the guy who is always masturbating," he confessed. "I brought

Kay Johnson, an artist who hangs out at the Bourbon House, home one night and read it to her. I think she wondered what kind of weird guy I was."

I asked him if he knew about Ayn Rand.

"Systems!" he said with a fling of his arm. "Life is too big for philosophical systems!"

Soon I was to meet Tom McNair's friend, another young writer named Robert Langley. From the north of England, Langley spoke with a Scottish brogue that women found, in addition to his bonny good looks, irresistible.

While it didn't work for me as well as for him, from Robert Langley the best advice about how to meet girls was forthcoming. "Me, I just go to the Bourbon House in the evening at about six o'clock. Before you know it, someone is buying me drinks. Next morning I wake up in bed with a lass, usually not remembering how the hell I got there."

"Then there is also Ivan's," Slim contributed on this all-important subject. "Every Friday night a gay fellow named Ivan holds a free-for-all discussion group at his pad. He don't bother you if you ain't queer, though. Provides jugs of cheap wine, Lots of women there, Discussion goes on until the wine runs out. A social clearing house is what I like to call it. That's what they both are Ivan's and the Bourbon House: social clearing houses, where folks go to find other folks with similar interests to their own."

I was quick to introduce Slim to my roommate, Greg Hill. During one of their first conversations, Greg happened to mention Burgundy Street, pronouncing it as most Yankees do at first, same as the wine.

"BurGUNdy!" Slim thundered in correction. "Hereabouts, you call it BurGUNdy Street!"

"I don't care how these people pronounce it," Greg retorted. "I'll be damned if I'm going to call BURgundy, 'BurGUNdy.'"

"Yeah, well. You might want to reconsider — for purposes of protective coloration," Slim said with a chuckle.

Greg admitted that was a point and, as I anticipated, they hit it off at once.

Both loved the same brand of humor. Greg would labor for hours, creating pen and ink designs of satirical coats of arms, with stripes of bastardy and cute anachronisms. In the same spirit, Slim would hunch over his table and draw painstakingly detailed navigational maps of a place he called Factitious Harbor, in the shape of a hand thumbing a nose and featuring points of interest like the Isle of Caprice and Snuggler's Cove, Both also tended to pursue an argument with intimidating zeal, only to suddenly abandon their point in favor of a disarming quip.

Many was the long, hot summer afternoon I was to enjoy sitting in Slim's room, sipping cold coffee from Mason jars and listening to him and Greg laugh as they lost disputes with one another at the drop of a syllogism for the sake of a bad pun. One overcast morning Slim decided Greg and I needed to find out where to buy the cheapest groceries, so he took us on the bus to a supermarket in Gentilly. Upon returning with wheels of cheese, a humongous bologna and long loaves of French bread, we spent the afternoon drizzly afternoon in Slim's pad consuming poor boy sandwiches and a gallon jug of grapey Italian table wine, making up riddles with existentialist punch lines.

Depending on the direction of the breeze playing in the plain curtains of Slim's open windows, you could smell the muddy Mississippi blended with the fragrance of malt from the Jax brewery, or sometimes fresh-roasting coffee clear from Magazine Street, or the lingering, damp aroma of mossy walls in the surrounding courtyards and that was fortunate, because otherwise Slim's room smelled like dirty clothes and dish water. Cockroaches played tag on the counter next to the wash basin and flies hummed lazily in the still air.

That such things made us uncomfortable was to Slim evidence of our sissified upbringing. To him we were "wide-eyed California boys, shockable and so forth, with a lot to learn about the world."

Slow and deliberate in his method of speaking, he made his voice deep and gruffer than usual to express displeasure. When he laughed it was often with considerable embellishment a spontaneous eruption that trailed off in a series of "har-har-heh-heh-yuk-yuk: I like that one; he-he-ho-ho; I like it; I like it." If Slim thought something was funny, he left you in no doubt whatsoever especially if you didn't see quite as much humor in it as he did.

In a glum mood, he could mutter and mumble with yet more persistence. And woe to the listener who turned an unsympathetic ear! Chief among his pet peeves was "the bifricated female of the species, with her artless wiles and innocent guile, her periodic and sporadic emotional instability, not to mention her downright goddamn bitchy disposition." Slim could rave that way for an hour about Margaret or his most recent lover when he deemed circumstances warranted "a non-stop, thoroughly cantankerous rumination on the subject." At such times he spat out his words with unmitigated venom and, if you weren't entirely supportive, he was as likely to shift targets and begin at once with an infinite catalogue of your own numerous shortcomings.

"Then there's also the goddamn, stupid coon-ass landlubbering indigenous personnel in this town. Order your coffee black and the dumb shits give you chickory with sugar. Order it any other way and you get coffee in your milk! It ain't fair and, besides that, it ain't civilized. God willing and weather permitting, I'll whip this case of consumption and get me my sailing papers one day soon and go back to sea, where folks ain't so narrow and all-fired provincial and so forth and so on and et cetera and the like."

Very early on in our friendship we decided that with his seagoing experiences and my writing talents we might collaborate in producing pulp adventure fiction for action-oriented men's magazines. Our hero's name for the first and only episode, which we never completed, was D. Daniel Diamond, a swashbuckling merchant sailor who missed ship in San Juan and proceeded thereupon to involve himself in an elaborate smuggling plot with a Puerto Rican bar owner who, "... said his name was 'Erman, but he looked more like a weasel to me." As I said, Slim used this reference to warn me about his brother-in-law a few days before introducing us, adding: "He was raised in the Midwest by a German family. Recently he went to Germany for a visit." That was the occasion of Slim's mention that, upon observing the effects of the Marshall Plan, Brother-in-law said: "And you say America won the war?

Bull shit!"

Frequently Slim reverted to a primitive version of the language that omitted most articles of speech: "Squaw don't like Brother-in-law. Says Brother-in-law's mean. This is true. But some mind he's got! Typical woman, though; no appreciation for brains. Squaw don't like him. Dumb female."

Once as we were strolling together up Saint Peter, Slim spied a man with a black beard across the street and called him over.

"Now this fellow is a poet from the old Fencing Master crowd. And his name is Frank S. Nothing. That's actually what he calls himself. You might like him." Then, as Frank S. Nothing approached, Slim said, "Frank, this is Kerry; Kerry, this is Frank."

Roaming the streets of the Quarter together, the three of us soon became involved in a heated discussion of philosophy. Frank was an existentialist who believed, loudly, in the virtues of intuition as opposed to reason. When I insisted he should read the works of Ayn Rand in order to find out why he was wrong, he countered that he had never heard of her and, what's more, he would now make it a point never to read anything she wrote,

Although I found him philosophically obnoxious, I loved lively arguments and throughly relished our shouting matches. We even argued about whether or not we were arguing. Frank insisted it was a discussion, not an argument.

We wound up at the pad of one of his poet friends whose last name was Holland. There we continued our debate as to whether feeling or reason should be the basis of epistomology, with Frank saying: "Like, man, it ain't reason. It's intuition. Your senses don't think things! They feel sensations. Everything is feeling. Dig it! Like, feel!"

Finally I made a point of one kind or another and Frank withdrew into silence.

Said Holland, "Frank is put down."

"Like, I ain't put down," he retorted.

"Frank *feels* put down," Holland replied.

All I recall about Holland was that he wore a black turtleneck and was clean-shaven, and that a number of years later I encountered his name again as publisher of a Washington, D.C., poetry journal.

At last, Frank entered the discussion again. "You know who you remind me of?" he asked rhetorically. "Thomas Wolfe. And I bet that, like, you could write that way, too. But you worry too much about where to publish, man! I listen to what you are saying to these cats about your book and most of it is about finding a publisher. That's nowhere, man Like just write! Don't worry. Just write."

To this I objected that it is necessary to eat.

"Forget about that. Fuck it. Don't worry about it. Just write! Some cat will dig what you write and he'll give you an apple."

When Frank and I grew tired of yelling at one another, we wandered with Slim from Holland's apartment on Jackson Square to Esplanade Avenue, where we ducked into a little cafe, Frank ordered apple pie and coffee for all three of us.

"Whenever you're strapped for bread and hungry," he advised, "order apple pie; it's, like, more nourishing than anything else at the price."

We discussed politics. Frank told me to read *The Republic* by Plato. "The best government," he added, "is a benevolent dictatorship run by a philosopher king."

I was argued out, so I changed the subject. "Slim tells me you call your self Frank S. Nothing."

"Like, man, I dropped that." Then he told me his last name which I only remember was Italian and began with S.

Soon I recognized that late-night wanderings were a part of Quarter life. Week nights the Bourbon House closed at two in the morning, unlike most other bars in New Orleans that were open around the clock. As we'd be sitting in one or another of these establishments, dawn would creep up unexpectedly and Slim would glance at the window and say, "Good God! There's a fire outside!"

Another night, as I led our way down dark alley, he said: "Follow me! I'm right behind you!"

Nothing seemed to delight Slim more than making introductions. In due time he took me to Ivan's. Shortly thereafter, he introduced me to Carmen and Ralph Babin. Carmen was a vivacious, plump Latin woman who seemed to me a fanatical socialist. Occasionally she would become irritated with Ivan and would hold an alternative Friday night discussion group at her house,

One morning, with great pride, Slim took me to an obscure restaurant tucked away in a dead-end alley near Canal Street where you could buy a cup of coffee for a nickel.

Newspapers and phone calls were also only a nickel, everywhere in New Orleans. (Most places, coffee had gone up to fifteen cents even in this town.)

"These friggin' coon-asses may be rude and crude and so on and so forth," Slim said of the natives whom he always called "coon-asses." "But they ain't entirely stupid, When the phone company tried to raise pay phone calls to a dime, they stopped making calls."

As for political philosophy, Slim's was Technocracy — a movement that enjoyed brief success in the Thirties, utilizing the Taoist Yin and Yang as its symbol. "Under that system nobody would have to work much, but absolutely everyone would work four hours a day, five days a week, That's better than what we've got now. Take for example the girl with the golden pussy who gets through school because all the guys help her with her homework and she might as well, because she ain't going to have to lift a finger all her life. By the time her looks fade she is collecting alimony. Or she just flat out works as a whore from the beginning."

At that point I stopped him. I had heard enough from Slim about the "bifurcated female of the species" to last me the rest of my days. While he resented and distrusted women, he also dismissed gays. In fact, at times he seemed nearly puritanical. Sex seemed a necessary evil which, while pleasurable, gave Slim far more inconvenience than satisfaction. Once he became angry when one woman told another he was good at cunnilingus! "No damn bitch is going to go around saying I eat pussy," Slim grumbled.

Moreover, Slim insisted he had joined the Navy in order

to escape a situation where he was living with more than one woman in the same house. "I had to get out of there; I was pussy whipped. There really is such a thing as too much of a good thing, you know."

Never having suffered any such tribulation, I was skeptical.

"Menstral cycles! Stockings hanging in the bathroom! Female complexity! Like 'Enry 'Iggins says: 'Why can't a woman be more like a man?'" he went on.

Among my boyhood heroes was Richard Halliburton, globe-trotting adventurer and author of *The Royal Road to Romance*. Of him Slim said, "His family lives in Algiers, Louisiana, and he was queer, you know." Mentioning Halliburton in passing conversation from then on, Slim called my former idol "that weird from across the river." Once he cautioned me, "If you take up traveling you won't be able to make it the way he did, with that third man theme working for him. Hell, he could always pick up spare change giving sailors blow jobs."

Such humorous wording kept Slim's listener charmed in spite of the pig-head ed wrongness of much that he said. And with his own tales of faraway places that rivaled Halliburton's, he never failed to find in me a ready audience.

"Now Finland is a place I like," he remarked one afternoon, adding that he flew into Helsinki once in circumstances I no longer recall. "Beautiful people! Tall, high cheek bones, blue and green eyes. But, but, but, but, but they are prejudiced against Negroes there."

"In the black hole of Calcutta" was where Slim caught his tuberculosis. "And that's exactly what it is, too — a black hole."

There were disadvantages to the wandering life, he often reminded me. "You know how you get homesick for Japan now that you're back in the States? Well, that predicament of a dilemma compounds itself the more you travel. No matter where you are, you get nostalgic for where you ain't. Hell, when I was in Tokyo get I'd get the blues for Hamburg. In Amsterdam I longed for the South China Sea. In some respects, it's a mournful misery of a life."

Another time he said, "You know, Kerry, I've been nearly everywhere. Let me tell you something: this world is very mundane place. That's the only word for it. Mundane."

Probabilities and possibilities of an impending nuclear holocaust were to Slim fascinating data. Likely targets in the U.S. of an atomic strike force were familiar to him as the names of the ports from which he had sailed. Plans for bomb shelters and fall-out shelters were among his possessions, most of them clipped from the page of pulp magazines.

"There was an article in *Popular Mechanics* or one of those other grease monkey journals," he told me once, "that illustrated the situation by picturing two neighbors, each with a basement full of dynamite and the detonator in the hands of the guy next door. They went on from there to calculate the odds that neighbor A would blow neighbor B to kingdom come so as to prevent neighbor B from doing the same thing to him first."

Why this subject so intrigued him always eluded me.

One day he mentioned to my friend Vic Latham that New Orleans was a high priority target area.

Disgusted at Slim's alarmism, Vic replied, "I doubt that very much."

"But, but, but, but. Are. You. Sure?" That was exactly the way it sounded, with long pauses between his words for effect.

"Let's put it this way," Vic snorted. "I'd stake my life on it."

From then on Slim never showed much liking for Vic.

As with all his interests, Slim's literary tastes ranged much farther in all directions than my own. Science fiction and light, witty humor were among his favorite themes. *Comfort Me With Apples* by Peter DeVries is the only book I remember him getting me to read. Another recommendation, a spine-chiller called *Kiss, Kiss*, I passed up. At this point I don't recall the author. I remember, though, that Greg read it and liked it.

When Greg and I initiated Slim into the Discordian Society, he took on a long, complicated Viking name and appointed himself Keeper of the Submarine Keys. "I like that one," he said, "because it brings up two questions. What submarine? And why is it locked?"

Unfortunately, whenever Slim came up with a good line whether by theft or originality — he was inclined to repeat it thereafter at every opportunity. This was not like Brother-in-law's method of mentioning the same item of seemingly irrelevant data over and over. Rather, Slim just had a quip for every situation, and no matter how often the situation arose the quip came out on cue. Far be it from Slim Brooks to feel any duty to be more original than fate.

For example, no one ever complained of their troubles to Slim without hearing him answer, "You think you got problems! My socks keep falling down!"

And of all the jokes in his store of prefabricated wit, Slim always seemed fondest of the corniest, such as: "There was once a fellow who sold another guy a friggin' jackass. And the one who bought the stubborn beast couldn't seem to get it going. So he went and lodged complaint with former owner. Former owner grabbed two-by-four and hit the ornry critter over head. Then he shouted, 'Gity-up, mule,' and jackass obeyed. New owner said, 'I don't get it.' And the fellow says to him: 'First, you got to get his attention!' Har-de-har-yuk-yuk, I like that one!"

"Slim," I would groan at every telling "that's not only the oldest joke in the book, but you tell it over and over again. Worse than that, every time you sound like you just now thought it up yourself!"

"But I like it, I like it. And, besides that, it's true. That's just exactly how people are. You got to hit them over the head to get their attention."

Since then I have often wondered whether he was already in on the plans of the assassins, understanding that killing the President was to be a way of hitting the jackass known as middle America over the head.

My favorite was his joke about two little black boys and their dog — not because of its racial stereotypes, for in spite of that I liked the point it made. "You see, one of them was fuckin' the dog when up walks this dignified gentlemen who stops and begins to lecture them on the evils of dog fucking. Little boy looks up without missing a stroke and says, 'Look, mister, it's my prick and this here is my dog.' Then he says to his friend, 'Hold his head, Willie!'"

Whenever Margaret or Slim either one felt the other was becoming too invasive with unsolicited advice, he or she would say: "Hold his head, Willie!"

Antics and tones of voice contributed as much to Slim's best humor as content. For that reason it is hard to translate into cold print some of his funniest and most original gems. I think of the Sunday morning he was searching without much success for the entertainment enter section of the newspaper. "There's one in here somewheres," he muttered, and then reached in quickly, grabbing a section at random and shouting: "Be one!" It wasn't, but I laugh about it still whenever I'm confronted with a similar problem.

That my friend Slim Brooks may have been a navigational consultant for the Bay of Pigs Invasion was something I'd never have suspected at the time. Yet he was perfectly adept at precisely such work, Something about the coffee stains on his charts seemed to rule out that possibility then.

Version II

I have a photocopy of a letter I sent my parents in 1961, wherein I mentioned that Slim Brooks gave me a haircut for my birthday on April 17th. In a tone of fascination, I added the remark that Slim had worked as a ship's barber, for it seemed this swashbuckling soldier of fortune knew how to do everything. In my letters to my father and mother, I shared all that seemed important, and even told them that Slim had good ideas about where to meet girls.

Since I was not keeping up with the news during that interval, I had no idea the fateful Bay of Pigs invasion was taking place the day I turned 23.

I am tempted to believe that Slim's cutting of my hair on the day of the Bay of Pigs invasion, coupled with the coincidence that it was also my birthday, was used to endow me with a peculiar significance to a secret society cloaked in a camouflage of Satanism and witchcraft. I hope it will become evident why I suspect this possibility as these recollections unfold.

> "Because of the power inherent in hair, great precautions were taken in primitive societies in the selection of a barber, in appointing an auspicious time for cutting, and in the disposal of the remains," says Benjamin Walker's *The Encyclopedia of the Occult, the Esoteric, and the Supernatural* (Scarborough Books, 1980).
>
> "Special days were set apart for the purpose and spells and incantations recited. Because hair could be used for many magical operations directed against the owner, care had to be taken that it should not fall into the hands of sorcerers. The hair was therefore buried in a secret place..." (p. 111) A hardback version of this book is called *Man and the Beast Within* (Stein and Day, 1977).

By his own account, Slim was a merchant seaman who happened to be in dry-dock with a bad case of tuberculosis. Towering over ordinary mortals like a derrick, his consumptive frame emphasized his height. By hunching sociably and quizzically grinning, he made up for this.

"You can remember my name real easy," he would say, "because I'm a long, tall drink of water: Slim Brooks."

Slim was the kind of individual who could have won anyone's trust, practically, at least for awhile. A funky, haphazard aspect of his personality made him seem like anything but secretive.

Personal tidiness seemed, in fact, to offend him deeply. Much of his barbed wit was aimed at people who thought they were too good to share his lumpen living habits. That he carried this characteristic to such extremes was also the reason what trust he won did not serve him in the long run.

I had first met Slim in a telephone soliciting "boiler room" of an aluminum awnings and siding company where I was holding down part-time work while writing *The Idle Warriors*.

He was hired about two weeks after I went to work there, and one day he doodled some Japanese ideograms on his desk, thereby catching my attention. When I told him I was just in from the Far East myself and was writing a novel about peace-time Marines overseas, he simply nodded knowingly and said, "Yeah."

After work that day, we strode back to the French Quarter together, enjoying the afternoon sunshine and chatting about his adventures and my dreams.

"I'm just in from Hammond, Louisiana," he told me, "where I was a hand on a river barge. I got along with those backwoods rednecks just fine. I like that about myself. I get along with about every kind of people."

Of Norse descent, Slim took pride in his Viking ancestry. "Hell, my people came over here, threw a party, got drunk and then politely went home. Your people still celebrate Columbus Day and you ain't even I-talian. Not only did you poison the country with your mechanical piss, but you hog credit for discovering the campsite in the beginning. And what's more, you won't even admit we're so much as the bastard cousins of your red-headed Irishmen — and before us Vikings raped 'em they was all black-haired virgins."

Then his lilting, soft and easy laugh assured me that he was not after all such a desperate individual.

A walking compendium not only of original proverbs and unique quotations, he was also well versed in the lore of the French Quarter.

Shortly before my arrival in New Orleans, there'd been a Beatnik coffee house on Exchange Place called the Fencing Master. "I was the fencing master at the Fencing Master," he boasted, and it struck me how his thin Douglas Fairbanks mustache lent credibility to the claim made otherwise ridiculous by his quixotic stature.

"When you spend months cooped up on a ship," he added, "and if you happen to be as ornery as I am, it behooves you to learn as many methods of arguing by hand as possible."

"Slimericks" was what I was eventually to dub these colorful embellishments of his. Most of them occurred in the course of conversation, though he also wrote homey couplets from time to time, such as this one, titled "Cortez:"

> With tongue in cheek and sword in hand
> We made Christians of this heathen land.

Occupying a large, mildewy second-floor room on Dauphine Street, Slim served his guests cold coffee in Mason jars, as the mud-moist Louisiana breeze blew at the curtains in the large, open windows.

A stack of rolled-up navigational maps filled the space beneath a card table in a corner.

Ornate French Quarter rooftops and garrets were part of the view, with the green tops of nearly tropical trees at a greater distance. Sitting here, you couldn't forget you were in New Orleans. Harbor horns bleated as Slim chuckled out phrases like, "God willing and weather permitting," while he spun yarns. A vivid memory remains from about the time of the haircut, perhaps within days afterwards. I recall Slim saying, "Now, my brother-in-law is coming to town in a in a few weeks, and I'm going to introduce you to him with the warning that he's kind of a weasel, like 'Erman."

In "San Juan Sinbad," a short-story upon which we were collaborating, the Puerto Rican villain was named Hermando, which Slim anglicized as 'Erman. "So don't trust him too much," continued Slim. "Just pay attention to him. He has a brilliant mind."

"Slim," I objected, "that sounds frightening!"

"No. Just keep your wits about you. You'll see."

Slim gave me that haircut in the new apartment into which Greg and I had moved, in a complex called The Buccaneer on Saint Louis near the Napoleon House. And I think it was just days or maybe weeks after April 17, 1961, that I met Brother-in-law in Slim's room.

I don't remember who got there first. Either Brother-in-law arrived while Slim and I were passing an afternoon together or I dropped by for a visit and Brother-in-law was already there. But I recall with full clarity what happened next.

Brother-in-law

SLIM introduced us as follows: "Kerry, this is Gary. Gary, this is Kerry." Then looking back and forth rapidly at both of us he said, "He doesn't like Kennedy either," laughing at his own joke.

"Yes," said Brother-in-law, "I think John F. Kennedy is a menace to the country and I think he ought to be assassinated."

We shook hands heartily.

"Oh goody! I was a catalyst!" Slim interjected.

We laughed, and I said, "At last, somebody in the French Quarter who isn't a Liberal!"

"Not only that," Brother-in-law retorted, "but I'm a Nazi and, actually, we won the war, Kerry. Did you know that?"

"Yeah, Slim told me you said the Marshall Plan proves it. That was beautiful."

"Yes, but that was only a joke. Kerry, have you ever heard of a company called I.G. Farben?"

Something in his voice scared me a little. That it may have been genuine bitterness beneath a National Socialist cover did not occur to me. But ever since arriving in New Orleans I had been putting up with nothing but Kennedy Catholics and Kennedy Democrats and Kennedy Liberals. It was refreshing to discover someone who hated JFK as much as I did.

"It's a German company that Hitler put together during the Third Reich, Kerry."

As was to become my habit with Brother-in-law, I probably tried to change the subject at this point.

But Gary persisted. "In the political realm only did the Germans lose the war, Kerry. In the economic arena, they won."

According to Peter Batty's *The House of Krupp* (Stein and Day, 1967): "Despite the efforts to break up the coal and steel empires into smaller units, most of them have in fact come together again. The one victory the Allied 'de-cartelisers' can point to is that the *Vereinigte Stahlwerke*, the notorious giant steel cartel that dominated the Ruhr before the war, has not been re-formed. But even that is only a hollow victory, for the Thyssen Group, welded in 1963 out of just two segments of it, is today far bigger than the old VS ever was. Similarly with I.G. Farben, the mammoth chemical concern, which was split into three by the Allied 'trust-busters' — now each of the three offshoots is larger than its former parent!" (p. 280)

To a more perceptive ear, Brother-in-law's words may have sounded like thinly veiled complaining. But since I bought the Nazi cover story without thinking, to me it sounded like right-wing delusions of grandeur — something like the hollow boast of a motorcycle gang member.

As I told Slim afterwards, I liked this brother-in-law of his more than I thought I would. "Why didn't you tell me he hates Kennedy as much as I do?"

"And spoil the surprise?" he said, laughing at the outrageousness of his humor. "Now I wouldn't do that. My name's Slim — not Scrooge!"

A bald head was Brother-in-law's most striking feature. In retrospect I wonder if he polished it. This is a serious possibility, for he must have been in disguise and may have shaved and shined his pate, wearing a toupee while on less clandestine missions.

The back of his head was rounded, protruding. I mention the shape of his head in hopes that his identification might be facilitated if he was in fact pretending to be someone else.

A somewhat nasal Midwestern twang could be discerned in his voice. Clipped words and abrupt sentences often dominated his speech patterns at the same time, however. Short giggles occasionally punctuated his sentences.

At such times he looked to me like a species of insect and his choice of words usually reinforced that impression. If what he said was not cruel it would disgust me in another way. "I like smoking a pipe," he told me once, "because it fumigates my mouth."

I gathered the perhaps erroneous notion that he avoided mingling with my Bohemian friends and acquaintances whenever it wasn't absolutely necessary.

His eyes were not a Germanic blue nor his eyelashes blond, I recall vividly, however, they were either hazel or green or blue-green, of a shade light enough that I was not moved to doubt his vaunted German ancestry.

Sometimes I would look at Brother-in-law's eyes intently, and he would meet my gaze grinning mysteriously, defiantly — as if to say what Lee Oswald said later to his brother, Robert, when he visited Lee in jail after the assassination: "You won't find any answers there, brother."

Gary's pupils were neither dilated nor contracted. There was no glint either. They were like closed solid gates.

With faint amusement, he would just wait patiently, returning my stare as if he could guess the questions in my mind, but knew that never in a million years of looking would I be able to guess the answers in his.

By and large I was tragically unimpressed by Brother-in-law.

I never thought much about him when I wasn't in his presence, except when Slim mentioned him. Once he told me that Brother-in-law had secured a job as a bouncer in a Bourbon Street night club owned by a colorful Mafioso thereabouts. Soon afterwards, he told me that Gary and Ola were now living together in an apartment in the vicinity of the Saint Louise Cathedral on Royal Street.

Ola Holcomb became Brother-in-law's lover shortly after his arrival. A month or so earlier I had myself tried to develop a romantic relationship with her, with disastrous results from the standpoint of my tender young male ego.

A mysterious woman to me, Ola professed to be an atheist but insisted on wearing a little gold cross around her neck. She rejected my advances for reasons she refused to fully explain. And now she was living with Slim's unusual Nazi brother-in-law, of all people.

In the middle Seventies when I first began talking about Gary Kirstein I began to sense something weird in the way people responded. There was a Gary Kirstein still living in New Orleans listed with information. A reporter told me he found Gary Kirstein's name in the resisters of some gun clubs. A magician in California investigating snuff films and other illegitimate practices among occultists said Gary Kirstein's name had turned up. I noticed that whoever I spoke to about him who seemed knowledgeable usually mentioned the

Trilateral Commission, as if to hint.

Anyway, it eventually became pretty obvious to me that whoever I had met in 1961 in New Orleans had probably been using Kirstein's name in order to set him up. Brother-in-law had in fact hinted at the time that he was "really more like a mad scientist" than the Nazi Kirstein was supposed to be and on one occasion he spoke emotionally of a scientist named Tom Miethe. So in 1977 and early 1978 I assumed I had been dealing with Miethe undercover as Kirstein. I found that Miethe was one of Hitler's rocket scientists who would up working for AVRO in Canada after the war. I met two individuals who claim they knew him as a teacher of nuclear physics at Georgia Tech in Atlanta in the middle Sixties. Still, people kept treating me like I was joking or crazy or trying to frame Miethe.

Then in 1978 somebody furnished me with what seemed like a hot tip that my man in New Orleans had actually been neither Kirstein nor Meithe but a Canadian businessman named Mortimer Bloomfield — mentioned in *Nomenclature of an Assassination Cabal* as one of John Kennedy's assassins. Since assassinating JFK had been one of our chief subjects of discussion, that seemed at least possible. Then, that same year, an assassination buff in California expressed the opinion that I had been talking to the Watergate burglar Edward Howard Hunt. So I read Hunt's autobiography *Undercover*. Not only did Hunt mention being involved in a number of CIA projects that the man I knew as Gary Kirstein discussed with me, a 1959 photo of E. Howard Hunt in the book exactly resembles the man I knew as Kirstein — except that Kirstein was bald and Hunt, at that time, wasn't. So for the past many years I've been more or less convinced was dealing with Hunt in disguise.

Greg Hill

SLIM Meanwhile I was preoccupied with the tasks and adventures of daytoday living in the French Quarter, where I shared my living space with a young man who had accompaied me from Southern California.

My roommate, Gregory Hill, was short in physical stature with curly black hair. Elfin blue eyes combine with his squat physique to give him a Pan-like appearance.

A lover of wines, cheeses, unusual tobaccos, exotic teas, strange blends of coffee, and anything else calling for subtle distinctions — including abstract optical effects in art and mindbending intellectual paradoxes — a connoisseur of everything quaint, particularly when he discovered for himself what was quaint about it, Greg would spend hours looking into something that most people would never notice.

Expressions of gratitude to and Huey P. Long for prayers answered among the personal classifieds of the New Orleans *Times Picayune*, Cajun jokes, French Quarter architecture, Irish Channel slang and crackpot cults all amused him enormously.

Our first outings together in El Monte, California, had in fact been to meetings of a far-out religion of flying saucer buffs founded by a man named Daniel Fry. The cult was called "Understanding" (except that it was spelled with a Christian cross where the "t" would ordinarily go).

Greg found in Slim an amusing and intellectually stimulating companion.

I took Greg to visit Slim's pad — where, in keeping with his notions of hospitality, the landlocked seaman immediately served up a Mason jar full of room temperature coffee.

Greg took a sip and wrinkled his nose. "This coffee's cold!"

Slim laughed. "Man, you don't drink coffee — you drink temperature!"

Always a pushover for utilitarian logic, Greg was to remark to me many years later: "You know something? From that day to this I have never once complained about cold coffee."

Greg and Slim met only once or twice. First on the Sunday before Memorial Day when Slim, Gary and Ola dropped into our Saint Louis Street pad for a visit. I don't recall much of the conversation that afternoon — only that Slim kept looking at Greg's typewriter, with which I was currently writing my novel about Oswald.

Hands behind his head, Gary tipped his chair back and stared at the machine with a loutish grin and began talking about a pawn shop on Canal Street where it was possible to have stolen goods fenced.

For my part, I spent most of the time observing the serene, resolute Ola, whose liberal cultural and racial views rebuked her Mississippi background. I was trying to figure out what she saw in a self-proclaimed Nazi, since in spite of her professed agreement with Ayn Rand, some of my own much more rational right-wing views seemed to annoy her. Slim had told me liked Ola because he deemed her red hair a Germanic trait.

In those days, we were inclined to leave our door unlocked, and the next day, Memorial Day of 1961, when Greg and I were out somewhere drinking coffee and arguing philosophy, somebody made off with the typewriter. Both of us suspected , but we didn't see how we could prove anything — the idea of checking with the pawn shop he'd mentioned never dawned on either of us.

We did call the police, however. Two cops came to visit us. They said from now on to keep our door locked. "Believe me," one of them added, "after you've been in our business awhile, you know better than to trust your own brother."

As for any hope of recovering our stolen property, the chances were, they allowed, slim.

Since I was drawing unemployment, retroactive from the period before I got part-time work as a phone solicitor, I gladly paid the greater portion of the price for a new typewriter — something which Greg commented at the time, was "more than generous," compelling me to explain that my motive was self-interest: "I want to finish *The Idle Warriors*.".

Later when the Foster Awning phone room closed down, Slim gave up his apartment to live for a while in a skid-row mission, and at widely spaced intervals he would use our shower. Sometimes he would make such a visit when neither

Greg or I were home, and we could always tell he'd been there because of the lingering stench. Slim would wear the same clothes, unwashed, for days at a time. This was not simply because of poverty, for he told me once that he actually preferred not to change clothes.

I Can Make You Famous

A few weeks later Slim and I went to visit in the ground-floor Rue Royal apartment he shared with Ola. Only Gary was there. A painting of a stripper with pasties stood at one end of the room on an easel, prompting me to comment that Gary was a good painter.

"So was Hitler," he responded. "In fact once an art critic complained that you could count the number of cobblestones in one of his street scenes. I don't think that was a very fair criticism. Do you, Kerry?"

"I should say not," I chimed in. "We Objectivists like realistic art that requires genuine talent. That critic was probably an abstract expressionist or something equally decadent."

"Precisely." He seemed very pleased with me.

Ola came in at some point. I was telling Gary how much I looked forward to finding out more about Papa Joe, his boss at the night club, because soon I was going to attempt a novel about New Orleans that would include mobsters among the characters.

Leaning forward, his elbows resting on his knees, began to tell me about Papa Joe, saying that he had many sons who helped him run the business. Unfortunately, either I changed the subject, or Slim said it was time to go, because the conversation went no further.

Somewhere around the same time, I became involved with an attractive nineteen-year-old Sophie Newcomb coed named Jessica Luck, and it must have been during July of that summer, 1961, that Slim invited both of us to ride with him and to look at some property on Jefferson Highway that Gary had just purchased and where he was going to build a house for his own use.

A long stone's throw from the brewery, with its aluminum kegs lined up in a row on the shipping dock, across the road the vacant land in question was grown over with tangled vines and small trees. I stepped forward into the swampy thicket, but cautioned me that there were poisonous snakes about of a species that would actually chase a human being — the cotton-mouth, I believe.

It was late in the day, the sun was setting, and I felt drained of energy, for to me it had been something of a pointless expedition. We piled back into the car and returned to the city.

started talking about Nazis and Russians during the Hitler-Stalin Pact, and asked me if I knew there had been a lot of "going back and forth from one side to the other" among them at that time. Having read as much in Eric Hoffer's *The True Believer*, I could say that I did.

By the time we pulled up in front of Slim's place we were involved in discussing the literal meanings of the names various Russian leaders had adopted for revolutionary purposes — "Molotov" meant "Hammer," and "Stalin" meant "Steel," and so forth.

Gary was next to me in the back seat, his hands clasped together, his elbows on his knees, in a posture I was coming to recognize as characteristic of him when he urgently wanted to be heard. "If I were to assume a revolutionary name, it would be 'Smith,' because a smith is someone who forges things—"

"You forge checks, money orders," guffawed Slim, beginning to list the small-time crimes to which frequently boasted.

Of course, Gary had been referring to the forging of political alliances, but he laughed with the rest of us.

Then I must have walked Jessica up to the Freret bus stop on Canal Street, because my next recollection of that evening is that only the three of us — Slim, Brother-in-law and me — were sitting in Slim's room, when at one point or other in the chatter Brother-in-law asked, "Kerry, how would you like to be famous?"

"I'd love it," I replied without hesitation. "I've always wanted to be at least famous enough to make the cover of *Time* magazine."

Suddenly very serious, hunching forward with his elbows on his knees, he said, "I can make you famous."

After listening to me rant about how famous I wanted to be, he stammered, "Kerry, in order to make you famous I'll have to k-kill five people."

"Sure," I said with false bravado, not knowing what else to say. "Go ahead." Perhaps he was planning to rub out some of his underworld associates. I didn't ask. The remark was disconcerting.

That night, safely home in bed, I thought before going to sleep that Slim's Brother-in-law was turning out to be weirder than I had at first supposed and that in the future it would be a good idea to steer clear of him.

As it happened I was not to encounter again for many weeks. Slim would make mention of him from time to time. He'd gone out of town to Mussel Shoals, Alabama. He'd gotten in a fight and come out of it with a black eye. He was going to write a book about the officials of the Third Reich. It would be called *Hitler Was a Good Guy*, and he wanted to pay me to help him research it.

I wondered what kind of book it was going to be; I wasn't sure I wanted anything to do with it.

Besides the Sunday afternoon before Memorial Day, Greg does not remember any further meeting with Brother-in-law. But in July of that year we moved to a larger attic apartment in the same building, and sometime thereafter — possibly late August — Slim and were very much present there one Saturday or Sunday morning. Slim and Gary and Jessica and I were going to the country for a picnic, and the place was noisy with our preparations.

Nothing significant happened that I recall, so perhaps Greg just didn't find it worth remembering. Or maybe he was bleary-eyed from a hangover and went back to bed afterwards and forgot about it. Since this time around I had the bedroom and it was he who slept in the living room, I'm sure he must have been awake, though possibly he had gone out early that morning.

Something had to be purchased to complete our provisions, so at one point Brother-in-law and I ran an errand together in his car. It was the only time the two of us were alone for more than two or three minutes that I can remember. Peter, Paul and Mary's then-popular *Where Have All The Flowers Gone?* was playing on his car radio.

"Heh, heh. I like that song," he said with what seemed like cynical relish. "It's so sad! Yeah, heh, heh — when will they ever learn?"

And so we picked up the wine or paper cups or sandwich bags or whatever we were supposed to get at Waterbury's Drugs and drove back from the corner of Camp and Canal to the apartment. I saw that Brother-in-law was in a wise-cracking mood today and seemed, in his sardonic way, maybe not such a dangerous character as I had briefly feared. But I wasn't inclined to bring up the subject of the five people he said he would kill to make me famous, and I hoped he had forgotten about it.

Then the four of us drove out into the backwoods of Jefferson Parish somewhere and sat under the trees eating poor-boy sandwiches and drinking wine.

How unusual for someone like Brother-in-law, in his neatly pressed slacks with his Mafia slang and Nazi jokes, to suggest an outing like this! But he seemed to be enjoying it all immensely. Now and again he would look at Jessica with an expression I can only describe as fierce satisfaction. Certainly he wasn't flirting with her, because his scrutiny would come when she wasn't looking at him. Vaguely disquieted, irritated with myself for feeling uneasy, unable to make any sense of his glances, I began to feel I was dealing with a man who was much too erratic or complex to evaluate.

Personally I preferred people like Greg, who belonged to a world I understood. Brother-in-law was from a world I didn't understand. I did not, in fact, know whether to fear or dismiss him as a cheap hoodlum's fabrication.

Slim belonged to both worlds. He would enjoy my labeling him a social amphibian. But he seemed predominately a creature of my world, and his fascination with this of his was hard to figure.

That autumn I heard from Slim that Brother-in-law's new house was now constructed on the property near the Anheuser brewery. Moreover, Brother-in-law was now respectably employed at the brewery. I don't recall whether he got the job there first and then purchased the land for his house or whether it was the other way around. What I do remember is that they were just beginning to produce a new brand of beer there — Busch Bavarian.

That he was no longer a bouncer in a Mafia strip joint I took as reassuring, for that would perhaps mean he was that much further removed from any present involvement with organized crime. Authentic New Orleans underworld figures were people I wanted to learn about — while staying as far away from them as possible.

And then there was the consideration that Brother-in-law was going to try his hand at becoming a writer. That was something I could identify with. Slim had assured me that Gary was going to keep his personal opinions out of *Hitler Was a Good Guy*.

"By God, he'd better," was my response, "if he expects to sell it to a decent publishing house."

It was to be an objectively written study of what the policies of various members of the Third Reich would have been, had they succeeded in their attempts to seize power from Hitler. The purpose was to argue that of all of them, Adolph Hitler was the least of many terrible evils.

So one morning, at Slim's prior suggestion, I met with him and Gary and we drove in Brother-in-law's car to the modest little flat-roofed house in Harahan, Louisiana, at the corner of Jefferson Highway and Plache. To the best of my recollection it was green stucco on the outside. Inside was a living room with an adjoining kitchen at the back separated by a structure resembling a breakfast bar. Upon a corner where a dirt or gravel road joined the highway, it stood far from any other residence. There was a bedroom off to the side opposite the main road. Or perhaps just a sofa in the living room that made into a bed — I don't recall exactly.

I remember thinking wistfully what I could do with a place of that size — a home base to which I could return after the numerous globetrotting adventures I was planning on having as soon as I became a successful writer. Surveying the living room for the first time, I noticed an unusually large number of cheap girlie magazines stacked here and there.

This was to be the first of perhaps a couple of dozen such visits, filling a two-year s from late in 1961 until November of 1963. Each of these visits took place at Slim's suggestion, and each time Slim was to accompany me. Sometimes we would meet in the French Quarter and all three of us would drive out to the house together; other times Slim would have already borrowed Gary's car and he and I would make the drive, with awaiting us at the house.

At the time, these expeditions comprised a negligible portion of my life, so it seemed to me, for they were isolated from my adventures among the Bohemians and hipsters of the French Quarter — the Quarterites, as we called ourselves. So to phrase it mildly, I wasn't taking notes.

So the conversational dialog I use in telling this tale is written necessarily with a certain amount of poetic or literary license, to capture the mood of each situation, as there is no way I am able to present a word-for-word transcript of what was said.

Most of my memories of these talks were repressed for many years until 1975, when I could recall at first only that Slim Brooks had a weird brother-in-law who seemed obsessed with Nazism and who spoke once or twice with me of killing John Kennedy. As I recalled it vaguely, I had decided afterwards he was just playing with my mind.

However, since 1975 I have thought about almost nothing but — literally, day in and day out. Times were many I thought my mind would snap from the emotional strain of having to dwell so constantly on anything so difficult to understand.

Gradually it occurred to me that possibly bizarre words and actions contain their own psychological camouflage. Police hasten to close cases like the John Kennedy assassination. Earl Warren said of the Dallas crimes, "This whole thing just makes me sick." Few Commission members bothered to attend the taking of depositions. When Jim Garrison reopened the case in the late sixties, reporters complained constantly about the bizarre nature of the probe's cast of characters.

In our society, distasteful matters are quickly disposed of with circumspection and minimal attentiveness.

The Manson Family

FOR many years *Warren Report* critics, as well as anyone who attempted to take a closer look at the Manson family, were popularly dismissed as "ghouls" and "vultures."

"Manson made many friends during his last seven years in prison," before his release in the middle Sixties, according to Ed Sanders' *The Family The Family*. "Some cell-mates say that Manson planned all along to collect an army of outcasts operating 'beneath the awareness' of the mother culture." (p. 32)

That Brother-in-law may have been involved in creating the Manson cult, as he must have been in on the John Kennedy assassination, was a notion that came to me slowly, very much intuitively feared before it was consciously acknowledged.

There is the nagging consideration that Robert Kennedy dined with Sharon Tate and Roman Polanski the night of his death and that Manson's people were very much involved with the "black-caped, black-garbed, death-worshiping Process Church of the Final Judgment" which, writes Sanders, "arrived on the Los Angeles scene in early 1968. They stayed in public view till a few days after Robert Kennedy's assassination in June of '68, after which they dropped from sight in Los Angeles." (p. 80)

We also read in *The Family* (p. 73) that Sharon Tate was initiated into witchcraft by a disciple of Aleister Crowley, who was technical adviser on the set of a horror movie she made in London, and that San Francisco Satanist Anton LaVey played the role of the Devil in *Rosemary's Baby*. (p. 77)

And we also read of Miss Tate that in 1966 "her father, Lieutenant Colonel Paul Tate, was doing his thing in Vietnam, capping a career in army intelligence." (p. 76)

Without the context of Brother-in-law's strange fascinations for both Satanism and military intelligence matters, such circumstantial oddities don't take on much significance. But Sanders makes a further observation that lends more weight to any hypothesis for investigation that might arise from these disturbing hints.

"It is possible that the Process had a baleful influence on Sirhan Sirhan since Sirhan is known, in the spring of '68, to have frequented clubs in Hollywood in the same turf as the Process was proselytizing. Sirhan was very involved in occult pursuits. He has talked several times subsequent to Robert Kennedy's death about an occult group from London which he knew about and which he really wanted to go to London to see."

And Process headquarters just happens to be in London, where they broke off from the local Scientology chapter the year President Kennedy was assassinated.

"There was one Process member named Lloyd who was working as a chef for one of the large Los Angeles hotels, either the Ambassador or the Sheraton. Lloyd was around fifty years old" and seems to have belonged to the branch of The Process called Jehovans.

"It is probably a coincidence that Sirhan seems to have visited a friend who worked in the kitchen of the Ambassador Hotel the day before he shot Senator Kennedy." (pp. 95-96)

Possibly, as paranoid as it may seem, it was not a coincidence. Could the Polanskis have been somehow involved in the conspiracy to murder Robert Kennedy? Many people with relatives or close friends in Communist bloc countries are perforce involved with the intelligence community, as may have been true of Roman Polanski, for if they don't follow orders, their loved ones in the old country are at the mercy of the secret police. And for that reason many join organizations consisting of exiles bent on liberating the homeland from Marxist rule.

Might the Tate killings have been a revenge crime for the assassination of Robert Kennedy? Might the murderers have been motivated at a more clandestine level by instigators working both sides of the fence? They would have been in a position to blackmail anyone conspiring with Manson or his followers, putting a contract out on Sharon Tate and her friends.

A somewhat far-fetched hypothesis, I grant you, but those are the kinds of notions about the disturbing links that kept occurring to me, sometimes in the form of nightmares.

Particularly since counter-cultural writer and publisher Paul Krassner was also announcing that his personal investigations had turned up numerous links between the Manson crowd, military intelligence, and the Kennedy assassinations, they were not possibilities I could easily dismiss — especially in light of what I was now learning about standard operating procedures in secret society combat within the intelligence community.

Hitler Was a Good Guy

BY the middle of 1976, it had become obvious to me in a thousand ways that my efforts to unravel the central mystery of my own life had attracted more than ample attention from someone. I could no longer afford the luxury of not thinking about Slim's brother-in-law and equally bizarre matters — as much as I would rather have been contemplating absolutely any other subject instead.

As a result I have permitted my mind to wander to the opposite extreme, that of endeavoring to remember everything about that unusual man, no matter how repulsive or insignificant, of allowing him to become the major focus of my thoughts — an individual I once found so boring and tedious that I actually wondered if he might not be prematurely senile.

Now and again I have received help from the mysterious forces that surround me in order to keep tabs on my actions. A key phrase mentioned by a stranger passing me on the street will trigger additional recollections about a conversation recorded incompletely in past notes — and I have been scribbling a constant stream of notes every day for years.

Sometimes I will discuss the case with a comparative stranger who, without admitting to inside knowledge, will ask a question so pointed as to appear quite well informed. Many is the time such a question renewed memory of another long-forgotten chat with Brother-in-law.

During the first visit to his new house, Gary asked me what seemed like an academic question: "Kerry, if one man saves the life of another man, would you agree with the notion that the first man then has the right to do whatever he wants with the life of the man he has saved?"

"I don't know," I shrugged, "but I read where the Chinese believe that if you save another man's life, then from that day forward you are to blame for any crimes he commits."

At the beginning of the next visit, he said:

"I'm interested in further discussing your opinion of this matter about one man saving the life of another man, Kerry. Now tell me: What would you say? Does the man who saves the life have the right to do whatever he wants with the life he has saved? Or not?"

I could not begin to imagine what possible difference my answer would make. "Yeah, I guess so," I finally said.

One of the first chats with Brother-in-law at his house centered around his projected book, *Hitler Was a Good Guy*, a name I loved for its shock value, but which Gary took pains to remind me was "only a working title."

"The secret to Hitler's power was that he had no power," he explained. "He was instead surrounded by powerful men — men with branches of the military, labor unions, police bureaus, organized criminal gangs at their commands. But he himself had no such direct base of power. He was a great orator who had written a book, but he possessed no direct access to a single organization. The Nazi Party was an alliance of the organizations under the men around him. Hitler was their compromise candidate because they could trust him when they could not trust one another, and they trusted him only because he had no power of his own. And that's why he was powerful. Many of the others held views much more extreme than his, but they didn't trust one another directly so they couldn't do anything about them."

A nonchalantly pedantic attitude dominated his mercurial personality as he spoke.

"I'm going to write a fictionalized chapter — a projection of what would have happened — if Martin Bormann had pulled a coup and taken over in Hitler's place, another chapter about what would have happened with Himmler in Hitler's shoes, and another one about Rosenberg. Now he was a beauty — he used to have anyone with the name 'Rosenberg' executed as soon as his troops took over a town. He was also the one who formulated the precepts of the Nazi religion, which has certain features to recommend it, incidentally."

I sat there not knowing how to react. I just didn't know how to take this guy.

"Hess was a stupid one. Literally of below average I.Q., he's the guy who parachuted into England to try to get the British to join the Germans — as Hitler, because of his racial theories, at first thought they would. Hess made that move on the advice of his astrologer. All the English did was put him in prison. He's rotting there to this day," he smirked. "Very unfair of them."

A mixture of horror and intellectual fascination left me in a state resembling paralysis.

"And when Himmler found out why Hess did it, he rounded up all the astrologers and killed them — including Hitler's astrologer — and Hitler got pissed off about that. God, was he ever pissed! Heh-heh."

That seemed to Brother-in-law a great source of amusement and he was to tell the same story many times; he seemed to find the follies of the Nazis as funny as he found their attainments admirable, which was disarming.

Later in the conversations he asked me once if I thought Rudolf Hess ought to be released from prison. I agreed that there was no purpose in keeping him jailed.

Over and over he was to remind me that there were many similarities between Nazi and Communist ideology, and that people attracted to one could frequently be recruited away to the other.

In my research, I found the diary of Paul Joseph Goebbels to be the most useful source of the types of quotations Brother-in-law said he wanted for his book — things that sounded worse than what Hitler had said.

He'd also told me to be sure to include anything any of them said against the Catholic Church, and these alleged writings of the Nazi Propaganda Minister were sufficiently anti-Catholic for that purpose.

In my own handwriting at the top of each folded-over page of letter-size paper, I dutifully wrote, "Hitler Was a Good Guy." Again in my own handwriting, I then proceeded to quote without comment all the most atrocious statements I was able to find by Goebbels and the other important Nazis. Unsuspectingly, I then turned these notes over to Brother-in-law. As I recall, he gave me ten dollars for my efforts.

Since in those days I was given to beginning writing projects with great optimism and enthusiasm and then abandoning them in favor of either a new inspiration or a more certain means of relating to the American economy, it did not strike me peculiar that Brother-in-law soon dropped further mention of his proposed magnum opus. For he seemed, if anything, even less reliable than me — what with his paranoid theories, his split personality, and his incessant repetitions.

Once or twice in our conversations he dropped a hint that he was actually "more like a mad scientist" than a Nazi or gangster, and he carefully planted the idea with me that his real name might be Tom Miethe.

Since then I was led to believe that his true identity was that of a Canadian associated with the Permindex Corporation named Louis Mortimer Bloomfield. Yet the most credible suggestion — one made by an individual named Joel Thornton — is that I was in fact talking to the Watergate burglar, E. Howard Hunt; my memory of Brother-in-law closely resembles a 1959 photo of Hunt to be found in his autobiography, *Undercover*.

> In their book, *Coup d'état in America*, Michael Canfield and Alan J. Weberman (Third Press, Joseph Okpaku Publishing Company, New York, 1975) describe an interview with Seymour Weitzman, an eye-witness to John Kennedy's shooting who ran into the parking lot behind the grassy knoll after the shots were fired.
>
> "In April 1975 Michael Canfield visited Weitzman in a home for aged veterans... Weitzman said he encountered a Secret Service agent in the parking lot who produced credentials and told him everything was under control. He described the man as being of medium height, dark hair and wearing a light windbreaker. Canfield showed him a photo of Sturgis and Barker. He immediately stated, 'Yes, that's him,' pointing to Bernard Barker."
>
> Bernard Barker, of course, attained notoriety in 1972 as one of the Watergate gate break-in gang under Hunt's direction. *Coup d'état in America* also contains reprints of the "tramp photos" of three suspects taken into custody by the Dallas police and then released mysteriously without record of arrest. These appear very much to resemble pictures of E. Howard Hunt and another Watergate burglar, Frank Sturgis, dressed in tramp clothing and walking across Dealey Plaza in police custody in the company of a third individual who could have easily been mistaken at a distance for Oswald and may have been used for that purpose, perhaps as sixth floor gunman.

Naturally I remain uncertain of his true identity. Strategies in the intelligence community are deep. Power is kept by carrying deception several steps beyond what any sane person might be inclined to suspect. Whoever he was, it is clear in retrospect that he employed all the professional techniques for covering his tracks.

Among the first and oddest things Brother-in-law was to bring up in our talks at his house were instances of freak radio reception. A woman had picked up a radio broadcast through her hair curlers. Every now and then, someone discovered their tooth fillings were sensitive to radio waves. "Things like that actually happen," he said, "although rarely."

"Yes," I answered. "I think maybe once or twice it happened to me. A few months ago, when I was living across from Lafayette Square in a little room over Fred's Inn, I seemed to hear radio programs as I was drifting into sleep during my afternoon naps — with station breaks, news, commercials, weather reports and music. When I woke up afterwards, though, I couldn't remember the call letters of the station."

Brother-in-law laughed and nodded — as if to indicate that, yes, he knew about that.

Since I had not discussed it with anyone, I dismissed his response as simply inappropriate. From such an unusual man I did not expect entirely comprehensible behavior at all times.

I neglected to add that I had also experienced audio hallucinations of a different nature when going to sleep at nights sometimes when I was in the Marines — during the interval I was serving with Lee Harvey Oswald in Marine Air Control Squadron Nine. I had written them off as a peculiar category of dreams. Nor did I tend to think that my radio program dreams experienced more recently had other than psychological causes.

I gathered early on that Brother-in-law had a penchant for the exceptionally bizarre, and that his mind tended to wander from one weird variety of trivia to another without the benefit of a healthy skepticism. Sometimes I considered the possibility that the whole works was the creation of a secret society consisting of bald-headed conspirators — for I have heard it second-hand that all the names Brother-in-law

used were those of balding men — a Fraternal Order of Bald
Eagles, if you will, bent on no less sinister a project than the
destruction of civilization.

> In the *Illuminatus!* Trilogy, (Dell Books, 1975) a series of
> farcical novels by Robert Shea and Robert Anton Wilson
> that presents an essentially romantic view of the assassins,
> but seems to be drawn from inside knowledge about con-
> spiracy politics, the hero named Hagbard Celine argues:
> "Civilization is privilege — or Private Law... And we all
> know where Private Law comes from... Out of the barrel
> of a gun, in the words of a gentleman whose bluntness you
> would appreciate."

Rich people like the Rockefellers, Gary took pains to remind
me, pressure the government to make laws designed to make
business difficult or impossible for their competitors.

I would acknowledge this, but was always quick to add that
such examples of Private Law, so to speak, were not what
was defined as pure *laissez-faire*, and I thereby dismissed the
actual as inconsequential because it was not an aspect of our
economic system Ayn Rand deemed worth defending.

> Ayn Rand's novel, *Atlas Shrugged*, (Random House, 1957)
> had made a lasting impression on me when I read it in
> the shipping-out barracks in Japan and on board ship on
> my way back to the States. Her arguments for *laissez-faire*
> economics, delivered by her characters in long philosophical
> speeches, convinced me that global prosperity absolutely
> required unrestricted production for profit.
>
> That view represented quite a jump from the vaguely
> Marxist position I had acquired serving overseas in the
> Marines, just previous to that, as a result of my experience of
> the conditions in nations supposedly under U. S. protection,
> namely in the Philippines and Taiwan, combined with the
> shock of the U-2 scandal — but not deeply grounded in
> reasoned economic analysis.
>
> My intense hatred — I cannot honestly call it anything
> else — for John F. Kennedy was largely based upon the
> startling similarities between New Frontier economic policies
> and those propounded by Wesley Mouch, the antagonist in
> *Atlas Shrugged* whose actions in government office destroy
> the American economy.

In these early conversations at his house, Brother-in-law spoke
to me frequently of Jesuits. What he said was easy to dismiss
as typical Ku Klux Klan anti-Catholicism.

That the Jesuits deliberately persecute people in order to "test" their adherence to Christian virtues, from which they themselves seem exempt, was something upon which he insisted. He added that one Jesuit ruse was to tempt their victims into blasphemy — into calling themselves Christ — and then to slay them.

> According to Peter Viereck in Metapolitics: Roots of the Nazi Mind: "Rosenberg reserves much of his most ferocious hate for the Jesuits and the Catholic hierarchy. Therefore his outline for the New Order consciously imitates Jesuit techniques and the Roman hierarchy."

In my mind's eye, that conjured up images of black-robed priests attacking unarmed victims with swords or daggers, and that seemed most improbable — but I held back from expressing doubt.

Sometimes when I appeared especially shocked by something Brother-in-law said, he would remind me that in the Vatican there is a Devil's Advocate whose job it is to present the arguments of Satan to the Pope, so the Pope can refute them. Then he would add that he himself was something of a Devil's advocate, in that he didn't adhere to all the ideas he was expressing.

Building secret societies that would employ some of the techniques of the Jesuits was an idea mentioned, perhaps conveyed from some other conspirator's discussions of plans in the manner of such an advocate, as Brother-in-law also warned, or promised, "The day will come when you will find yourself surrounded by Devil's advocates; if you answer all their arguments, you will become philosopher-king."

The Philosopher-King

GARY said many times over again that the best government was that of the philosopher-king. At great length he would go on about the traits a philosopher-king should possess — such as being able to distinguish between coincidence and conspiracy. Another trait he mentioned was not punishing messengers for bringing bad news.

Surrounding a man with liars until he became so disgusted with lying that he would not tolerate an untruth was one of his ideas for preparing the philosopher-king for the job. On a separate occasion he told me that someday I would be surrounded by liars, and if I could find a way to make them tell me the truth I would become philosopher-king.

"Kerry, there are tribal secret societies that surround their king with beautiful women all his life and watch him make love to them — then they sacrifice him."

That sounded like a dubious honor.

"Kerry, do you think a philosopher-king should have a good enough memory to remember something for thirteen years?"

Of course.

"Rosenberg should not be accused of wanting dictatorship as a principle," Viereck tells us in *Metapolitics*, adding soon afterwards: "He follows the spirit of Wagner's complicated distinction between King and monarch. Rejecting alike government by parliament or by kaiser (monarch), Rosenberg demands the Volk-king, the hero-dictator risen from the ranks, whom Jahn and Wagner prophesied.

"The qualities and justification of the Volk-king are outlined in the Führer section of the chapter on Wagner's metaphysics. This Wagnerian concept is basic to Nazism. Rosenberg says: 'We want to see in a German king a person like ourselves... But yet the incarnation of a hero myth... '

"The gist of the Führer myth is that the Führer is (incarnates) the Volk, instead of ruling it detachedly like monarch or economic class or representing it like a democrat. The Führer is an organic part of the Volk instead of a detached atom. This myth is absolutely basic to Hitler's rule today. Of course, it is only a myth...

"Kerry, I think the philosopher-king should be a very gentle person, someone with the soul of a poet, but that he ought to be surrounded for protection by mad dogs — the worst and meanest badasses around."

Though wondering what type of administration that would produce, I kept my speculations to myself.

"Kerry, you know at the end of the war Hitler came up on the radio and gave a speech calling for the werewolves of Germany to come to the aid of the Nazi cause."

"Yes, you have mentioned that before," was my response after the first telling.

"Do you believe the saying that power corrupts and that absolute power corrupts absolutely?"

"Yes. It's like Ayn Rand says, 'Who will protect us from our protectors?' That's an old Roman saying, but it's in Latin."

"You've also heard the saying, 'Curiosity killed the cat.'"

"Yeah, that's a bunch of shit, though. More cats have been killed from lacking the curiosity to look both ways before crossing the street, probably, than by too much curiosity."

"You might just want to keep it in mind anyway. Someday you may find yourself in a situation where it is true."

"I doubt that very much."

"Well — just don't forget you could be wrong."

I was not inclined to persist in arguments with a man who might be both armed and dangerous, not to mention insane.

"Kerry," he once said, "one good way to construct the government of the philosopher-king would be to arrange it so that whoever was king didn't know it, and in such a way that he would be used for decision-making purposes while standing in line at the store and places like that."

So incomprehensible a notion seemed academic to me, but I saw no reason to say as much. A stupid idea anyhow, this philosopher-king jazz, because even if a dictator managed to rule benevolently, what was to guarantee an equally kind and wise successor? That objection expressed, Slim and Gary both answered, "Yes," and looked smug, as if they had already thought about that one and solved it.

As for our unwitting philosopher-king, Slim contributed something now about that idea: "As one good way to do it. Not the only way."

"Sure," I said, eyeing them both with a mixture of skepticism and boredom, "that sounds like one good way to have a philosopher-king."

"What do you think about the ombudsmen they have in Scandinavian countries to help ordinary people gain access to government? What about having people like that in our nation? Do you think that would be a good idea?"

I did.

Once Brother-in-law also asked me if I didn't agree that the philosopher-king should also be someone who could keep "state secrets."

I routinely concurred.

E. Howard Hunt writes in *Undercover* that he once received a cable signed jointly by Richard Bissell and Tracy Barnes summoning him to headquarters:

"Bissell had succeeded Frank Wisner as chief of the Clandestine Services, and after hospitalization brought on by overwork Wisner had been assigned to the relatively relaxed post of London chief of station. As a special aide to Allen Dulles, Bissell had created the concept of the U-2 aircraft, then managed that successful program. I had held several perfunctory meetings with Bissell during consultation periods in Washington and a lengthier one during a Latin American chiefs of station conference in Lima, Peru.

"As principal assistant to Bissell, Tracy Barnes told me, I was needed for a new project, much like the one on which I had worked for him in overthrowing Jacobo Arbenz. My job, Tracy told me, would be essentially the same as my earlier one — chief of political action for a project recommended by the National Security Council and just approved by President Eisenhower: to assist Cuban exiles in overthrowing Castro. Representative Cuban leaders were grouping in Florida and New York, and my responsibility would be to organize them into a broadly representative government-in-exile that would, once Castro was disposed of, form a provisional government in Cuba... "

Such an assignment might have given Hunt the opportunity to experiment with unusual forms of government.

Witches Against Cæsars

So hideous were many of Brother-in-law's fascinations as to defy every shred of taste or morality. Not only did he seem to relish the atrocities of the Nazis, but tortures and brutalities from any other period of history were of equal interest to him.

He would often repeat a platitude, and I would reply by mentioning yet another one; he would tell a joke, and I would and try to top it with one of similar taste; he would tell me something horrid and I would think of something just as gory to say to him.

Jessica had related to me a particularly ghoulish story she had heard in history class, about warfare between Renaissance clans, where a family invited an enemy to a feast and served him the flesh of his own child. Predictably, Brother-in-law seemed quite pleased with that story when I repeated it to him.

I wondered what kind of implacable hatred could underlie such gleeful ferocity.

But when Gary spoke of his "philosopher-king" it evoked in my imagination visions of an old man in trunks on a blanket with his legs crossed, surrounded by an orderly circle of Devil's advocates of restrained and gentle nature, presenting formal arguments with incense burning in the background. It was an image from a Hindu holy picture, quite distant from everything ugly — except for the unavoidably relevant tales of human perfidy. Because of his training, my imaginary king was able to resolve all disputes in the manner of Solomon. Not then understanding anything about the S.N.A.F.U. factors involved anywhere there is not communication between equals, I thought of it as a helluva nicer way to make a living than telephone soliciting.

If he really didn't have me in mind for the job, I didn't want to seem so low as to envy anyone else who might be appointed — to resent the line of work itself — like some raving anarchist who was bitter at everyone and moreover had the nerve to look smug about it.

If perhaps the idea Gary dreamed of wasn't functional, there were still always the aesthetic considerations. Omar Khayyam never wove such fantasies as these in the minds of his Sultans. And that was so unusual for Gary, who generally preferred to discuss something ugly.

That there was hope for the Jesuits was among his moderating opinions; they were intelligent people who could be reformed and made useful, "If only the Pope could be proved fallible."

> In 1975 I received a press release from Robert Anton Wilson stating that Pope Paul had been granting audiences to a spirit medium named Matthew Manning, who claimed to have placed him in communication with the souls of a number of Catholic saints.

"Kerry, the Jesuits say, 'Give us a child until he is seven, and we will make him ours forever.' Hitler said the same thing. I wonder who would win in a contest between them."

Darkly, he spoke of building Satanic secret societies within the Society of Jesus, cults that practiced human sacrifice and conjured up the old Saxon fertility deities. During these conversations, whenever I complained about Christianity for any reason, he assured me that Hitler was planning to "do in" the Christians as soon as he took care of the Jews — that the actual faith of the Nazis had been a resurrection of the old pagan "religion of the soil."

> Vincent Bugliosi reported in *Helter-Skelter*, written in collaboration with Curt Gentry (W. W. Norton & Company, 1974): "The Process, also known as the Church of the Final Judgment, was a very strange cult. Led by one Robert DeGrimston, t/n Robert Moore — who, like Manson, was an ex-Scientologist — its members worshiped both Satan and Christ." (p. 244)

There were times when I would complain to Brother-in-law about the irrational brutality of the Nazis, or their authoritarianism, and he would remind me that "the German family unit, with the importance of the German father — its patriarchal structure — is probably to blame for much of that."

"Maybe so," I conceded.

"The original European tribalists did not even worship a father-god as their primary deity. Why do you think the

Mother of Jesus is so much more important to European Catholics than Christ or Jehovah? The Church never could have won their ancestors over without the cult of the Virgin. And with the Church came Roman imperialism, Kerry — so it was imperialism that introduced patriarchy to Europe."

What exciting possibilities came to mind! Druids forming ancient secret societies to combat the foreign oppressor from Rome, leading to the organization of alliances between tribes of Visigoths and Vandals — gradually surrounding the heart of the empire with raging colonial peoples who would bring it crumbling to its foundations.

The witches against the Cæsars! It was a saga belonging beside the legend of Spartacus in the annals of history.

One thing Brother-in-law often mentioned the concept of the scapegoat. He told me that it was originally termed "escape goat" and that it was derived from a tribal ritual mentioned in Leviticus. "The custom was to take two goats and to kill one of them and to sprinkle the altar with its blood, and then to take the other goat and bestow upon it the sins of the tribe," he said. "Then they let the escape goat go, to wander in the wilderness."

Once I responded that there was a novel called *The Scapegoat*, as I would say for lack of anything more appropriate, that there was a novel called *The Devil's Advocate* when he would touch on that subject.

Of one or the other of these books, I think the latter by Taylor Caldwell written under a pseudonym, he would always reply, "And that is a very good book, too."

With a demented gleam in his eye, he also spoke once or twice of building a secret society where "at a certain point in time, all the members have to kill each other."

To my mind it sounded like an expensive way to purchase cheap thrills.

There are many respects in which I look back in astonishment at my own stupidity. Sitting there entertaining the notions Brother-in-law presented, I never for a moment thought to connect anything he said with my own actual future, much less with the present.

Yet this was a time in my life when I was a vocal atheist in a city about ninety-five percent Catholic.

Most of my friends in those early days in New Orleans met at a Friday night discussion group in the Quarter. Among the regulars was a quiet, very intellectual painter named John Kamus.

Both Ola and Jessica had arrived there upon different occasions, in John's company, the first time I met them.

"No wonder she's an atheist!" exclaimed Ivan, the discussion group's host, when he learned Jessica's father was president of the Holy Name Society and her mother belonged to a number of Catholic auxiliary organizations.

Later I'd convinced John Kamus to read *Atlas Shrugged*. We then met in a restaurant to discuss, over coffee and sandwiches, Ayn Rand's philosophy, which he didn't find very compelling.

Not long afterwards I mentioned to Gary that John Kamus at least agreed with Ayn Rand in that he also liked Aristotle.

Brother-in-law said, "Now, Kerry, that is a Catholic idea — that admiration of Aristotle."

"Look, I'm sure John Kamus isn't a Catholic."

Brother-in-law indicated that perhaps my certainty might be out of place.

I probably tried to change the subject, because I recall his annoying persistence in pointing out to me that the Society of Jesus had plainclothes spies.

I was very uncomfortable about that idea. I would have felt disreputable even suspecting John Kamus to be a Catholic spy.

As much as I detested religion, accusations like that sounded little different to me than the racist remarks Gary made with chronic persistence.

So You Want to Be a Spy?

"KERRY, what do you think of snuff movies?" Brother-in-law was seated in his characteristic elbow-on-knees position upon a footstool near the center of the living room. I was sitting at my usual place near the door. It must have been between ten and eleven on a Saturday morning. We had just arrived at the house.

"What are snuff movies?" I asked.

"Those are films they make in Mexico," he said, "where a woman thinks she is going to be shot with a fake gun as part of the script, but they shoot her with a real gun, instead."

I could tell right away it was going to be one of those days when I wished I'd never met the sonofabitch.

"I think that's a great idea," I lied. My enthusiasm now was entirely sycophantic. Humor the crazy bastard, I figured. That way at least I would minimize my own chances of winding up as a star in one of his bloody productions.

I added for good measure that killing was natural and that it was my ambition before my life was over to break every single one of the Ten Commandments — nihilistic thoughts I had actually entertained from time to time, but which were thoroughly inappropriate to the discussion.

Gary and Slim looked at one another and grinned, communicating great delight with my response.

In addition to *The Idle Warriors*, I was attempting to write another novel. My rationale for continuing this harrowing relationship was to gather precisely this type of information about the local Mafia, in order to lend authenticity to *The Color Wheel*, a book I was writing about all the different kinds of characters in New Orleans. But the trauma was starting to get the best of my curiosity.

Glaring at me with evil glee, Gary ended the discussion of snuff films by saying, "Yeah, I'm going to get people into murdering other people on film, and then I'm going to build a network of blackmailed murderers."

Says Ed Sanders in *The Family*: "Once this writer was in Los Angeles posing as a New York pornography dealer with Andy Warhol out-takes for sale. There was an opportunity at that time to purchase seven hours of assorted erotic films including Manson porn collected during the pre-trial investigations. But the price was $250,000. Then there was a note which was written to a reporter by a person named Chuck, a friend of Gary Hinman, claiming possession of films of 'Malibu and San Francisco axe murders.'

"Later it turned out that a Los Angeles dope dealer allegedly sold a film depicting the ritual murder of a woman to a famous New York artist whose name will not be mentioned here." (p. 228)

Sanders not only links the Manson Family with the making of snuff films, but finds reason to think The Process Church was involved with them in such activities.

Another exchange in which I responded fearfully because of Brother-in-law's fierce attitudes, I regret as much as the chat about snuff films.

Once he said to me: "Kerry, the Cubans are mostly of Spanish blood, and Spaniards are white people. So if there is another war, and if there is some way of influencing where it occurs, I think it would be good if that war was against somebody other than the Cubans — such as an Oriental race. Don't you?"

"I think there should be a war against Communism," I commented.

He also used to say, "You know, Kerry, occasionally Fidel Castro turns up at bars right here in Jefferson Parish."

"You're putting me on!"

"No. He sneaks into the country and visits bars in Jefferson Parish, and sometimes he and his friends beat up on a bar girl and kill her."

I didn't know whether to believe that or not, but there didn't seem any point in arguing about it. On subsequent repetitions of the story I would just say, "Yeah, you said that already."

"Kerry, do you realize that professional spies never look like spies? That they don't always even try to remain inconspicuous?"

"Yes, I read a book called *So You Want to be a Spy?* once. Sometimes the best cover is to be very conspicuous — to walk through the front door with a duchess under each arm."

"Yes. And another cover is to look ordinary."

Never did the conversational theme veer from Nazism for long.

"You know, there were assassination plots against Hitler." We would discuss these at great length; he was extremely well informed about them.

"Something else happened near the end of the war, when Hitler could no longer hide from himself that he was losing. He gave orders that all the German stockpiles of nerve gas be released into the air. He wanted to take everybody with him, but Nazis under him in the chain of command quietly refused to carry out his orders." That was another one he brought up again and again.

Sometimes Gary came off as a wizened pipe-smoking social philosopher and it seemed ungracious to think of him as anything else.

About the roots of Nazism he spoke intelligently.

"Nazism, Kerry, is a reactionary ideology — but it is in reaction against something. And it's worth thinking about. What is this thing it is reactionary against? Roman imperialism — its heritage in culture, resulting in colonialism in politics!"

For as we both knew, neither Germany nor Italy had empires of colonies sending them cheap raw materials, until they undertook their fascist rampages. "Kerry, it was a reactionary movement against imperialism — not a pure one, but those were its roots."

Another time he asked me what I thought of recruiting people of various, conflicting anti-imperialist ideologies to the same organization — a secret society constructed for the purpose of destroying imperialism. Not only did it then seem to me an excellent idea, but in spite of all that has happened since then I cannot quarrel with the basic concept.

Hideous Dynamics

W^E sometimes went places together, all three of us, before or after talking at Brother-in-law's house. Usually Slim and I would ride along with Gary as he took care of his mysterious business.

Once we went into Waterbury's drug store at the corner of Camp and Canal, and Slim and I sat at the counter of the soda fountain while Brother-in-law excused himself to "run an errand."

About the amount of time was involved that it would have taken to go next door and borrow, say, a pocket wire recorder from Guy Banister's office, where all FBI and CIA anti-Castro activities were coordinated with exile training operations.

> If Brother-in-law did borrow a wire recorder from Guy Banister that day, it is an important clue in the assassination, and also serves as further indication that he may have actually been E. Howard Hunt.
>
> Guy Banister was Director of Division Five of the Federal Bureau of Investigation, the anti-Communist department. In those days we now know he was working closely with Hunt and the Double-Check Corporation of Miami, a Central Intelligence Agency front working with Cuban exiles.
>
> Brother-in-law never mentioned Banister by name to me, though he repeatedly reminded me of the function of Division Five of the FBI. However, I was already acquainted with Banister. For the woman who was finally hired to type the last draft of *The Idle Warriors* manuscript, Joyce Talley, introduced me to her literature professor at Louisiana State University in New Orleans — a gentleman named Martin McCauliffe — who in turn introduced me one evening in the Bourbon House to Guy Banister, calling him simply "a friend." This occurred during the summer of 1961 after I was working full time at American Photocopy Equipment Company and no longer had sufficient time of my own to put the finishing touches on the draft of the novel.
>
> Both Martin McCullough and Guy Banister were chiefly interested in my book, and in reading sample chapters of it, on what was probably a pretext that Joyce Talley's praise had aroused their interest.
>
> Banister's office first came to public attention in the summer of 1963 when Lee Harvey Oswald was to use that address on the Fair-Play-for-Cuba leaflets he distributed on Canal Street. Unfortunately, since I was out of town at

the time, I did not learn about this event until after the assassination.

After conversing at Brother-in-law's house that day, we returned to Waterbury's in the evening and again Slim and I sat waiting while Gary "ran an errand."

During either the first or second of those intervals, *Where Have All The Flowers Gone?* was playing on the fountain jukebox.

"Brother-in-law likes that song," Slim said with a chuckle.

"I know," I answered. "That's what he told me."

"You know, that's how he makes his money — stirring up wars for suckers like that to die in. He's that kind of guy. He hires himself out to people who make munitions, etcetera and so forth. And he's right, they never do learn."

To myself I remember thinking: Yeah, maybe.

Possibly that day we sat waiting in the drug store was the same day that I was endeavoring to obtain from Brother-in-law some abortion-causing pills for Jessica, illegally. Jessica thought she was pregnant and her staunchly Catholic parents were not even aware we were making love.

I was anxious to obtain the pills Slim said his brother-in-law could supply, and it seemed like we went everywhere in town first. To a restaurant for coffee at one point, to an anonymous house in the suburbs at another.

Brother-in-law went inside for a minute as Slim and I waited in the car. Gary seemed to be enjoying my dependence on him and seemed to be drawing it out as long as possible.

At long last, we went way out in the country and near a clump of trees somewhere he gave me the name of a druggist who "even sells paregoric to little children — he'll sell you anything." As we stood there he also described in rather nauseating detail how the abortion pills worked — gradually poisoning the woman's body until it rejected the fetus, because it could not support both life systems at once in that toxic condition.

So dangerous did it sound that I never went to the druggist. Instead, I tried an experiment in psychological medicine. From a Katz and Besthoff pharmacy I obtained an envelope meant for mailing a credit card application. Then I obtained some Hershey's "M & M" candies (because they looked like pills and that brand carried no markings on the candies themselves), sorted out the white ones, and slipped them into the envelope.

They worked perfectly: Jessica had her period within an hour of swallowing the first placebo. As I hoped and suspected, she had been suffering only from tension brought on by the fear of pregnancy.

> In retrospect, though, it seems to me that Brother-in-law probably accomplished his purpose. In his possession was very possibly a recording of our conversation, useful for inflaming Catholics against me whenever so doing suited his purpose — as it may have five or six years later when Jim Garrison first tried to recruit me as a witness against Clay Shaw, only to suddenly become suspicious of me in a way that admitted to no effective reply.
>
> Such a recording, together with my handwritten quotes of the Nazi Propaganda Minister discussing the desirability of eradicating the Catholics, once the "Jewish problem" had been solved, would have served not simply to alienate Garrison, but also to give people like Jessica's father fits of holy rage. That would have been a perfect means for throwing a monkey wrench into a probe being conducted in a heavily Roman Catholic city about predominantly Roman Catholic Cuban exiles.

One of Brother-in-law's oft-repeated statements was: "You know, Kerry, the Nazis had flying saucers towards the end of World War II."

> "The real story on 'flying saucers' is finally coming to light," asserted the 7 April 1950 *U. S. News & World Report*, and I mentioned to Brother-in-law having read in the early fifties an article to the same effect in *Reader's Digest*. "What the saucers are, how they operate, and how they have been tested in U. S. All can be told in detail at this time," continues the *U. S. News* piece confidently.
>
> "That story, without violating present security regulations, points to these basic conclusions by engineers competent to appraise reports of reliable observers:
>
> "Flying saucers, seen by hundreds of competent observers over most parts of U. S., are accepted as real. Evidence is that they are aircraft of a revolutionary type, a combination of helicopter and fast jet plane. They conform to well-known principles of aerodynamics. An early model of these saucers was built by U. S. engineers in 1942, achieved

more than 100 successful test flights. That project was taken over by Navy in wartime. Much more advanced models are now being built. Just where present saucers are being built is indicated by evidence now available.

"In more detail, the story pieced together from non-secret testimony of responsible U. S. scientists, private observers and military officials is this:

"Early models of the flying saucer, pictured on this page and the next, were built by U. S. government engineers of the National Advisory Committee for Aeronautics. Similar flying-saucer projects were begun in Germany and Italy at the same time, in 1942." (p. 13)

Another article ascribing flying saucers to the U. S. Air Force appears in an early Fifties back issue of *Reader's Digest*, in addition to the article mentioned above.

But searching the *Reader's Guide to Periodical Literature* for the years since those pieces appeared, one looks in vain for any contribution to flying saucer lore that attributes such a mundane origin. Conspicuous, in fact, for their absence are any speculations that flying saucers might be government aircraft of any type.

In recent years the mass media, not known for paying much attention normally to the notions of cranks, has given enormous publicity to the dubious idea that U.F.O.'s have existed since prehistoric times and even that the Garden of Eden may have been populated by a couple of space cadets from other planets.

Books about flying saucers are the same way, although in one that soundly debunks the so-called archaeological evidence for cavemen from outer space there appears a photograph of a U. S. government flying saucer as well as the following sentence: "During April 1950, radio reporter Henry J. Taylor claimed that flying saucers were highly secret American inventions, and for a short time a satisfactory explanation seemed to be available." But no mention is made of why such a thesis was only viable for "a short time" in Morris Goran's *The Modern Myth: Ancient Astronauts and UFOs* (A. S. Barnes & Co., 1978).

A thinking student of this popular media flying saucer literature cannot help but wonder if the invisible hand of very stringent intelligence community censorship did not muzzle free debate at some point in the early fifties. Thereafter, providing the motivations of the censors were sufficiently strong, as they appear to have been, any other crime, such as an assassination, could be assured of a powerful cover-up if only its perpetrators could somehow involve it inextricably with truthful data about flying saucers.

And I would say, "Yes, you mentioned that already. They also had developed the jet airplane by then."

Looking at me with a grin, he would say, "Yes they had. Furthermore, they were very close to having an atomic bomb."

"Yes. I heard, in fact, that they were working with something called 'heavy water,' used in hydrogen bomb development."

"We can say they were on the verge of arming themselves with nuclear power," he concluded with a sense of satisfaction that I took for Nazi boasting.

I do not know why the obvious possibility that Brother-in-law was recording these sessions did not occur to me.

> In *Appointment in Dallas* (Hugh McDonald Publishing, 1975) by Hugh C. McDonald as told to Geoffrey Bocca, on page 165, a mysterious CIA-KGB hit man known in the book as "Saul" and allegedly one of the John Kennedy assassins describes Oswald's behavior during an interval when "Saul" claims to have been tailing Lee in Mexico City during the summer of 1963:
>
> "He was always alone at mealtime, and he talked audibly to himself, all the time. His snatches of conversation were not rational. He seemed obsessed with 'Marina' — I know now, of course, that that was his Russian wife — and kept saying the words 'shining hero,' and giggling to himself."
>
> Had Oswald by this time discovered that there was an eavesdropping device concealed on his person, it is possible that his chatter was more rational than might be supposed, particularly if he was using the same type of intelligence community cant that might also explain seemingly nonsensical passages in Sirhan Sirhan's journal. While such a hypothesis may seem far-fetched at first glance, it is not at all inconsistent with the things Brother-in-law said to me about possible uses of electronic surveillance.

Brother-in-law brought up the subject himself at the beginning of one of the conversations — telling me that the European wire recorder was much superior to the method popular in the U.S., particularly for the clandestine recording of a conversation.

"You know they can also edit and doctor recorded materials to make it sound like you said things you did not say."

I always pointed out that such fakes could be detected technologically. "That's right, Kerry," he would say in a tone of inexplicable sympathy. "They can."

All these chats contained a sense at the time both of desolation and desperation, in that they seemed to be the brainchild of desperate individuals.

Sometimes, for a glimpse of a moment, I would wonder if Slim and Gary had maybe murdered both their wives, allegedly sisters, and were now "on the lam" in a terrible Leopold-Loeb crunch that required an entire, cumbersome, hopelessly complex conspiracy to explain their actions to the world.

Upon those fleeting occasions, my psychological defense was to forget about it as unlikely — and then to dismiss lingering remnants of the unpleasant possibility with the probability that no such conspiracy would succeed anyhow.

In other words, a combination of intellectual cowardice and irresponsibility for problems I felt unequipped to solve permitted me to lock the whole experience away somewhere in the unvisited archives of my memory.

Over and over he asked me if I thought there could be any such thing as the perfect crime. I was extremely skeptical of any such possibility, for in those days I understood almost nothing about the nature of practical politics.

Brother-in-law would say to me, "I think I can commit the perfect crime."

My mental context contained images of Carlos Marcello and his friends. I believe, but am not certain, that Gary said he had grown up in Kansas City in the neighborhood of someone involved in the Ma Barker gang. I envisioned him as having in mind something along the lines of the Brinks robbery.

"Maybe," I said, "but I doubt that you'll get away with it." Not only was my perspective distorted by his cover, but also by years of cops and robbers movies and television programs such as *Dragnet*.

Yet it also passed through my mind that a crime wave launched by Brother-in-law would be characterized by the bizarre — embellished with Nazi mystique, perhaps, and possibly involving "snuff movies" and weird religions.

Partial Enlightenment

WE met in spirit in a black, moist, gnomic forest, fertilized already so tragically by means of such methodically cruel methods as to sometimes frighten even Hitler himself. We seemed to stand there at times in misty heartbreak, and commented to one another about the forbidden beauty of the flowers they had fed themselves upon the decayed flesh of those millions of victims.

Serenely superior to the trauma, Brother-in-law had the fierce willingness to admit to the mayhem, to discuss it in as much detail as any normal person. Then he would insist that you look with open eyes at the quaint drama of these bizarre foreigners who combined science with superstition, politics with astrology, police brutality with unorthodox epistemology — to somehow produce something hideously dynamic.

Sometimes he was like a brilliant chemist, prowling through the exploded ruins of the laboratory of a colleague who had hovered at the instant of his unfortunate tragedy upon catalyzing the Holy Grail. This fellow knew better than to believe in the efficacy of ancient philosopher's stones, but the possibility of synthesizing one had occurred to him.

Our political scientist took a cold, curious attitude towards others. His colleague's experiments upon *homo sapiens* evidenced in the debris did not disturb him, but only seemed silly in their extravagance. Why cause millions of people to suffer when with a fraction of the number of victims, tormented conspicuously enough, one could probably perform the equivalent sociological alchemy? The only misfortune, it seemed to him, was that the state of the art was that of alchemy, not of nuclear physics.

Whenever Brother-in-law was not boring, he was terrifying — yet somehow he seemed, perhaps because of the simple protective effects of trauma on my part, to be more boring than anything else.

Another psychological phenomenon took place within me in his company — a perceptible draining of energy through the bottom of my stomach or spine.

Upon reading Omar V. Garrison's *Tantra*, a book of Tibetan
sexual yoga, I discovered that such an effect is produced
in victims of Tantric black magic. According to the Avon
paperback, *The Occult Reich*, Hitler often seemed to visitors
and associates to function as a human energy vacuum —
with a parasitical vigor that just sapped every room of its
energy when the little man strode in. Every now and then
I continue to meet an individual who has this effect on me,
independent of any personality traits, and I have talked to
others who have at one time or another felt the same awful
drain of energy in the presence of a mysteriously enervating
individual.

I have heard this phenomenon can be produced with drugs,
particularly with belladonna. As I recall, Brother-in-law was
a host who served a lukewarm cup of weak instant coffee when
I first arrived and then dispensed with hospitality altogether.
The cup was made of plastic and shaped like a tea cup. It
seems I was always sitting there, drowsier than I wanted to
admit, though by no means heavily drugged, if drugged at all,
wishing to hell the creep would at least offer me some decent
coffee.

It is also a distinct possibility that upon other occasions I
was placed in a formal hypnotic trance. Once Brother-in-law
discussed the Bridey Murphy case with great enthusiasm and
asked me if I thought further examples of reincarnational
memory uncovered with hypnosis should be researched — but
adequately, he emphasized, by someone with resources.

When I objected that I did not believe in reincarnation,
he replied with sympathetic approval, "Neither do I, Kerry,
but I think the possibility should be investigated anyhow,
by someone with more money than those guys who wrote
the Bridey Murphy book, someone who could conduct a very
thorough investigation."

He made sure to obtain my agreement. But I do not
remember personally volunteering to be the subject of any
such probe.

I do possess a distinct memory of sitting with Slim, late
one afternoon, close to twilight, in a corner bar in some
podunk Louisiana town, waiting for Brother-in-law to return.
All I remember is that we were sipping beer in a place that
resembled in structure the Napoleon House, with openings to

the street instead of walls on two sides, but plainer — with Seven-Up signs instead of wrought-iron frills. I cannot at this point recall how we got there or where we went afterwards.

Possibly related to an earlier time is a memory of breakfasting with Slim one blazing morning in a tiny restaurant on Lake Pontchartrain, with Brother-in-law inside a houseboat just across the narrow dock from the front window of the café. Again I don't recall how we got there or where we went afterwards.

More than once I have wondered, though, if I was hypnotized aboard that houseboat that day, perhaps by means of drugs, and then methodically programmed. For I have a number of memories which are dreamlike in quality and seem unrelated to anything else that ever happened to me, except that they are vaguely associated with Brother-in-law.

Woody Guthrie singing about the "arch and the stones" in one of his albums reminded me vividly of these disassociated fragments of memory, pertaining to images of myself as the "first post-revolutionary man" of uncharacteristically utopian and romantic Marxist rhetoric, and as a lonely anarchist harmonica player wandering through America.

Also I seem to recall having received instructions regarding a future mission of saving the U. S. from a Russian invasion. I have a sense of being told that I would be able to rely on the radio for help, just by listening to the music.

Such things cause me to speculate that Brother-in-law may have been a high-level double agent who sold projects to hypnotically program me to both Russian intelligence and Division Five of the FBI — without anyone but Slim knowing what an outrageous practical joke he was playing on us all.

Swept up in the beauty of an abstraction, I was not paying any attention whatsoever to what was happening with this man in this room in this particular here and now — so I freely granted him permission to brainwash me.

Zen Masters call that the danger of partial enlightenment!

A scene I recall vividly took place as the three of us were returning from a trip somewhere, walking across the gravel in front of Gary's house. I had been discussing the building of a mass movement, a great Objectivist army of tax protesters marching into Washington, singing songs and shouting slogans in the manner of a Civil Rights demonstration.

"No," said Brother-in-law as we approached his door, "that isn't what you want. To overthrow the government takes an organization that is neither fish nor fowl — something that cannot be readily categorized, with some of the aspects of a bureaucracy and others of organized crime. That way, it will be nearly invisible to the average person."

Lacking the necessary color and flamboyance to interest me, and sounding rather sinister besides, that idea turned me off. I tucked it away in the back of my mind as a warning.

Once we talked at length about the time a few years earlier when the U. S. intervened secretly in Guatemala to overthrow a leftist regime. Brother-in-law asked me if I didn't think that was a good policy, and of course in those days I did.

I went on to recite a few facts about the incident I'd read in a national magazine, something which seemed to gratify him, and thereupon he spoke knowledgeably about the operation in the manner of someone who had troubled himself to become quite well informed about it, but I don't recall his mentioning the CIA in that respect.

We also spoke of the capture of the Soviet spy, Rudolph Abel, and of what a brilliant victory for U. S. espionage that had been. I do not remember, however, whether or not we ever discussed the trade of Abel for our U-2 pilot, Francis Gary Powers, made by the Kennedy Administration. However, since the U-2 planes took off and landed at Atsugi when I was overseas in the Marines, in an aura of official mystery until the U-2 incident involving Powers, the subject of the U-2 was of personal interest to me.

> In *Undercover*, E. Howard Hunt mentions that many of the uniformed officers working with him at one time had been in private life attorneys. "Among those I came to know," he writes, "were Navy Lieutenant James Donovan, who was later to defend GRU Colonel Rudolf Abel, the Soviet spy, and who was instrumental in exchanging him for U-2 pilot Gary Powers." Hunt also discusses the U-2 project in his book, mentioning those involved in its development, etc.

Haunting Fanaticism

BROTHER-IN-LAW liked to grin and chew on his pipe and allow a considerable silence to pass before changing the subject from one of his little reminders to the next one.

"You know, Kerry, there is a member of the Rockefeller family who travels around the country making Satanist human sacrifices. And he has a whole set-up, like a traveling road show, he takes with him for that purpose. His name is Tracy Barnes. Can you remember that, Kerry? Tracy Barnes."

In the quiet that followed I wondered if such a fantastic story could be true. Certainly the rich could not be murdering the common people in the most outrageous of all possible manners and be getting away with it simply because they were the rich, and not the poor! That seemed highly unlikely, to say the least.

But then, if by some quirk in our system of government or economics it were true, there was nothing I could be expected to do about it, anyhow. So why this urgent insisting to remember?

As an Ayn Rand Objectivist I thought it my rational duty to assume innocence without hard evidence of guilt, particularly when rich capitalists were the objects of accusation. For as Ayn Rand incessantly pointed out, there were swarms of envious parasites under every rock, just looking for safe ways to snipe at the rich and productive industrialist.

> Writes E. Howard Hunt in *Undercover*, "Then to my welcome surprise I was summoned to the office of C. Tracy Barnes, a wartime associate of Allen Dulles, Wall Street lawyer and brother-in-law of Joe Bryan. Barnes swore me to special secrecy and revealed that the National Security Council under Eisenhower and Vice President Nixon had ordered the overthrow of Guatemala's Communist regime. If I accepted the proposed assignment, Barnes told me, it would be as head of the project's propaganda and political action staff, and he added that naturally no clandestine project had higher priority than this."

Brother-in-law was to tell the same story about Tracy Barnes and the Satanist human sacrifices a number of times. That I should not forget it seemed especially urgent to him.

> According to Carl Oglesby in *The Yankee and the Cowboy War*, "It was in reality such 'hard-nosed liberals' as the CIA's Tracy Barnes and Edward Lansdale (for whom Ellsberg worked in Vietnam) and Kennedy's chief military advisor Maxwell Taylor who advocated clandestine war, or Special Forces warfare, as an alternative to conventional military and diplomatic options and thus got the U. S. involved untenably in Cuba and Vietnam."

"Tracy Barnes is a little man, Kerry," he added with what seemed like genuine anger in his voice. "Don't you agree that little men are subject to Napoleon complexes, that they tend to compensate for their deficiency in height by abusing their power?"

"Yes," I said, going on at some length about all the examples of little men who shouted orders and made unreasonable demands in high school ROTC and the Marine Corps.

> "At headquarters I paid protocolary calls on Allen Dulles and General Cabell, Frank Wisner," at this point in *Undercover*, Hunt inserts a footnote ("A diminutive personal assistant to Frank Wisner was known as the Ozard of Wiz.") continuing with, "and his principal assistant, Tracy Barnes. Freed from the parochialism of OSO, Dick Helms was now chief of operations for the entire Clandestine Services. In each other we discerned kindred spirits and formed a friendship which, though sporadic, due to my extended absences abroad, continued until the summer of 1972, when my name was first mentioned in connection with Watergate."
>
> Since then, in recent years, I have learned that twitting Tracy Barnes about his stature is a favorite CIA pastime, as also is resistance to "parochial," or Jesuit, influences, which tend to dominate the intelligence community, often by indirect means. Hunt's wife, Dorothy, for example, was Catholic, and therefore the statement about his relation to Helms may contain some subtle allusions.

Very much as Brother-in-law mentioned Tracy Barnes and the Satanist sacrifices, he remarked also that the notorious bombing of the Sunday school in Birmingham had been the work of Griffin Bell, a name equally unknown to me at that time.

"Griffin Bell is a judge, Kerry. He is judge of the Fifth Circuit Court. That means he travels from one place to another, hearing cases. He's a circuit judge. Can you remember that, Kerry?"

"Yes, I can remember that because Marryin' Sam in *Li'l Abner* is a circuit judge and I knew a guy in elementary school named Clifford Bell."

"Kerry, remember that slogan, 'There's a Ford in your future?'"

"Yeah, in a crystal ball. It used to be in ads in my grand-father's *National Geographics*."

"Well, keep it in mind. There may be a Ford in your future."

"I doubt it." I wasn't much into cars.

At that point Slim spoke up: "Listen to this man, Kerry. He's trying to tell you something."

Yeah, sure. I hated it when Slim became paternalistic like that.

Brother-in-law also spoke of the classes in anti-Communism that General Edwin Walker gave in Germany. "He was trans-ferred for it, and a bunch of his fellow officers resigned when the Army reprimanded him."

"Good for them," I said of Walker and his friends. "Some-times I wonder if this country even wants to win the Cold War."

"And you know about the case of the Air Force general, Billy Mitchell?"

"Yes, I read about that in *Reader's Digest*."

"I don't think what they did to Billy Mitchell was fair. Do you?"

"Certainly not. He was like Rickover. He wouldn't tolerate red tape. That was his problem."

These were all things he brought up more than once and I became adroit at using them as excuses to change the subject. A Ford in my future? "They used to say you could have any color of Model T Ford you wanted, so long as it was black," I would say.

"Yes, that's called a Hobson's choice. You know, Kerry, the anti-Communist department in the FBI is called Division Five."

"Yeah, you've told me that before." "Kerry, five is a very important number."

In 1964, living in Shirlington, Virginia, and corresponding
with Greg Hill, I suggested that our satirical religion, the
Discordian Society, which Greg and I had originated in
California before going to New Orleans, needed a dogma —
or , as we called it, a catma.

Brother-in-law's comment was in the back of my mind
when I therefore determined that it should be the Law of
Fives: Everything happens in fives — or can in some other
way be connected with the number five. Slim Brooks was our
fourth convert to the Discordian Society and, as might be
anticipated, Brother-in-law was the fifth person to join that
facetious cult devoted to the Greek goddess of confusion,
Eris — known to the Romans as Discordia.

Although I was soon to forget Brother-in-law's reminder,
I remained fascinated with the "law" it inspired, as with
the Discordian Society in general, most particularly because
of its rapid growth in membership. For in the late sixties
and early seventies both Greg and I began encountering all
manner of people calling themselves Discordians, including
that other man whose weird ideas about Nazis seemed to
so much resemble those of Brother-in-law, Stan Jamison,
whose Discordian name was Coman-Ra.

How Coman-Ra entered the loosely knit Discordian network of friends and acquaintances I'm unaware, but I recall
that I first began receiving mailings from him in about 1970.
These ranged from instructions about how to grow bean
sprouts to racist right-wing hate literature that both Greg
and I thought was rather alarming. Not until 1975 did
Coman-Ra intimate to me that he knew something about
the John Kennedy assassination.

"There is Division Five of the FBI, Griffin Bell is with the Fifth
Circuit Court," Brother-in-law continued, and he may or may
not have mentioned, in addition to perhaps two other things
related to the number five, that there was an intelligence
community organization called the Defense Industrial Security
Command with five front groups.

When I encountered that information in William Torbitt's
unpublished manuscript, *Nomenclature of an Assassination
Cabal*, it seemed to stimulate my memory, but I have never
been certain of that much.

"Have you ever noticed, Kerry, how by just pulling one thread
you can unravel a whole sweater?"

"Yes?"

"Keep in mind that is also true in politics: you might find
it very useful someday."

"All right, fine."

"How do you feel about this idea? What if things were to become worse in this country, for a time, and then to improve enormously? Do you think that would be okay?"

"Sure, I guess."

"Kerry, have you ever heard of a game called 'Freeze?'"

"No."

"Well first you turn the lights out in a room. Then everyone starts doing whatever they want. Then someone yells, 'Freeze!' and everyone has to hold still as the lights are turned on."

I must have looked rather puzzled. I remember feeling very afraid. Insanely, it seemed to me, Brother-in-law chuckled, and said: "That's a very good way to deal with people who are doing all kinds of bad things."

"Have you ever heard of 'Splooie?'" I asked in determination to keep up my end of the conversation.

"No. What is 'Splooie?'"

"A game they play with pledges in fraternities during Hell Week. They assemble them in a dark room and tell them all to start jacking off and for the first one who ejaculates to holler, 'Splooie!' And then they turn on the lights, and there is always one guy who was stupid enough to believe them and go along with it — and there he is, all alone among them with his pecker in his hand and cum on his trousers."

"There was a man who went to Heaven. And he found himself all alone on a cloud. Sailing past him were clouds with guys on them who were surrounded with wine bottles and women. So he sailed his cloud up to Saint Peter and said, 'Hey, what gives with those guys?' And Saint Peter said, 'They're in Hell.' And he said, 'Oh yeah? Then why the wine and women for them, and me sitting here all alone?' Saint Peter said, 'The Hell of it is, the wine bottles have holes in them and the women don't.'"

Then the discussion would drift off in another direction that seemed almost as inane. We spoke of the intelligence of dolphins and also of their extreme sociality — of how one dolphin would throw itself into a net so the rest of the school could escape.

More than once he mentioned that in Germany during World War II, armament factories owned by the Krupps were spared deliberately by Allied bombers, though whole civilian populations nearby were decimated.

To me that sounded like an awkward, top-heavy conspiracy theory. In those days most people seemed to believe that Roosevelt's New Deal had proved that governments were stronger than big business.

Only Crazy David, the paranoid, thought cartels existed that were above history in their chosen obscurity to the average person. But then he even suspected the politicians of rival nations conferred with each other about how to best destroy one another's people.

Crazy David said that only sixty families controlled most of America's wealth. That sounded like a hazy legend left over from the Gilded Age or one of the stories my dad used to tell about the Great Depression in order to rationalize voting against Eisenhower.

Certainly Brother-in-law was just a deluded psychopath caught up in the grandeur that was the Third Reich, boasting of the power of the Nazis. A dark, Wagnerian opera in a flop house.

But then there was always the inconvenient unpleasantry that such had been the predicament of Hitler in his early years.

Squalor and majestic themes had combined with national chauvinism to produce the dark Jungian shadow-roots of the next haunting fanaticism of our age.

According to *The House of Krupp* by Peter Batty, in February of 1956 Alfried Krupp "made an extensive tour of the Far and Middle East, dropping in to talk to business-heads in such capitals as Cairo, Bangkok, Delhi and Karachi. He was in fact the first major German industrialist to set foot in the area since the war. At the outset the trip was described as 'a serious attempt' to counter the Soviets' economic offensive in the underdeveloped countries of Africa and Asia, but on his return, discovering the Russians were now interested in buying from him, he changed his tune and hastened to deny that he was waging 'a private crusade against Communism' — to the chagrin of many American diplomats whose blue-eyed boy he had recently become... Within a few months he was off again to Canada — though... Canadians were not so ecstatic at having a convicted war criminal in their midst and showed their discontent by staging demonstrations everywhere he went in their country. Alfried's reason for going there was his participation along with Cyrus Eatton, Khruschev's famous capitalist friend from Cleveland, Ohio," in a conference. (p. 254)

Significantly enough, it is noted elsewhere in the book that it was John J. McCloy, who was later to serve on the Warren Commission, and who has also been linked to Morgan banking interests, who rescued the Krupp fortune after the Nuremberg trials: "He had also to many people's surprise decided to cancel the order confiscating Krupp's properties — it had not been expected that he would go quite that far. McCloy's justification for his generosity was that no other war criminal had been punished in this way: 'Confiscation of personal [sic] property does not belong to the practices of our legal system and in general is in contradiction of the American conception of justice. I am not able, on the basis of the evidence against the accused Krupp, to find any degree of personal guilt which would put him above all the others sentenced by the Nuremberg courts.'" Batty goes on to say on the same pages, 233 and 234, "Later, when challenged by a number of eminent Americans to explain himself further, McCloy described his decision to release Krupp as the most 'wearing' he had ever had to make. But to his eternal shame, in my opinion at least, he also endeavored to play down the charges of slave-labor brought against Alfried at Nuremberg."

We also learn from *The House of Krupp* that "Alfried's first major Russian order came in 1957, after he had exhibited at the Leipzig East German Trade Fair the previous March — an action which at the time shocked many West Germans." (pp. 257, 258) It was a contract worth just over four million pounds for chemical works and three synthetic fiber plants "which ironically he was making under license from an American firm. This quickly led to closer and warmer relations between Moscow and Essen. Indeed when Mikoyan, the Russian Trade Minister, visited West Germany in 1958 he went out of his way to talk to Alfried's general manager, assuring him that 'the products of Krupp have an excellent reputation among our people.' A few weeks after this remark of Mikoyan, Khruschev, then Russia's Prime Minister, declared in a speech to the Central Committee of the Soviet Communist Party in Moscow that 'the Soviet Union has in the past entertained good relations with the Essen firm of Krupp.'

"Later that same year, a group of Krupp senior officials headed by their general manager were feted in Moscow;

Mikoyan called them 'the first swallows of commerce from the western world.' The Russians were evidently very eager to do business with Alfried's men, but negotiations broke down on credit terms — though rumor had it that the real reason was that Alfried had been hobbled at the last moment by the Americans.

"Khruschev himself took a hand in the next stage of the wooing when, at the Leipzig Trade Fair in the following March, that is March of 1959, he made the East German press drop their usual denunciations of Krupps as warmongers, and of Alfried in particular as a convicted war criminal. Moreover, he visited the Krupp stand at the Fair and drank a toast to the firm out of a Krupp stainless steel tumbler filled with French Cognac, expressing regret that the head of the House was not there in person, but sending Alfried his good wishes all the same. Today, Alfried's name no longer appears on the Soviet list of war criminals and until quite recently the House of Krupp maintained a permanent office in Moscow: perhaps the two most remarkable, and at the same time the two most paradoxical, facts in the whole post-war rise of firm and family."

Possibly it was such maneuvering by Moscow that caused Mao Tsetung to denounce Khrushchev's policy of "peaceful co-existence" with the West as political revisionism — not, as many Americans were led to believe, any tolerance by the Russians for American democracy, or any particular hostility by the Chinese toward peaceful relations with the U. S.

But the most disturbing question plaguing me is why, with a record like that as American High Commissioner in Germany, was the Honorable John J. McCloy later appointed to the President's Commission on the Assassination of President John F. Kennedy?

In light of such data, one can only conclude that Brother-in-law was not deceived in believing there was a conspiracy on behalf of the Krupps in the highest levels of the U. S. government and that it was responsible during the war for sparing their armament factories from Allied bombing.

another subject he discussed in a way that made him seem, temporarily, more like

a leftist than a fascist. Merriment at the torture-murders of Il Duce and his

woman dominated his mood at such times.

There was only one way I could take it: this Nazi brother-in-law of Slim's

was weird, and Slim's fascination with him was weird, and that's all there was

to it.

"Kerry, there are bureaucrats in the C.I.A. who okay things without reading

them. Don't you agree that that kind of behavior should be punished?"

"Yes," I exclaimed. "There is such a thing as criminal negligence. In

Manila there were people living in pasteboard hovels who were starving to death,

and the Philippines was a U.S. possession until the late Forties. That's an-

other example of something made possible only by criminal negligence."

My hypothetical interpretation of the remark about C.I.A. employees is as

follows:

Assuming Brother-in-law was a high-level C.I.A. operative, he or someone

he knew -- possibly Richard Nixon in his Vice Presidential capacity as director

of planning the invasion of Cuba -- discovered that agency officers routinely

okayed project proposals handed them by trusted underlings without first bother-

ing to read them. Thereupon the person making this discovery invented the rat-

ionalization for taking advantage of such behavior, that it should be punished,

in order to create his own virtual government within the U.S. security apparatus.

Confirmation for this possibility comes from these statements in the following

article reprinted in the March, 1974, issue of The Yipster Times from either the

Los Angeles Star or the Boston Real Paper:

"A number of top secret and politically dynamite documents link President Nix-

on to a plot to kill former President John F. Kennedy, according to private re-

searcher Sherman Skolnick of Chicago. Skolnick referred to one of the documents

during a five-hour radio talk show broadcast October 15 over WLS Radio Station

in Chicago.

"Skolnick, speaking in the early morning hours on WLS Radio talk show Point-

Page 87 from the serialized edition of *The Dreadlock Recollections* (1989).

Maybe They're Crazy

SLIM and I, entering after Brother-in-law answered the door, found ourselves places to sit. For reasons possibly having to do with unconscious fears, I preferred the chair just inside the door, right next to it. Slim usually sat on the opposite side of the intimate living room, or somewhere in the middle, sometimes, to my right or my left.

"Would you like a cup of coffee?" Gary asked.

We both said, "Yes."

After handing me a weak concoction of instant-smelling stuff in a pastel blue plastic tea cup, Brother-in-law took a seat in the chair to my left and fiddled with his pipe and a pouch of Half & Half tobacco, exchanging comments with Slim about things pertaining to the mundane logistics of their relationship. A girlie magazine cover briefly attracted my attention.

Brother-in-law announced, very excitedly, "Kerry, I want to find out if the pen really is mightier than the sword!" Such were his opening words, and it was immediately obvious that this would be one of his days of striding about the room. "Do you agree that it is?"

"Yes. I was just thinking the other day that many people probably resort to violence because they lack the ability with words to express their anger any other way."

"Excellent! And do you think that if your life depended on it you could articulate the anger of others, of people who are more oppressed than you?"

"Definitely!"

"Wonderful! Then we shall find out which is mightier — the written word, or the force of arms."

"Have you ever seen a copy of the Diego Rivera painting called *The Scream?*" Another of those questions.

"I'll tell you what I fear as a writer," I responded. "It is the people like Smerdyakov in *The Brothers Karamazov*, the people who miss the point of what you write, by taking it too literally or not literally enough, use it to justify actions you aren't actually recommending. Ivan Karamazov wrote an essay arguing that since there is no God there can be no crime, and Smerdyakov, his bastard brother, read it and murdered their father. Then later on he confessed to Ivan and said, 'But Brother, it was your idea!' Knowing that there will always be people like that, somewhere, reading what I have written, terrifies me."

"Yes, well, the author was trying to put across the idea that people need to believe in God whether or not there is a God, because otherwise they would become criminals — that if God didn't exist, then it would be necessary to invent Him," Brother-in-law explained.

"I understand that, but it's rot. Robert Ingersoll refuted that notion magnificently in his writings, and also by the example of his own life. On the other hand, more murders and tortures have been committed in the name of God than for any other reason."

That Brother-in-law would frequently bring up things that seemed related to nothing whatsoever was something I found peevishly irritating. "Have you ever noticed how a saxophone works, Kerry? It is a very complicated instrument. You have to be extremely physically coordinated, and that takes considerable practice and skill. Yet it is something that can be learned."

Then he added that agents in the intelligence community could use similar techniques for conveying data upward in a bureaucracy in such a way as to manipulate their superiors on different sides of a conflict — "just like working a saxophone. Especially double and triple agents can use it, deciding which information to give which boss, and thereby influencing men in power from a position below them."

Another thing he said was, "You know, Kerry, many of the people that serve as espionage agents are not doing it by choice; they are being forced to work against their will by means of extortion — including people who work for our government!"

I explained that I was aware of that much. I had seen a movie based on a true story starring Ernest Borgnine called *Man on a String* where an American of foreign descent was forced to return to the old country on a "vacation" and spy for the U. S.

"Kerry, have you ever heard the story about the little Dutch boy the one who saved Holland by plugging the hole in the dike with his finger?" Another irrelevant comment. It seemed to me to rate an irreverent reply.

"Yes. A gay friend of mine in high school used to say, 'Did you hear about the little boy who stuck his finger in the dike? She didn't like it.'"

"Tell me something," Brother-in-law replied without laughing at my little joke. "What would you do in a situation like that? That little boy saved his country. But he also starved to death, because nobody found him till after he was dead. How would you handle that type of predicament?"

I answered that I would probably sit there with my finger in the dike constantly thinking of some way to signal for help.

That reply seemed to please him very much.

"And there is also the fable of a king," he continued, "whose people were forbidden to speak to him by a rival monarch, so he worked out a code where every article of clothing and every gesture stood for something, so they could tell him what was going on. Do you think you could do something like that in a similar situation?"

Another time he said, "Kerry, you know, one of the symptoms of schizophrenia is that they develop whole languages of their own — using ordinary words, but ascribing their own private meanings to them."

"Yes, I read that in one of Loy's psychology textbooks from nursing school." Loy was a French Quarter friend, one of my closest, a serene woman with long black hair who made her living as an artist.

"Well I wonder what makes them invent their own secret languages. Why would anyone, especially a crazy person, go to all that trouble?"

"Maybe because they are crazy. One kind of paranoia is paranoid schizophrenia."

"But you know, Kerry, there are some people who have exhibited the symptoms of paranoia who were taken to psychiatrists, and when they began investigating their backgrounds and their life situations they found out the patient was really being persecuted."

"Yeah, you've mentioned that a couple of times before. There are also actual paranoids, though. Not all of them are really being persecuted."

"No, Kerry — not all of them."

One of Brother-in-law's recurring themes was the origin of the word, "Hollywood."

"It is from the holly plant or, to the pagans, the holy plant."

"Yes, there is holly growing in the canyons near Hollywood, California."

> Something else he said about Hollywood is vague in my memory now — but it concerned the importance of not remaining in a political condition, having to do with pagan secret societies, that would be called "Hollywood."

Another time he spoke sympathetically of the "Hollywood Ten" — the screenwriters who were blackballed for their suspected Communist connections. That was one of those inconsistencies in his politics I found so disconcerting. What business had a Nazi like him worrying about the civil liberties of accused Reds?

What the Communist underground in Italy did to Mussolini and his mistress was another subject he discussed in a way that made him seem, temporarily, more like a leftist than a fascist. Merriment at the torture-murders of *Il Duce* and his woman dominated his mood at such times.

There was only one way I could take it: this Nazi brother-in-law of Slim's was weird, and Slim's fascination with him was weird, and that's all there was to it.

"Kerry, there are bureaucrats in the CIA who okay things without reading them. Don't you agree that that kind of behavior should be punished?"

"Yes!" I exclaimed. "There is such a thing as criminal negligence. In Manila there were people living in pasteboard hovels who were starving to death, and the Philippines was a U. S. possession until the late forties. That's another example of something made possible only by criminal negligence."

My hypothetical interpretation of the remark about CIA employees is as follows:

Assuming Brother-in-law was a high-level CIA operative, he or someone he knew — possibly Richard Nixon in his Vice Presidential capacity as director of planning the invasion of Cuba — discovered that agency officers routinely okayed project proposals handed them by trusted underlings without first bothering to read them. Thereupon the person making this discovery invented the rationalization for taking advantage of such behavior, that it should be punished, in order to create his own virtual government within the U. S. Security apparatus.

Confirmation for this possibility comes from these statements in the following article reprinted in the March, 1974, issue of *The Yipster Times* from either *The Los Angeles Star* or *The Boston Real Paper*:

"A number of top secret and politically dynamite documents link President Nixon to a plot to kill former President John F. Kennedy, according to private researcher Sherman Skolnick of Chicago. Skolnick referred to one of the documents during a five-hour radio talk show broadcast October 15 over WLS Radio Station in Chicago.

"Skolnick, speaking in the early morning hours on WLS Radio talk show *Point-Counterpoint*, said the documents were among those being used by E. Howard Hunt and his wife Dorothy to blackmail President Richard Nixon. Skolnick said Mrs. Hunt was carrying the documents with her on United Airlines flight 553 when it crashed last December killing Mrs. Hunt, CBS Newswoman Michele Clark and forty-three others. Skolnick has charged the jet was sabotaged.

"One of the documents the Hunts were using to blackmail the President, according to Skolnick, is a top secret National Security Council memorandum bearing the signature of then President Dwight D. Eisenhower. The memorandum is dated November 22,v1960, just weeks after Kennedy was elected President and while Eisenhower was filling out his term as the nation's chief executive. "..." '...' "The memorandum says, according to Skolnick, that in the opinion of the Eisenhower National Security Council John F. Kennedy's ascendancy to the office of the Presidency was not in the best interests of the country. 'The Eisenhower National Security Council took it upon themselves,' Skolnick said, 'to declare Kennedy a threat to the national security.'

"The private researcher said the NSC document recommends 'in so many words' that JFK be dealt with so he could not hold the office of the Presidency. The memorandum, according to Skolnick, 'recommends that Kennedy be murdered... '

"In November of 1960, the date of the top secret memorandum, Richard Nixon was Vice President of the United States and thus a member of the NSC. If the NSC document is authentic, as Skolnick says it is, then Nixon was one of those who recommended that Kennedy be murdered."

Further insight as to how such a thing is conceivable is provided in *The Secret Team* (Prentice-Hall, 1973) by Fletcher Prouty, as he explains how the automatic okay process was facilitated: "Once the CIA had become involved in a series of clandestine operations, it then would make a practice of going back to the NSC... and ostentatiously brief the next operation as a series. As they hoped, after awhile the important and very busy members of the NSC or of the NSC subcommittee would plead other duties and designate someone else to act for them at the meetings. This diluted the control mechanism appreciably. Further, the CIA saw to it that men who would always go along with them were the designated alternates." (p. 108)

"And in building our secret society to fight imperialism I think we should follow the policy of not letting the right hand know what the left hand is doing. Is that okay, Kerry?"

"It's okay with me," I said innocently.

"And I think one of the legitimate functions of government ought to be the enforcement of contracts. How about you?"

"Yes, definitely. That's one of the only proper functions of government, according to Ayn Rand."

"And I think any contract made by anyone over the age of twenty-one ought to be binding. Is that okay with you?"

"Yes."

"Yes! And I also think oral contracts ought to be binding. A man's word should be as good as his bond."

"Yes," I replied, wondering to myself why Slim seemed

suddenly so excited. As usual, he wasn't contributing to the discussion, but he seemed almost beside himself with glee — grinning in admiration at Brother-in-law, looking at me with a very pleased expression in his eyes.

> The National Security Council is empowered by law to direct CIA actions, but was gradually lulled into approving actions initiated within the CIA, instead. After that it was easy for empire builders within the CIA to turn both the upper levels of the agency and the National Security Council into a rubber stamp operation for their policies.
>
> With Nixon and Hunt working together in anti-Castro activities, and in light of allegations that Hunt was in a position during Watergate to blackmail Nixon, it is probable both men were among the perpetrators of such ruses. Once any proposal such as the John Kennedy death warrant — and who knows what else? — was written up, perhaps all that remained necessary was to place it in the "IN" basket on the desk of a bureaucrat who routinely okayed all projects.

Of course it did not occur to me that I had just okayed something without examining it, and had moreover set myself up so that every time I agreed with Brother-in-law thereafter he would possess the power to make it a binding contract. For as far as I was concerned at the time I was only humoring the pipe dreams of a maniac, for fear that if I offended him he would become dangerous to me — or, as with the above, because I happened to agree, but thought my agreement was only academic.

Upon other occasions Slim became incomprehensibly excited when Gary was talking of things that seemed utterly irrelevant, and his silent eagerness was distracting. For example, when Brother-in-law was talking about the roots in mythology for the meanings of the names of the days of the week, Slim was almost bouncing up and down in his seat.

"Kerry, you know among sheep they have a ram with a bell around its neck, to keep the others from straying from the flock. Well in the Chicago stockyard they have a belled ram like that also, and it is trained to go to the area where the sheep are slaughtered. So the other sheep follow the lead ram from the railroad cars to their doom. And that happens over and over again, every time a new batch arrives and is unloaded."

A splendid new addition to my trivia collection.

Sometimes he could really seem mundane and pointless. "You know, dog is 'god' spelled backwards."

Then there were his ridiculously low-brow jokes. "You know what they call a man who likes womens' breasts? A chestnut."

"Did you hear about the old maids who had a beer party at the beach and got sand in their Schlitz?" I would reply, drawing from my Marine Corps experience.

"There was a nigger in the hills of Tennessee," he would tell me, "who read *Mein Kampf* in the late thirties or early forties and thought it was the greatest book ever written. And then heh, heh — he found out that Hitler regarded Negroes as a subhuman species. More inferior than Jews."

Now and then he would chat with me about the possibility of building a universal language based upon the Jungian notion of the collective unconscious, utilizing associational symbols and unconscious archetypes.

I remarked to him that Freud insisted that in the analysis of dreams trains were always symbolic of death, and mentioned that Jessica's psychology professor had said that rubbing one's nose was a negative sign while stroking one's hair was a positive sign.

That such a language would resemble the cryptic chatter of schizophrenics and therefore would be useful under certain circumstances for dismissing those who spoke it as insane was another relevant possibility that did not occur to me.

That several such cant languages have been developed within the intelligence community and conspiracy politics and that at least one of them was in use as far back as the Fifties is something known to those familiar with neo-Nazi Satanism and witchcraft.

Can You Remember That?

SOMETIMES Brother-in-law spoke as if he had in mind a very definite plan that would come to fruition at a set date and that I would have to recall certain items of information in order to survive.

"Kerry, keep in mind that the Communists will try to make you a martyr for their cause."

I would assure him I maintained no illusions about the Communist doctrine of the ends justifying the means. I had read for myself the words of the Third International.

Then at other times he would say with a smirk: "You know, Kerry, if you walk down the street talking to yourself in public, people are going to think you are crazy."

Obviously. What a strange thing to say! "Of course," I would agree. "I think people who walk the streets talking to themselves are crazy. Who the hell wouldn't?" And then I would begin belaboring my pet peeve:

"There are more people in New Orleans who act crazy in precisely that way than anywhere else I've ever been. Then they've got the nerve to call California 'the land of fruits and nuts.'"

Brother-in-law would then look disappointed or annoyed, as if I had missed some kind of point.

Again, the subject would shift for no reason I could discern.

Upon one occasion he said, "Thirteen years from now will be the American Bicentennial. Kerry, I want to give this country a Christmas present!" He sounded angry.

"And I think the Communist Party ought to be legal, just like any other political party."

"Yes," I staunchly agreed. "J. Edgar Hoover says that outlawing Communism only drives it underground and makes it harder to deal with."

"And I think there ought to be places where sadistic people and psychopaths can go, designated national parks or something, where they can fight one another to the death if they want."

"A place for people like me," he added as Slim laughed, as if the two of them were sharing a secret joke.

Such legalized dueling seemed logical, considering the alternatives these dangerous characters might otherwise have in mind.

In the long run, the most disquieting thing about Brother-in-law was his implacable cheerfulness in the presence of the most heart-rending topics of discussion.

"Kerry," he said one day, "why is it that people are apathetic to mass murder and yet not to the murder of one person?"

"I don't know! I've been going crazy about that one ever since the Katanga massacre. Had it been an axe murder, it would be making front page news for weeks or months afterwards."

Gary looked so amused about it, rather pleased. "Yeah, we double-crossed Tshombe's faction and they were the ones who supported the United States. It wasn't even in our national self-interest to support the Congolese!"

As nationalistic as I was in my Ayn Rand days, that was hardly the traumatic message of women being hoisted on bamboo poles crammed into their vaginas, little boys and girls being burned alive in piles of wood by a United Nations police force.

I agreed with Brother-in-law's point also, though, as far as it went. It was alienating that no cruelty seemed to disturb him.

One day he compared himself to a character in Romain Gary's novel, *The Roots of Heaven* — the sociopathic gun-runner who was content to live in the world as it is and exploit its misery. "But perhaps there is some way we could work together," he added, after being kind enough to observe that I wasn't that way.

"Tell me, Kerry, would you be afraid to go to jail?"

"In a revolutionary situation," I said, "jail can be just another station house on the way to political power. That's something else a Romain Gary character says. I've read about Mahatma Gandhi's imprisonments and of how he made a yoga discipline of them, and I could also do that. Sometimes that's how I handled being in the Marine Corps."

"Kerry, there are some people called Scientologists who want to create a society based on human sacrifice. Did you realize that?"

"Slim has mentioned them. That's L. Ron Hubbard's new religion, isn't it? But he didn't say they were into human sacrifice."

"Well, they are. And it would be a good idea for you to keep that in mind. You might be in a position to keep them from taking over someday."

Then there was the time he talked at length about Frederick Demara — a Canadian con artist who had passed himself off as a doctor and performed successful brain surgery. "He sounds like a pretty smart man. Wouldn't you say so?"

I contributed to what seemed like an exchange of trivia at this point by saying: "They say that con men generally try to establish that there is some larceny in the hearts of their prospective victims before they bilk them."

Slim and Gary looked at me and nodded, a slight smile playing on Slim's lips, a twinkle in Brother-in-law's eyes, as if that were a much more relevant statement than I realized.

"Kerry. What do you think about the idea of building a secret society that uses the methods of Communism to fight Communism?"

We both expressed sympathy from time to time for the John Birch Society, though neither of us agreed completely with its politics. In those days, however, the mass media — particularly the Liberals — were misrepresenting the Birchers as para-military subversives. With encouragement from the White House, the media were attacking all extreme political positions. Rhetoric labeling intellectual minorities as dangerous, simply for being out of the "mainstream," regardless of their positions on violence, seemed itself both dangerous and irresponsible. That was one of the chief reasons I hated John F. Kennedy as much as I did: I valued dissent; he considered it unpatriotic.

"Kerry, you aren't the kind of person who is likely to give up and commit suicide in a difficult situation, are you?"

"You'll never meet anyone less inclined to suicide than me," I retorted. For at that age I had not thought much about my own thinking, riddled with contradictions as it was. I was attracted to every possible sort of dangerous adventure. Quite literally, I did not expect to be alive thirteen years in the future, when Brother-in-law's political timetable was supposed to activate his revolution.

Yet nothing seemed sicker to me than deliberately taking sleeping pills, for example — a depressingly popular activity among Quarterites. As a good Objectivist, I despised with Ayn Rand all that was "anti-life."

Yet as an aspiring soldier of fortune and globe trotter, I felt only contempt for pedestrian and plodding individuals who did not agree with me that life was to be measured "not by its length, but by its intensity." How much you could cram into your lifespan was what counted, not how long you endured. To me the first only was living; simple contentment with nothing more than survival was merely existing. Secure in the feeling I was preaching to the converted, I explained my philosophy of life to Brother-in-law here very often.

"Kerry, how would you like to be placed in danger every day of your life?"

"Great! I'd love it!"

"I can arrange for that to happen — if that's what you want." A hint of warning colored his tone of voice.

"That's exactly what I want. Life means nothing except when it is seen in contrast to its background of oblivion. That's the message I got out of that Tennessee Williams play they made into a movie — the most recent one, *Suddenly, Last Summer*. Death is the face of God — the only God there is: absolute nothingness."

Slim said, "Kerry wants to live fast, die young — and leave a beautiful corpse. That isn't my philosophy, but I can understand how he feels."

"That's right."

Occasionally, I would share short-story or novel ideas with Slim and Brother-in-law. One of them was for a story called *Apex: God of the North*, about a great iceberg with a computer operations center concealed within it, secretly controlling all history from its submerged location close to the North Pole.

I was also contemplating a sequel titled *AnaPex: God of the South*. Gary seemed mildly entertained by these notions. At least he didn't dismiss them as unwelcome digressions.

And Slim was so interested in my writing projects that sometimes he would ask me for my notes when I was through with them, with the flattering words, "Someday you'll be a famous writer and they'll be worth something."

At times I even suspected Slim of swiping notes from me — although it was difficult to imagine a motive for going to that extreme. Since I tend to be absent-minded about my personal effects, I usually wound up depreciating the latter suspicion as routine paranoia.

> Among notes that vanished mysteriously about the time of one of Slim's visits were some about an idea I had been playing with since my Marine Corps days, for building a secret society of assassins to kill foreign dictators.
>
> They featured a diagram shaped like a Maltese cross. At the center was the leader, who would then appoint one assistant in each of four areas: administration, intelligence, operations and logistics — the organizational divisions of Marine Corps activity.
>
> Each assistant would then appoint followers whose identity would remain unknown to the leader, as would his to them. Every follower was to recruit two more followers and so on, in descending levels of authority, creating four pyramidal wings.
>
> In the service I had once gone so far as to appoint another Marine, Raul Gayon, my chief of intelligence. Shortly thereafter, though, we quarreled and stopped speaking to one another.
>
> I remember clearly that my suddenly missing notes were in pencil. I don't recall how thoroughly they explained the diagram. I think they were probably rather scant, with just enough information to convey the general notion and no more.
>
> Vanishing at about the same time were jottings about a publishing business I was thinking of establishing, called Thor Thunderpress. Slim had said Thor was the Norse god of thunder; his name consisted of the first four letters of my last name. I don't believe he further mentioned to me that the symbol of Thor's hammer was the swastika, nor that Hitler took that insignia from the Finnish Air Force.
>
> In fact, I think Brother-in-law told me the swastika was favored by Hitler because it was the symbol used by the Aryans in conquering pre-Vedic India.

Brother-in-law seemed attracted to any idea that smacked of clandestine administration. Once he said: "Hitler was a clown. He never should have gone public. He should have lived as an ordinary citizen, ruling from behind the scenes."

Another example of how Brother-in-law paid attention to ideas that fascinated me occurred when he once warned: "There will come a time in your life when one of your friends will begin to behave exactly like Francisco d'Anconia in *Atlas Shrugged* — inexplicably seeming to abandon ideals both of you shared. Can you keep that in mind? His motives will be similar to Francisco's in Ayn Rand's novel — infiltrating the opposition."

I assured him that I could, although in fact I was not endeavoring to remember anything this weird, repetitive man said. Slim could think Brother-in-law was brilliant and competent if he wanted; I was certain the man was just a bullshitter, though possibly a dangerous one.

"And if there was a Nazi takeover in this country, a fascist takeover, don't you think it would be better just to torment one man — instead of a whole minority, like the Jews?"

"Yes, but how much would this one man be tormented?"

Slim chuckled.

Brother-in-law smirked and said, "Not very much," waving his hand in a depreciating gesture.

Sometimes Brother-in-law could appear competent enough to give me pause. Briefly, I would worry that I was underestimating him. An isolated visual memory sticks in my mind of Gary standing next to his car in sunglasses, chewing the stem of his pipe, looking like a most efficient Nazi general. In that instant he seemed to be contemplating me as if I represented to him a valuable prize — someone who would be useful in his plans.

Once he asked me what I thought of creating numerous factional conspiracies, consisting of secret societies, small countries and so forth, like pieces of a puzzle — then, at an appointed time, drawing them together in a powerful organization large enough to conquer the world. I think one of the examples he mentioned was Poland. In any case, references to Poland were frequent in his talks with me — the

Polish Corridor in World War II, Hitler's contempt for the Poles, etc. Brother-in-law seemed to mention Poland as often as he spoke of Germany.

All in all, he seemed as conscious of Europe as of the United States, mentioning often the poem about Flanders Field, for instance, and the sinking of the Titanic. Once, in fact, he posed the theory that the Titanic was wrecked deliberately in order to get rid of some important person or other. Contemporary European affairs were also much in his mind. We shared an admiration for a French rabble-rouser who was at that time stirring up a revolt among small shop keepers in Paris with the slogan, "Hang the tax collectors!"

Perhaps that explained why his opposition to Communism was more qualified than that of the average American anti-Communist patriot of that day. "Kerry, do you agree with the Marxist-Leninist theory of historical responsibility — that people should be held responsible for the results of their actions, regardless of their intentions?"

"Yes," I barked. "Nothing is truer than the saying that the highway to hell is paved with good intentions. If nearly half the world is not to continue starving to death, then ethics has to be geared to what will actually change the present situation. What will work, what will feed people has to be the standard of morality — not what seems fair in the eyes of spoiled intellectuals who've never been outside the United States. Like the poet Robinson Jeffers says, this country has a national introversion complex. So does Japan. Neither country really believes the outside world exists. People watch a newsreel or read something in the papers, but subconsciously it is only entertainment to them."

That Brother-in-law just loved to hear me talk like this was evident from the look in his eyes. "And these Liberal professors, these intellectuals you speak of — did you ever notice how they talk? They say, 'I feel' this and 'I feel' that. Not, 'I think' — but, 'I feel.' I believe that's what's wrong with them, don't you? They don't think, they feel. Don't you agree that reason should prevail over emotion at all times?"

"Yes — that's just what Ayn Rand says."

That this alleged Nazi's politics were riddled with contradictions was something I found puzzling, but not very interesting. In my all-American way, I figured he was just some kind of nut.

Humanity's actions were replete with examples of illogical behavior. Ayn Rand said that the only free will consisted of the decision either to think or not to think. To me it was obvious that most people thought only when immediate, everyday problems confronted them. When it came to philosophy and politics, faith and wishful thinking took over. Nothing else could explain to me why, for example, there were so many otherwise intelligent people who believed in God.

That I was often as contradictory as he was never dawned on me. I would sit there asserting that when there is a contradiction in anyone's thinking, they ought to check their premises. Then, unconsciously, I would answer a question by contradicting something else I had just said. Not only was I, an author, simply humoring this man in order to gather background material for a book, I was also young and brash. Rationality appealed to me as much because Ayn Rand's novel romanticized it as for any other reason.

Destiny's Tots

ONE of Gary's favorite war stories was about how the Germans had once tricked Stalin into purging all his best generals.

"During the Hitler-Stalin Pact, when the Nazis were making preparations to break with Stalin and attack Russia, they took him a list of all his most brilliant generals and told him they were plotting treason against him. Not only did Stalin believe them, he said, 'How much do you want for this information?' The damned fool actually paid them for it!" Gary must have told that story nearly a dozen times.

"You see, the Russians knew Hitler thought Jews were inferior. That was no problem to them because Russians themselves have been traditionally anti-Semitic. In Czarist times they used to round 'em up and kill 'em in what were called pogroms. What they didn't understand about Hitler, though — heh, heh — was that he considered Slavs a subhuman race. Heh, heh — he hated them! In fact, Rosenberg used to measure the skulls of Slavic execution victims to try to prove they had smaller heads, and therefore smaller brains, than Germans."

My policy during such discussions was usually to maintain a tactful, frightened silence. Something about the way he laughed awakened the possibility that he was not sincerely a racist, that it was all part of his swaggering, 'bad guy' image. I didn't want to take my chances by provoking unnecessary arguments, though.

I was more comfortable when he spoke in terms of American Conservatism, a philosophy with which I disagreed but was in sympathy in that it opposed socialism.

"Have you ever heard of the Hoover Institution for the Study of War, Peace and Revolution?"

"As a matter of fact, yes. I was reading an article about it recently."

That article probably appeared in *The National Observer*, to which I subscribed. Although he didn't say so, Karl Hess was obviously an admirer of Ayn Rand. As publisher and editor of that publication, he always took the proper Objectivist position in relation to every issue.

"What do you think of that organization, Kerry? Do you approve of the Hoover Institution?"

"Yes. I like the things I read about it."

Brother-in-law seemed enormously pleased — as if my favorable response here were crucial.

That was a question he only asked once. Another such inquiry was, "What do you think of developing nuclear power for peaceful purposes? The Atoms for Peace Program?"

"I think it's a good idea."

Then he said something about an atomic power plant in Oregon. In those days splitting the atom in order to create electrical energy was something that seemed like a very progressive idea, since theretofore it had only been a source of explosive power for weapons.

Also, he spoke of a demonstration against the testing of the hydrogen bomb at Bikini. A protest took place in Times Square. Goats had been used as guinea pigs in the H-bomb test, so "they mounted a stuffed goat on roller skates and wheeled it around Times Square with a sign hanging from its neck that said: 'Today me — tomorrow you!'" That story he told two or three times.

That this Nazi seemed to approve of a peace demonstration annoyed me, again because it was out of character. I was not so radical as to believe in peace marches. What business had he taking a position to my left?

Like all Objectivists, I opposed conscription. Yet, in Ayn Rand's view, both war to protect American investments and advanced weapons technology were justifiable. Blind pacifism, though, was regarded as whim worshiping. Worrying about The Bomb was for fuzzy-minded socialists like Bertrand Russell.

"How to you feel about conservation, Kerry?"

Unlike other Objectivists, I was concerned about pollution of the natural environment.

"When I was a teenager I used to sneak up into the Puente Hills above East Whittier, early in the morning before sunrise, and pull up the surveyor stakes in a construction site for a subdivision they were building there. I love nature."

Brother-in-law gave me the impression he was about to become involved in a dynamic new ecology movement. In this connection, I think he also mentioned he had been initiated into an Indian tribe in New Mexico.

"Someday, Kerry," Brother-in-law said excitedly, "you will find yourself in a position of great power. You will not, however, be aware of who is supporting you."

Striding about the small room, wheeling and turning, he said: "No one will be able to touch you. It will be as if you are elevated upon a high pillar — and," he paused dramatically, "there will be assassins at your disposal."

Whenever he became that dramatic, Brother-in-law was especially difficult to believe. To this day I think that speech was preparation for a time I would be deluded into thinking I possessed great power, in order to test my true loyalties. I think such a routine may be a regular feature of CIA "false flag" recruitment.

Another time he asked, "What do you think of a government composed of many philosopher-kings, like sages on the side of a mountain, who are moved up and down this mountain of power according to their wisdom and abilities?"

Stripped of its majestic embellishments, this very much resembles the methods of the CIA in supporting rivals to the power of a government slated for overthrow. Various individuals will be selected who for one reason or another are more or less incompetent — making them easy to topple in turn when necessary — but for whom considerable popular support can be marshaled. Then one faction is played against another in order to keep the Agency in control of the overall situation.

"And one other thing, Kerry. You know, if you expose the assassins — you won't become philosopher-king."

"Of course not," I answered, figuring as usual I might as well humor this grandiose burglar with all these wild daydreams until I could get back to the sane people in the French

Quarter. "I wouldn't expect anything else. I mean, it wouldn't make any sense for a king to expose his own guards."

That I would ever repeat anything in these discussions was the last thing I wanted this man to believe. After all, should he be serious — no matter how deluded — he nevertheless probably did have friends in the underworld. I was given to understand that if he suspected I would become a stool pigeon, Brother-in-law could arrange to dispose of me in short order.

Since I tend not to be much good at keeping secret whatever is on my mind, notorious blabbermouth that I am, I handled this problem by forgetting all about these discussions as quickly as I could.

Telling myself these thoughts were both unpleasant and improbable, I consoled myself by thinking that if by some chance they weren't, I was then already in so much trouble that worrying about it wouldn't do any good.

"Kerry, there are some men who are content to think of themselves as quite ordinary. There are other men who feel greatness within themselves from the day they are born."

"Destiny's tots."

"Exactly. What kind of man are you?"

"I've always felt that way — that I am destined for great things. My friend in high school, Bob Doidge, used to call it megalomania. But I think that is what drives some people to rise above the common herd. Like Howard Roark in *The Fountainhead* — he knew he was great. Without that sense of confidence, nobody would ever amount to anything."

"You know, Kerry, Hitler used to create myths about himself. For example, he said that before the war he was once walking in the forest and an old woman appeared who told him that someday he would be the ruler of all Germany. He said things like that," Brother-in-law asserted with approval, "to make himself more acceptable to the German people."

On another occasion he mentioned that when Hitler found himself involved in a struggle, he wrote a book about it. "That's something you might try when the time comes."

My ambition at that time was to become a novelist and a short-story writer. After becoming wealthy that way, I planned to travel the world engaging in dangerous adventures, in the manner of my heroes Richard Halliburton and John Goddard. Then I intended to write non-fiction books about my adventures.

Writing a book about my political oppression seemed like an awkward, and lengthy, way to deal with it.

Like most Nazis I have known, Brother-in-law was also forever speculating that maybe Hitler was still alive and well in Argentina. Moreover, he claimed Martin Bormann had been spotted by someone after the war in the Swiss Alps, and that he had been briefly pursued.

In the Anteroom of History

URING one of the Saturday or Sunday morning visits Slim
and I made to his cottage, Brother-in-law asked me if I
thought people ought to be free, legally and socially, to form
any kind of family structure or group living situation they
wanted.

My answer was one he could easily have anticipated, since
I was thought odd even among the Bohemians of the French
Quarter for my outspoken devotion to free love and group
marriage. This was previous to the time when Robert Hein-
lein's novel, *Stranger in a Strange Land*, popularized that
notion among hipsters. One of my novel projects was a humorous fictionalized account of my own unsuccessful attempts
to attract converts to join me in a group marriage.

After obtaining my enthusiastic agreement about at least
that much, Brother-in-law looked at me with a glint in his eye
, and said: "I'm sure you recall that Omar Khayyam verse
about smashing this sorry scheme of things."

That I was very much into Omar Khayyam was something
else he knew. "Yes! Something about if we could conspire
to shatter this sorry scheme of things and mold another
one, nearer to the heart's desire! That's one of my favorite
quatrains."

"Kerry, how would you like to conspire with me to shatter
this sorry scheme of things?"

"Great. When do we start?"

"It's going to take years. And I can't tell you much about
it, because it's going to have to be very secretive. You are
going to have to work on a need-to-know basis, just like you
did when you had a security clearance in the Marines. You
will receive only enough information to perform your part of
the work." Then he paused and looked at me and asked, "Is
that okay?"

"It's okay with me," I answered eagerly.

"I don't think jails should exist. Do you? I think society
should find a more humane way of dealing with criminals."

"Yes. I think they should be confined comfortably and
studied to find out what makes them criminals, so crime can

be prevented. As Robert Ingersoll said, 'Men do what they must do.' Everything anyone does always seems to them like a good idea at the time. We should find out why criminals are attracted to antisocial behavior, instead of punishing them."

"Exactly. And don't you think it would be better if our technology were oriented more toward the exploration of outer space than to the production of war materials?"

"Yes," I said, not certain I was telling the truth. I hadn't thought much about that one before.

"Now I know you agree that both forced segregation and forced integration are wrong. What if people were allowed to form their own communities? What if white racists could live in segregated communities while others were free to form racially mixed communities? Black separatists could also form their own communities. That way we Germans could maintain our racial purity, you Beatniks could intermarry, Malcolm X and his friends could go off and live by themselves — and everybody would be happy."

"That sounds like a good idea," I said. Silently, though, I wondered if he simply wanted to divide us into neat geographically distributed categories in order to make the job of exterminating the rest of us easier for him and his Germans.

I agreed wholeheartedly though to the idea of free trade among nations with no tariffs restricting international commerce. "Yes, that's one good thing about our President," one of us said. "The 'Kennedy Rounds' to negotiate the gradual reduction of tariffs."

"And I think we should return to a limited, Constitutional government."

"Yes," I agreed. "Government should confine itself to its proper functions: preventing force and fraud. There should be no bureaucracies except the police and the military. And the military should only be used to defend our shorelines and to protect American investments abroad."

"Kerry, I don't think we should defend the foreign holdings of Americans. I think investors should place their funds at the mercy of foreign governments at their own risk. Otherwise there are too many excuses to get involved in foreign wars."

We agreed to disagree on that one.

"And I think there ought to be sanctity of the home. I think a man's home is his castle and that's the way it should be."

For a brief, mad split second I wondered why this Nazi wanted privacy like that. What was he planning to do in his castle — Bavarian Gothic as it was sure to be?

Then I thought about the quartering of British troops in Colonial American homes and the Bill of Rights and the principles of Objectivist individualism, and I felt ashamed of allowing sinister possibilities to distract my mind from such a refreshingly rational discussion with Brother-in-law. For if these were his true politics, how could I take seriously his stuff about being a Nazi?

"Kerry, I think Robert Kennedy's Justice Department was wrong in jailing and fining those business executives for Anti-Trust Law violations. Don't you?"

"Yes. That's what Ayn Rand says in one of the Objectivist newsletters. Of course, the Marxists are wrong, and so are the Kennedys. Punishing the great producers of the world is not the answer to insuring adequate production."

> Mixing government and business, Rand says, is a form of fascist-socialism. Whether the businessmen or the government bureaucrats wind up ruling the economy, either way you've got one group of men running everything. I considered Roger Blough and those others to be great, persecuted heroes, and it appeared to me that the Kennedy brothers double-crossed them. Besides that, I found the Anti-Trust Laws to be vague and irrational.
>
> At that time, I believed that only unregulated, unrestricted production would ever be able to feed everyone in the world — like the starving people in the Intramuros sector of Manila, the City of Walls, as they call that bombed-out slum. That was why I became a Marxist, temporarily, before I read *Atlas Shrugged*, because of the sight of starving people. It's one thing to read or hear about something like that and quite another to actually witness it.

"Yes," he said. "And I think it would also help if we returned to a predominantly agricultural economy."

"Certainly. Between the United States and Canada, there is enough fertile land and right weather conditions that both countries together could feed everyone. We could be the breadbasket of the world. Instead, our criminal bureaucrats pay farmers not to grow things."

"And I think unions ought to be free also. If workers want to form a radical labor union, I think that is their right."

"Yes, I can agree to that. It's in keeping with the idea of separation of the government and the economy."

"But I don't believe in the general strike."

"What is the general strike?"

"That's where the workers take over a factory and run it themselves."

"Yeah, I don't like that idea either. Great organizational skill, perhaps genius, is required to administer a productive corporation. Talent like that deserves whatever rewards it cares to demand. If workers tried to run things, they'd do it inefficiently. One of the problems is most people think 'profit' is a dirty word. Kennedy is always calling on people to make sacrifices to the national interest. According to my philosophy, that's immoral."

"Ah yes," he said, looking at me steadily. "What if we could give the word saysacrifice such a bad name that no one would ever again listen to talk like that?"

I wondered what he had in mind, but I think I was afraid to ask. "That sounds okay, I guess."

"What do you think of local police? Don't you think it would be a good idea to recruit local police to a revolutionary movement? They would be in favor of local control of government institutions, of keeping political power closer to home."

"Yes, that might work. One of our worst problems in this country is the centralization of power in the hands of the Federal Government."

> Also, he mentioned various civil organizations. He said that they were involved in politics much more than the public suspected, and that in the future they were going to become yet more involved. Among them, I think he included both the Elks and Eagles.

"You know, Kerry, before his death John Dillinger wrote a note insisting that he had never harmed anyone. Why do you suppose he felt that way?"

"Who the hell knows? How could I answer a question like that?"

"I think central banking ought to be abolished. Don't you agree?"

"What is central banking?"

"That's where bankers have got the power to inflate or deflate the value of the currency in order to manipulate the economy."

"Debasing the coinage. Yeah, Jessica says they were doing that at the fall of the Roman Empire. If that's what you mean, I agree. That's a form of fraud. I don't think we should let them debase the coinage either."

"Kerry, I think the best person to solve a complicated political assassination would be an anarchist — because he wouldn't be partial to any of the many political factions involved."

"Yes, but anarchy isn't practical."

A smug smile brightened his expression. "Don't be hasty in passing judgment on the writings of the anarchists. They had some good ideas, no matter how you feel about the need for government. For example, Bakunin and some of the other anarchists said some very perceptive things about money and banking."

His evident amusement puzzled me at the time.

"There's a guy who hangs out at the Ryder Coffee House on Rampart Street — Ernest or Irv or something like that — who says he's an anarchist. I asked him about anarchy. I said, 'Explain to me how the hell anarchy could be made to work.' You know what his answer was? 'We live in a very complex society.' That's all the dumb sonofabitch would say. Over and over again, to each of my questions: 'We live in a very complex society.' That's all I could get out of him!"

Brother-in-law's private amusement seemed to increase.

"Kerry," he said, groping for words, "there is a game where the people form a large circle and hold hands — and then they choose a person to be in the middle of that circle, to be what they call saythe goat. Now, for the goat, the object of this game is to break out of the circle. For all the other participants — the people who make up the circle — the object of the game is to keep the goat from breaking out, at their particular point in the circle."

I sat there, annoyed at the way he constantly changed the subject.

"Getting back to that anarchist and the Ryder Coffee House," I said, trying to hide my annoyance at Gary, "he's got a lot of other weird ideas besides anarchy. One night I overheard him talking to somebody about how if there was an older man who loved a younger man very much, then maybe there was a way the older man could transfer all his thoughts and experiences, his whole mind, to the younger man. That, he said, would constitute a kind of immortality for the older man — maybe, he said, the only immortality possible. What an absurd notion! How impractical can you get?"

Brother-in-law looked at me as if he wanted to say something but, for some reason, could not. For a moment it occurred to me that maybe he knew the person in question — that both of them belonged to an occultist-anarchist conspiracy. But that was too bizarre. I quickly dismissed the notion.

"I think the only kind of immortality there is, is fame. They say Omar Khayyam lit up the sky of the Persian Empire like a comet. Everyone knew who he was when he lived, and remembered him after he died. That's how I want to be."

My every intuition confirmed that I would accomplish my goal. Sitting in the Bourbon House, swilling coffee and smoking cigarettes, or debating the "whim-worshipping existentialists" at Ivan's or the Ryder, I felt like the young Lenin of rational capitalism.

Every hour of my life seemed spent in a dressing room just before curtain call; I sat forever twiddling nervously in the anteroom of history. Everything was a matter of being aware enough to seize the opportunity that would inevitably present itself.

About the only time I did not feel that way was during those long, meandering talks with Brother-in-law — except now and then, when I allowed my natural optimism to get the better of my judgment. But then something he would say would always convince me he was deluded, or impractical, or joking. "I'm only kidding, Kerry."

As he spoke, he displayed a funny little mannerism from time to time of moving his hands, back and forth, as if he were administering holy water or playing the piano, his fingers wiggling. Usually, this gesture was indicative of multiplicity — such as of all the many conflicting political factions in a complicated assassination conspiracy, almost as if he felt they were at his fingertips.

I Would Risk My Life

IN Louisiana, during the summer, in the afternoons, when it is not raining in a heavy, steady rhythm, it often seems as if it is about to rain, even when the sun is shining brightly. For hours the air just hangs, stagnant and muggy.

I recall that it was on one such afternoon that Brother-in-law mentioned that his family traced its lineage back to the Crusades. Kirstein means in German "follower of the Christ."

When I asked him what "stein" meant, taken alone, Brother-in-law said it was translated as "cup."

In the Marines I had known a man named Steinknopf. I mentioned that and Brother-in-law said it meant "cup head."

In German beer-drinking fraternities, he told me, "they use the top of a human skull for a stein, and that's what that name means."

I shuddered.

"Do you know what Germans call a battleground? A rose garden — because of the red wounds of the soldiers."

Conversation lagged. This afternoon's discussion was not intense. I kept wishing Slim would say it was time to go. I asked Gary what branch of the service he was in.

"I was drafted into the Navy. During World War II they were drafting for both the Army and the Navy."

Slim mentioned previously that his brother-in-law, as well as most Midwestern Americans of Germanic background, had been shipped to the Pacific instead of Europe — for fear their national loyalties would tempt them to spy for the Germans.

"My dad was in the Navy," I said. "He worked on a landing barge."

"I was in Naval Intelligence," Brother-in-law remarked.

"Where were you stationed?" That a pro-Nazi second generation German-American should be assigned to intelligence, anywhere, was not a peculiarity I thought to question.

"I was on Guam," he answered.

"My dad was stationed on Okinawa," I told him.

"Kerry," he said for the third or fourth time, "there are only three people in the world who understand Einstein's theory of relativity. Do you realize that?"

"Not really."

I wondered if he was trying to hint that he was one of them. In retrospect, I think he wanted to draw attention to the identity of those three individuals.

"Do you know that it is actually possible to trisect pi?"

"In high school geometry they said pi was indeterminate, and therefore could not be trisected."

"That's what they say, Kerry. They are wrong, though."

I shrugged. Mathematics had always bored me. I wished Brother-in-law would offer me another cup of coffee.

After one of the times he reminded me that he was "more like a mad scientist" than the person he seemed, he added, "and I think people like me — people who are more intelligent than others — are persecuted and enslaved because of our superior intellect. And I think it ought to be the other way around. I think people like me should be able to do whatever we want with people of lesser intelligence. Don't you agree, Kerry, that that is a rational attitude?"

I felt like a mouse engaged in a dialogue with a cat. That he was playing games with me for his own amusement seemed obvious. His motives, though, were terribly obscure — assuming there were any, besides passing a dull afternoon telling lies to a gullible young man from the French Quarter.

I thought about what he said. "Yes," I replied hesitantly, "that does seem like a rational viewpoint." I would have preferred not to answer at all. Altruistic societies unfairly exploited genius and talent. That was one of Ayn Rand's central contentions. I had never thought about whether or not that gave exceptionally intelligent people the right to exploit the mediocre in return.

More to the point, it seemed at the time, was whether or not Brother-in-law really was a "mad scientist." As unlikely as it seemed, it was no more preposterous than his internally inconsistent Nazism.

"Kerry, even Ayn Rand says there are times when self-sacrifice is justified. For example, when the society you live in becomes intolerable, she says, it makes more sense to give your life than to suffer oppression. Do you agree with that? Wouldn't you rather give your life," he emphasized the words, "than live under an intolerable system?" At this point he was up and about, becoming animated again.

"Well," I said, "let's just say I would be willing to risk my life."

"Yes! Yes! To risk your life. That's what I'm talking about."

"When a society becomes totalitarian, though, I think it is the average man who is to blame, the second-rater, as Ayn Rand calls him — like Peter Keating in *The Fountainhead*."

"I agree," he snapped, and Slim laughed.

What was Brother-in-law up to? He may have been devil's-advocating the opinion of a brilliant scientist connected with the intelligence community who saw me as precisely such an average, mediocre person. Or that may have been his own opinion of me. Either one would explain Slim's laughter.

Yet at other times Brother-in-law seemed to disagree with my contempt for ordinary individuals with no ambition to become great. "You know, Kerry, Carl Sandburg has written a poem celebrating the life of an average, undistinguished man. Don't you think there might be something to that idea after all?"

"Definitely not!"

A Chance to Find Out

"You know, Kerry, the Jews in Germany didn't put up much resistance to the Nazis."

"Yeah, that puzzles me. I met another writer one night in the Quarter, Henry Avery, who lived in Israel, fighting Arabs. He talked about that."

"It is difficult to figure out why they just obligingly marched into the ovens singing religious songs, isn't it?"

"Henry Avery says there were exceptions. In Czechoslovakia, young blond Jewish men infiltrated the SS and kept their people informed about Nazi plans. And in Germany one old Jewish rabbi stood in his doorway and boldly scolded Hitler's police, telling them they could take him and his family, but that they had better not lay a hand on his sacred books."

Genuine admiration seemed to light Brother-in-law's eyes. "Yes!"

Once he gave me his mellowed-out hoodlum grin and said, "I think there ought to be absolute sexual freedom. I think people ought to be able to fuck in the streets, if they want to."

"Certainly. I think we ought to be at least as rational about sex as we are about eating. There are cultures with taboos about food that are as silly as ours about sex. That goes to show how subjective it all really is."

"Kerry, do you think the average person has within himself the potential to be a genius?"

"That's something I've always believed. Maybe a combination of educators and scientists and other geniuses could take someone of average intelligence and cultivate brilliance in them — providing, of course, there was no organic damage to the brain."

"Or perhaps you could create genius in anyone by breaking down all the emotional blocks and sexual inhibitions."

I hadn't thought of that. It seemed logical enough. Many of my own learning disabilities in early elementary school had been emotionally grounded.

However, whenever I would become exceptionally enthusiastic about sexual freedom, Brother-in-law would put a damper on my zeal by pointing out proudly that National Socialism had practiced sexual freedom by maintaining breeding camps for the S.S.

That wasn't what I had in mind.

"Kerry, why are so many rich people attracted to the doctrines of Communism?" In tone his question seemed both agonized and sincere.

"I've been wondering about that myself. I think maybe it is because the Communists are not actually against the rich. What they are always objecting to is the middle class. So possibly the Communists and the rich have got a common enemy."

"The same thing has occurred to me," he said. "And another thing you should keep in mind: in Russia they've got an 'American town' where they train spies and assassins for work in this country. Don't forget that."

> In his book, *Conspiracy* (McGraw-Hill, 1980) Anthony Summers writes: "FBI Director J. Edgar Hoover was one day to wonder aloud to the Warren Commission about the rumored existence of 'an espionage training school outside of Minsk.' In fact, the CIA had been told there was a spy school in Minsk as long ago as 1947, and information since the Kennedy assassination has confirmed the existence of a training school with one-way windows protected by a high wall. This establishment was located close to the Minsk Foreign Language Institute, and in one set of his notes Oswald seems to have gone out of his way to obscure the fact that he had been to the language school..."

He was forever instructing me what to remember and quizzing me about what I knew.

"Did you know that Stalin had a great number of doubles, so as to confuse any would-be assassins?"

"Yeah, an FBI man who belonged to the Mormon Church that I interviewed for a high school term paper told me about that. Also, he gave me a bunch pamphlets by J. Edgar Hoover. You know what Hoover calls Communism — Red Fascism. I think that's a good name for it."

"Yes, Kerry — so do I."

During one conversation like this, he injected the question: "How would you like it, Kerry, if I put you in a position where the people of this country would have to overthrow the government in order to save your life? Is that okay with you?"

I suppressed a laugh. For a two-bit hood, this man sure had big ideas. "Yeah, sure, that's all right with me."

"You will be all alone," he warned.

"I am not afraid of solitude," I said, trying to sound like a hero in an Ayn Rand novel.

"Tell me something: Do you believe familiarity breeds contempt?"

"No. I've never agreed with that saying. I think familiarity breeds love."

"Kerry, you know, people like Fidel Castro — who had to struggle for their causes — aren't going to respect you unless you also go through a struggle."

"Who the hell cares about the respect of Fidel Castro?"

Brother-in-law and Slim just locked at one another and grinned.

Many times he said, "During the Thirties the Rockefellers, the Morgans, the Mellons, the duPonts and a handful of other rich families got together and tried to overthrow the government so as to neutralize Roosevelt. And General Smedley Butler, a retired Marine, exposed the plot."

From time to time he would also ask me if I realized the Rockefellers were Communists.

"I wouldn't be surprised."

"But the Rockefellers are basically idealistic people, Kerry. They are not as mean as many rich people."

A frequent habit of his was to balance one opinion with another like that.

"Kerry, I think your problem is that you are a good writer, but you don't have anything to write about."

"I agree that that's my problem."

"How would you like me to arrange things so that you've got something to write about?"

"I'd like that very much!"

"Tell me: Do you think ignorance is bliss?"

"No."

"You might have a chance to find out for sure." His voice seemed to convey ominous undertones.

"Yeah, we've argued about this before. I most certainly do not agree that ignorance is bliss."

"Remember Cox's Army, Kerry? Did you study that in history?"

"A bunch of farmers who marched to Washington to protest hard times. In boot camp our drill instructor used to compare us to Cox's Army when we marched out of step."

"Marching to Washington like that is a good way to capture the imaginations of the American people. You might want to keep it in mind."

Exactly when he thought I would need to march to Washington was unclear to me. Vaguely, it is linked in my memory with the Smedley Butler story.

> A complete account of the fascist plot exposed by General Smedley Butler is to be found in Jules Archer's *The Plot to Seize the White House* (Hawthorn Books, New York). On page 213 Archer quotes John J. McCormack, who probed Butler's charges in 1934: "There is no doubt that General Butler was telling the truth... We believed his testimony one hundred percent. He was a great, patriotic American in every respect."
>
> Details of the plot and excerpts from General Smedley Darlington Butler's testimony are also included in *A Man in His Time* by John L. Spivak and in *1000 Americans* by George Seldes, as well as *Facts and Fascism* by Seldes.

Switching Signals

"**K**ERRY, I think a revolutionary ought to be able to make it with no help at all. Don't you? You know, it is not going to be easy for someone who wants to overthrow the system to get a job. He's going to have to learn to live with no help at all. Do you think you could cope with a situation like that?"

"Yes," I lied. Since I had already been down and out more than once, to me it wasn't an academic proposition, and I knew damned well I couldn't make it with no job without at least writing my parents for money or borrowing "bread" from a friend.

"And can you keep your sense of humor under persecution?"

"Yes — at least I didn't lose my sense of humor during fraternity hell week."

Both of them seemed inordinately excited at this response.

"A day will come, Kerry, when you will find yourself in a struggle against very powerful bureaucrats. But the agents they send to harass you will not be loyal to their bosses. They will say and do things to give themselves away, as if by accident. And when you counter-attack — those above you will give way."

That seemed extremely improbable in all respects.

"I've got another suggestion for you. You know, a lot of fascists admire General MacArthur. Heh, heh — you might take up smoking a corn cob pipe."

Once, he spoke to me of something called "a process." It did not, however, sound much like the Process Church. As best I could gather, it was the plan of a fascist think-tank to create a society of docile conformists by means of "processing" each and every citizen.

"That's horrible," I responded.

"True, though. They are already discussing it."

Once, in chatting about cant and syntactical ambiguity, he said, "Someday you are going to encounter people something like Jesuits who speak a secret language where the most literal possible meaning of every idiomatic sentence is the true one.

That way, they will be able to talk to you without being understood by outsiders. Kerry, do you think it's possible to learn a language just by being exposed to it long enough, with no formal lessons?"

"Of course, that's how we learned to speak English as children."

I had read somewhere that assuming control of important symbolic buildings was the key to overthrowing a government, since the people are conditioned to look in that direction for leadership.

> An examination of the strategy used by Nixon at the Watergate Plumbers seems to indicate precisely such thinking dictated many of their decisions: possession of the White House seemed more vital to them than any illusion of fair elections, any pretense of Presidential honesty or the least shred of respect for the Constitution.

Ideas like that seemed more practical than devious secret languages and I mentioned my observation to Brother-in-law.

"Yes," he said as if he had already thought about it, "that's true."

Occasionally, apropos of nothing in particular, Gary would begin discussing how scientists went about creating nervous breakdowns in laboratory mice.

"They keep switching signals on them. First food behind one door and an electric shock behind the other. Then the opposite. Then back again to the first way. You know what happens? The mouse becomes rigid in his behavior. Sooner or later, he just begins hitting at one door repeatedly — no matter how many shocks he receives."

This discovery seemed a source of morbid fascination to him. In fact, he seemed happy about it.

"Kerry, you know California, Arizona, Utah, Colorado, New Mexico and Texas — all that land once belonged to Mexico." This man's attention span didn't seem very impressive.

"Yes, I'm aware of that. I grew up in California — that's part of our history. We stole that land from the Mexicans, and they haven't forgotten it, either."

"And I think we should give it back to them. What do you think?"

"Hell, yes! That's a great idea. I think Mexico is a sleeping giant anyhow — just like they used to say about China. Someday, it's going to be an important modern nation."

Then I laughed and said, "One of my short-story ideas is that Mexico is first to send an rocket to the moon, and they cover its surface with an Aztec calendar! Can you imagine something like that?"

Brother-in-law nodded and laughed.

From time to time he would remind me he still planned to kill the President. Once he said: "I'm going to talk to everyone in the country who wants Kennedy dead about the idea of assassinating him. Then I'm going to do it. Then I'm going to pay a visit to each and every one of them. I'm not going to say anything. I'm just going to look at them and smile, so they'll get the idea. After that, I'll feel free to call on them for favors."

Think of Me as the Devil

SOMEWHERE among the conversations mentioned previously, there was one in particular that seemed incredible to me at the time. One morning Slim took me out to the house in Harahan, and Brother-in-law opened things up by announcing that he had just read *Atlas Shrugged.*

Always in search of converts, I perked up. "Isn't Ayn Rand a genius?" I said.

Snorting, he said, "She's a woman."

"So what? She's the greatest mind of our age."

"Nothing great is ever produced by a woman."

"But — "

"However, I found Galt's motor fascinating — the one that did not require fuel, but ran instead on static electricity from the atmosphere. Kerry, did you know that there already is such a motor, and the oil companies are suppressing it?"

"That's what my dad says. He never read *Atlas Shrugged,* though. I tried to read him Galt's speech once, but he just kept saying, 'When is this guy going to get to the point?'"

"And, Kerry, that motor was invented by Nazi rocket scientists working for Hitler — and it is the motor that is now used to power flying saucers!"

I should have known Brother-in-law would say that. Naturally, I was disappointed. Expecting a convert to what I thought was the most rational philosophy in all the world, I was instead confronted by the same old, raving paranoiac Nazi maniac as always.

> According to personal correspondence to Stan Jamison from a man named Crabb of the Borderland Research Foundation in Vista, California: "An ex-Marine here in Vista told me that he personally saw operational Flying Saucers at Edwards Air Force base in California in 1967 when he was on temporary duty there. So the Air Force has anti-gravity machines and a radical, cheap, universally available, nonpolluting source of power which would solve all our pollution problems, and make obsolete the oil industry; so anti-gravity will never be made available for public use as long as the oil majors control policy here in the U. S."

Brother-in-law was pacing up and down. With a dramatic pivot he stopped, looked at me and said, "Don't you agree that if such a motor exists, it ought to be made known to the world?"

"Of course."

"And do you agree that there could be no greater crime — no greater crime in the world, Kerry — than the suppression of that engine?"

"Yes."

"No greater crime," he repeated solemnly. "I agree. If there is a motor like that."

"Ayn Rand speaks of Prometheus, who brought the fire of the gods to humanity. Remember what happened to him? He was chained to the rocks and vultures fed on his entrails forever. You know, Kerry, if you try to expose that motor, that will happen to you. The world will tear you apart."

"I can imagine."

Somehow, nothing he said seemed to ring true. More than a matter of content was involved: Brother-in-law seemed so excited with his pacing about and gesturing that it was out of character. Slim sat there silently, as usual, looking much too amused.

"Another thing: one of the scientists that invented that motor went to work in Canada after the war for the AVRO Company. Until the Diefenbaker government drove them bankrupt. Diefenbaker was a Liberal, Kerry. You don't like Liberals, do you?"

"I certainly don't."

"Kerry, that scientist was just like John Galt in *Atlas Shrugged.* And when that company went bankrupt — he vanished. Just like John Galt!"

I was not at all comfortable with this notion of a National Socialist behaving like an Ayn Rand hero.

"And you know what else? That man had designed a flying saucer for A. V. Roe — and when he disappeared, he took his flying saucer with him!"

Sure.

Brother-in-law now turned and crossed the room in my direction, saying in what seemed a very angry tone of voice: "And, Kerry, that man's name was Tom Miethe!" He pronounced the name with frightening bitterness.

Slim was nearly in stitches, though.

I was to hear from a friend, Cid Norris, in Atlanta in 1975 that there was in the sixties at Georgia Tech a professor of nuclear physics named Tom Miethe. Moreover, he was known to frequent the Catacombs Coffee House at the corner of 14th and Peachtree.

During that time period, a man identifying himself as a runaway CIA agent, bleeding from gunshot wounds, arrived at the Catacombs without warning and left what he claimed were tapes pertaining to a JFK assassination conspiracy with David Braden, proprietor of the Catacombs.

No sooner had this alleged CIA maverick departed, in great haste, than there arrived a detachment of suited men with badges who, according to the tale told by Ms. Norris, thoroughly searched the premises. "It was weird," she told me, "because they said they were looking for an escaped fugitive, but they were looking under mattresses and in drawers — like what they really wanted was the tapes."

David Braden is thought by Cid Norris to have contacted Art Kunkin of the *Los Angeles Free Press* and New Orleans District Attorney Jim Garrison about the mysterious information contained in the tapes. Not long afterwards, Braden told Norris he had been warned to leave town, and not long after, he did.

As for Tom Miethe, who wasn't present the night of the incident, he is alleged to have also departed from Atlanta, suddenly and mysteriously, with no word about where he was going — after designing a car engine that did not use gasoline.

Most of what Cid Norris told me was confirmed independently by another Atlanta woman, Anita Teel, who claims to have lived with Miethe for a time. Ms. Teel claims Miethe spoke at least one foreign language, was addicted to collecting guns and binoculars and displayed an impressive ability to pull strings with a phone call to this or that anonymous contact.

"Kerry, there also appear to be flying saucers that are from outer space." At this point he mentioned a name I do not recall, saying, "He met some flying saucer people on the rim of the Grand Canyon. They were dwarfs with enlarged heads and they communicated by means of telepathy with him."

I looked at Slim. "It's true," he said, with a smirk.

Techniques involving the use of high-frequency sound waves exist, and are used within the intelligence community, to produce thoughts from the outside in the mind of an unsuspecting victim. According to a news report based on data released under the Freedom of Information Act, the CIA once induced a Soviet agent to leap out a window to his own death by this means. It occurs to me that the same method could be used to produce an illusion of telepathic communication.

"I went to high school with a guy who believed in flying saucers from other planets," I told them. "You would've liked him," I added, looking at Brother-in-law. "Our Senior English teacher asked us to write essays about our politics and he wrote one, insisting that he was a 'Military Fascist.' What surprised us most, though, was that our Liberal teacher gave him a A+ on it. No shit! His name was Hickman. In the essay, he said he expected the flying saucer people to help him take over the world. I couldn't believe it when he got an A+. The teacher, Mr. Surface, even had him read it to the class. He said it was well-written and provocative. I found it so unusual that I borrowed Hickman's essay from him and copied it in my journal."

Brother-in-law responded as if this was something he already knew about, with a pleasant, confident nod.

"Hickman didn't have many friends, and he used to always dress completely in black. Only one guy — another social misfit named Dennis — used to hang out with him."

"Kerry, you know Hitler used to talk about what he called 'the Superman.'"

"Yes, I remember reading something about that. Hitler admired 'the Superman,' but was also afraid of him."

"There was a mysterious man named Gurdjieff, Kerry, whom Ouspensky wrote about."

"Under the initial, 'G.'"

"Yes, that's him."

"Gurdjieff went to Tibet and was functioning as an emissary of the Dalai Lama. There's a theory that he contacted the Nazis by short-wave radio from Central Asia, Kerry, and that it was he who was 'the Superman.'"

In 1978 I found a more complete version of this theory in an Avon paperback called *The Occult Reich*.

"There is going to come a time when all these things will be very important to you, because you are going to have to deal with them. At that time it will help you to read a book by Peter Viereck called *Metapolitics: The Roots of the Nazi Mind.* Can you remember that?"

> This particular statement would have been made in or after the spring of 1963, although I'm not certain it was included in the discussion of Tom Miethe.
> At this point a sense of chronology eludes me. I recall, though, linking it to a book I read in April of 1963, *Psychotherapy East and West*, in which the Latin term, meta, was explained in connection with a discussion of the meta-Freudians.

"Metapolitics," I said. "Yes, I can remember that."

"Metapolitics: The Roots of the Nazi Mind," he repeated. "It may come in handy in understanding someone you're going to be up against."

I must have looked frightened, because both Brother-in-law and Slim laughed.

"You know, in this generation there are two Dalai Lamas. There is usually only one. That is because — "

"I know, and one of them is sympathetic with Marxism — the sonofabitch!"

"Yes, he is open to Marxist ideas, Kerry, but that doesn't necessarily make him a villain." "I don't know about that."

"Kerry, have you ever heard that song: 'I'm a ramblin' wreck from Georgia Tech and a heck of an engineer...?'"

"Sure. Everybody has."

"You know, Kerry, Ockham's Razor doesn't always apply to every problem to be solved."

"What is Ockham's Razor?"

"That's the idea that the hypothesis making the least number of assumptions is most inclined to be the valid one."

"Oh yeah, I remember now."

Occasionally he would launch into a long discourse of Zeno's paradoxes. "You know, from a logical point of view an arrow can never reach its target."

"Why not?"

"Because if it keeps halving the distance between itself and the target it will continue to halve that distance on into infinitesimally."

I didn't like arguments against logic. "Reason is more than just logic; it also requires observable facts; it is a combination of logic and facts. And it is a fact that arrows hit targets."

"If a barber shaves every man in a village, but does not shave himself — yet does not have a beard — then who shaves the barber?"

As best I recall, the answer was that the barber was a woman. But I hated talking about philosophical riddles. For a man who showed such irritation at facetiousness in others, Brother-in-law certainly seemed indulgent of his own digressions.

"Have you heard the story of the riddle of the Sphinx, Kerry?"

"Yes." Whoever this man was, he definitely possessed a classical education. In the French Quarter it was not unusual for college graduates to be working as barkers on Bourbon Street, so — at the time — it didn't occur to me that all this fondness for ancient fables was inconsistent with a gangster's career.

Appropriate to the situation, he often mentioned Faust, and seemed to view himself as a Mephistopheles. "Just think of me as the Devil," he would say with a laugh. "I go around making pacts with people."

As in everything else, his preference in mythological themes seemed heavily weighted in the direction of death and suffering — or, sometimes, power.

"Remember the sword of Damocles?"

"Yeah."

"Remember the Greek mathematician who said, 'Give me a lever and a place to stand and I will move the world?'"

"I like the one you told me about Hitler. About how he said nobody should ever make the mistake of assuming people are any stupider than they really are."

"Yes, Hitler. did say that."

"That's so true. A certain amount of rationality is needed just to work at a job and survive. People aren't near as stupid as these politicians think they are."

"Kerry? Do you know that line from that Tennessee Ernie Ford song: 'I got one fist of iron and the other of steel; if the right one don't get you, then the left one will...?'"

I chose to interpret that as a warning of some kind.

Once, I told a tale that may have given Brother-in-law an idea. "I heard a story on the radio about a French financial genius. A doctor came to him and offered him fifty francs to will his brain to medical science, so they could cut it up and find out what made him so smart. But when the man died and the doctor came to collect his brain, it turned out he had sold it for the same price to fifty other doctors. Nobody got it. His brain was buried with him."

California Mind Control

As sophisticated as he could seem, Brother-in-law was never above platitudes. "Remember the story of the little boy who cried wolf?" Patiently, as if imparting great original wisdom, he repeated the whole story to me. "And so when a real wolf came, nobody believed him."

"They used to read that to us in grammar school," I said coldly.

"Remember the story of Cæsar's wife? About how she couldn't afford even the appearance of lacking virtue — because she was Cæsar's wife?"

"Yes. I saw the movie with Marlon Brando and Greer Garson, based on the play."

"That's an important lesson to keep in mind."

"We went to a sneak preview when I was in junior high. Our drama teacher got us free tickets."

"Do you recall Louis XIV? They called him the Sun King and they built a cult around him. He said, 'I am the State.'"

"Yeah, people used to even stand around and watch him take baths. There was a picture of that in one of our history books."

"You know that saying, Kerry, about the exception that proves the rule?"

"Yes. That didn't used to make sense to me. If there is an exception, that proves it is not a rule. Then I read somewhere that people use that saying wrong. It means the exception that tests the rule; they are using 'prove' in the sense of testing. I think that was in *Reader's Digest*."

"Remember Mendel, Kerry, who discovered genetics? His accomplishments were never recognized within his own lifetime. Wouldn't that be horrible? To make an important discovery and yet to remain anonymous and unrecognized?"

"A fate worse than death," I replied.

"You wouldn't let that happen to you, would you?"

"Don't worry. I wouldn't."

What made these discussions seem unimportant, more than anything else, was the way they wandered from one topic to another. Swirls of organic verbal coherence would build up to the point where we would seem to be getting somewhere and I would become excited, then Brother-in-law would either seem to change the subject for no reason, or he would make a remark so horrid as to turn me off. As a small boy he must, I figured, have gone around knocking down sand castles and sticking firecrackers in ant hills — for he seemed gleefully delighted with acts of destruction.

"Remember what Priscilla said to John Alden?"

"Yeah, 'Speak for yourself, John.' I read the *Classic Comic* of *The Courtship of Miles Standish*. A guy I've known since the third grade had a whole collection of them. That's how I learned to read."

"She wanted to hear what he had to say, not what the man who sent him told him to say."

"Yeah, I bet I would never have learned to read in school. I just wasn't much into Dick, Jane, Sally and Spot."

"Kerry, I think the philosopher-king should be someone who doesn't blame messengers for bringing bad news."

"I agree. Once in a *Captain Midnight* radio show an evil king had someone shot for bringing him news he didn't like. That seemed awfully unfair."

"You know, that was one of Hitler's shortcomings. Toward the end of the war, when the Germans were losing, he instructed his intelligence people not to give him any bad news."

"That figures."

"Did you know, Kerry, that Hitler and most other great dictators kept a copy of Machiavelli's *The Prince* at their bedsides?"

"Eric Hoffer's book, *The True Believer*, seems to be written in the same style as *The Prince*. He says that one of the sources of recruiting for fanatical causes is the bored, because if your own business is worth minding, then you usually mind it. I like that saying. I think one of these days I'll print up business cards that quote it. New Orleans is just full of people who don't understand how to mind their own business. Total strangers are always walking up to me and giving me free advice. I hate that."

Slim shared my feelings about the provinciality of New Orleaneans and was always ready to discuss the subject. Brother-in-law was not the same way. Avoiding my glance, he would say nothing.

Lulls in the conversation were not unusual. But they would always pick up again.

"You know, in the Mayan culture of Central America they used to raise virgins from birth for the sole purpose of sacrificing them to the gods when they came of age."

"Yeah. What a waste! There was this documentary film about that they used to show us in school. It was about Guatemala. It must have been one of the only films in the library, because they showed it nearly every year. They kept the virgins in a gigantic well until it was time to cut their hearts out."

"Kerry, do you believe in the greatest good for the greatest number?"

"Yes. But I believe the greatest number is Old Number One here."

Brother-in-law cracked up. He liked that one. It was a statement he could identify with.

One of his trite repetitions, spoken always with a cheerful, tight little grin, was, "You know, Kerry, it really is a dog-eat-dog world."

"That's what my dad used to always tell me."

"It's true."

"I think that depends on how you look at it. Ayn Rand would say that's a parasitical attitude."

"Kerry thinks everything Ayn Rand says," Slim injected to Brother-in-law, "is about ninety-nine percent more true than anything anyone else says."

"Not exactly. There are things in Ayn Rand's writings I disagree with."

"Kerry, imagine a movement based on a man, instead of an idea. Consider the advantages. A man possesses many ideas. He is more flexible than an ideology," Brother-in-law went on in a voice filled with warmth and emotion. "People can identify with a man as they cannot identify with cold, abstract ideas. Think of that — a movement based on a man."

"Yes," I said, "I think that's probably true," unsure of whether or not he had changed the subject again.

"You know, Kerry, the duPont family is very large; there are hundreds and hundreds of them."

He had changed the subject.

Then there was something he mentioned once or twice that seemed even less credible than flying saucers powered by German secrets of perpetual motion.

"In the state of California, Kerry, there is a plan to begin performing mind control experiments on people who live there. I. G. Farben, the economic arm of the Third Reich is involved in it. They are going to put surveillance devices in the heads of their experimental victims, in order to monitor them, and then they are going to subject them to mind control. So, if I were you, Kerry, I would think maybe it would be a good idea to stay out of California in the future."

I looked at him. I didn't say anything, except to acknowledge that he had spoken. A picture was conjured up in my mind of thousands of puppets on electronic strings being manipulated by a vast, hidden cartel — of people in psychological torment that seemed too horrible to be possible. This guy was wasting his talents as a cheap hood employed in a brewery; he should be writing novels.

A couple of other times he spoke of what, perhaps because of the way it was phrased, sounded more credible. "Kerry, the Fascists are now experimenting with advanced thought control techniques. You know, there are Fascists in this country. Among them is Henry Luce, who publishes *Time* and *Life* magazines. They are planning to build a society comprised of nothing but human robots, with transistors installed in the backs of their heads, so that they will be absolutely obedient to subliminal messages."

"Yeah. There are people who say it can't happen here. But I guess it can."

"Remember the saying about how you can lead a horse to water, but you can't make him drink?"

"A friend of mine in high school used to say, 'You can lead

a horse to water, but a pencil must be lead.'"

With characteristic unfairness, Brother-in-law seemed annoyed at the irrelevance of my remark.

He found my comments about Germans equally irritating. "Every now and then we have German tourists at work, where I wait tables at the Sheraton-Charles. They're so rude and crude," I said, borrowing one of Slim's favorite expressions. "They blow their noses in the cloth napkins and leave olive pits in the ash trays. When they want a waiter, they snap their fingers. They talk loud. I don't like Germans very much," I added, feeling brave.

"You cannot, however, generalize about a whole race from a few examples."

I couldn't believe my ears!

"And there are things about the Germans, Kerry, that are quite admirable. They are very precise people, in both their music and their devotion to science. In that sense they are highly civilized — real sticklers for perfection."

"Yeah, I guess that's true."

"Kerry, one of Nelson Rockefeller's sons went on an expedition in the jungles of New Guinea and vanished. I wonder what ever happened to him?"

I shrugged my shoulders.

"Kerry, you know, criminologists say that a strand of hair is a more certain method of identification than a fingerprint."

"I read that in *Dick Tracy's Crimestopper's Textbook*," I replied, adding that I had also learned from the same source that the best murder weapon was an icicle, because it melts afterwards and cannot be used as evidence.

Once he spoke of the People's Republic of China — a very mysterious, bellicose foreign power in those days. "You know, Clare Booth Luce is in favor of diplomatic recognition for Red China."

"No, I didn't realize that. Hell, she supports Goldwater. I don't get it."

"It's true, though." After a pause, he added, "You know, loyalty to the State is expected above loyalty to your own family there."

"Yeah. I saw a picture of a statue once in a book in the library of a little boy in Communist China who reported his own parents to the secret police."

"Those are the values they foster there. They've got so many millions of people to work with that their values have to be different than ours."

"I don't see what difference the number of people makes. That is altruism at its worst extreme, if you ask me."

"Kerry, I've got a close friend in the New Orleans police department. He knows I'm a burglar. If I ever get in trouble, I can rely on him for favors."

"Yeah, they ought to call the New Orleans police the Blue Mafia. Did I tell you about the time I got put in jail for nailing posters to telephone poles? I never saw such rotten conditions and such open corruption in my life. I'm tempted to write a book about it."

"Kerry, when I take over the country, how would you like to be Secretary of Defense? You are a strong believer in national defense. You would be able to travel everywhere in the world, and that's something I know you would like. I think you'd make a very good Secretary of Defense."

"Yes. I'd probably like that job."

"Then it's settled. When I take over, you will be my Secretary of Defense." Slim was looking at me and laughing.

"And who do you recommend for President — after we kill Kennedy and Johnson's term expires?"

"Barry Goldwater," I answered without hesitation.

"Don't talk to me about that raving Red," Brother-in-law said with a laugh. "I think Nixon ought to be our man, because Nixon is unprincipled. A man without principles is easy to manipulate. We want somebody we can control, Kerry."

I was amused to hear Goldwater called a "raving Red." Brother-in-law seemed to be making fun of himself — of the extremity of his own paranoia and right-wing views. Little things like that always made everything else he said seem less menacing.

There were many subjects of discussion about which my memories are vague due to distaste. Barracudas and moray eels were among the themes he would dwell on much too long for my comfort. Among the only undersea creatures that attack humans without provocation, they seemed of particular fascination to him, as I would sit there fidgeting and trying to change the topic to a more pleasant one.

Another depressing subject was Hughes Aircraft, of which he spoke quite often, although I do not recall the details of what he said — something, I think, about a project invasive of human rights. All that remains in my mind here is a surrealistic visual impression that seems purely imaginary in origin, though associated in his words somehow: greasy airplane parts and scraps of aluminum in a vacant lot. Brother-in-law was forever dwelling on the mundane when he was not preoccupied with the depressing or the bizarre.

"Kerry, have you ever heard the saying, 'Let George do it?'"

In retrospect I wonder if this was a veiled reference to George De Mohrenschildt who, according to his own statements just previous to his death, was involved in the assassination conspiracy.

At that time I was unaware that a man named George De Mohrenschildt was involved in Dallas in discussions with Oswald that could easily have resembled Brother-in-law's talks with me. At least, Oswald seems to have talked with De Mohrenschildt alone at length, and he seemed to come away from those discussions with an attitude that was as ambivalent toward him as mine was toward Brother-in-law.

Sometimes I was successful in returning digression for digression, particularly in the realm of stories about weird people. My tales of Southern California's ample lunatic fringe seemed to entertain Brother-in-law.

Besides Daniel Fry's UFO watchers, there was a religious cult in Box Canyon under the leadership of a Messianic ex-convict calling himself Krishna Venta — until his followers assassinated him.

> "Another input into the mind of Manson was provided by a religious cult, The Fountain of the World, located West of the Spahn Ranch in Box Canyon near the Santa Susanna fire department. He was very impressed with the Fountain

and spent a lot of time visiting it.

" ...The Fountain was formed by a holy man named Krishna Venta who died by violence. The family grooved with the violent history of the Fountain. The religious retreat occupied subterranean chambers and caves wherein they did their thing. As the cult progressed, dissension ensued and parties unknown blew up the founder, Krishna Venta, and nine of his followers — with forty pieces of dynamite placed in the catacombs. This occurred in 12-10-58, whereafter the Fountain struggled onward and was still thriving when Manson discovered it," according to Ed Sanders on pages 110-111 of *The Family*.

As I remember it now and told it to Brother-in-law then, Krishna Venta had been blown away by the very men who died with him, whose wives he had been making it with. An eerie tape recording explaining their motives was headlined in the newspapers as "voices from the dead" — a gift to history the assassins had been kind enough to contribute before destroying themselves and their Messiah.

"That man had it made," I said. "Not only was he fucking all the women, but he had required all his converts to sign over to him all their earthly possessions when they joined. He said he was not born of woman, because he didn't have a belly button. I figured he must've gotten plastic surgery."

"Kerry, you know how in old Westerns they run the bad guys into a box canyon before rounding them up?"

Also among the more well-known luminaries of Southern California's more eccentric attractions was a television personality named Criswell whose predictions about the future were made in sing-song tones that I found easy to imitate. A close friend of Mae West, he once prophesied she would become President of the United States.

Then there was a tale told by a woman who had lived across the street from us about a strange lady she met at a Tupperware party who had purchased tickets to Venus from the author of a then popular book called *The Flying Saucers Have Landed*.

Among the most notable lecturers Greg Hill and I had encountered at Understanding were Reinholt Schmidt and Jimmy Valaquez. Schmidt amused us because he said the interplanetary aliens spoke to him in High German and that the numerals on the dials in their saucer were "just regular numbers." When Greg asked, "Why do you suppose they use Arabic numerals just like us?" Schmidt said, "Why, I don't know what other kind of numbers they would use."

Valaquez was a more convincing speaker, but then his story of encountering UFO people was so far-fetched as to require the utmost rhetorical skill. All his aliens dressed like Jesus and wore sandals that were made of living protoplasm that glowed in the dark.

"Remember Eisenhower's farewell address, Kerry, about the danger of what he called the military-industrial complex?" was a question Brother-in-law only asked me once.

"Yeah, I figure Ike was senile by the time he made that speech."

"No, Kerry, there really is a military-industrial complex, and you had best keep that in mind."

"That's right," Slim added. "He ain't lyin'."

"Kerry, if the society you are living in begins to become totalitarian, you will be able to tell," he said more than once, "because, when you attempt to uncover the past, they will say: 'Don't bother with the past; only the future is important.'"

"Yes, William F. Buckley tells a story about Mussolini saying something like that to an American general once." My information was slightly confused.

Mentioned in Buckley's *Up From Liberalism* in connection with an attempt to officially "muzzle" General Smedley Butler, the incident is also reported in Jules Archer's *The Plot to Seize the White House*. General Butler invoked the wrath of Herbert Hoover some years previous to his effort to expose a ruling class conspiracy against Roosevelt by repeating a story told him by a reporter in which Mussolini's chauffeur-driven car ran over a small child without stopping afterwards.

Page 116 of Jules Archer's book says: "... The wire services carried journalist Cornelius Vanderbilt's revelation that he had been the one who had told Butler the true story about Mussolini. He corrected a few details. After running down the child, Vanderbilt said, Mussolini had observed the journalist looking back in horror and had patted his knee reassuringly, saying, 'Never look back, Mr. Vanderbilt — always look ahead in life.'"

"You will know it is happening — when your society is becoming totalitarian — as soon as they start saying: 'Yesterday's gone. Don't stop thinking about tomorrow.'"

"Just like Mussolini."

"And another thing, Kerry: Do you know where the expression, 'swan song,' comes from? A swan sings its most beautiful song as it is dying."

> In the aftermath of Watergate, when Martha Mitchell died of cancer of the bone marrow, I recalled Brother-in-law's words here. Of everyone involved in that scandal, she was by far the most talkative. A book called *World Without Cancer*, circulated by the John Birch Society, claims there is a Rockefeller-Farben conspiracy that disposes of its enemies by means of artificially giving them cancer. Jack Ruby, Clay Shaw and Werner Von Braun were among persons allegedly connected to the John Kennedy murder plot who died of cancer. David Ferrie, one of Jim Garrison's suspects, was known to have at one time experimented extensively with inducing cancer in laboratory rats.

"You know the angel in the Book of Revelations that rules the world for a thousand years with a rod of iron? What do you figure that could symbolize?"

"Anything you want it to," I replied casually. "That's the advantage of predicting things in vague language: they are bound to come true — one way or another, sooner or later, if someone interprets them with sufficient ingenuity."

"Rods are used in nuclear energy reactors. They are also used in computers."

"Like I say." I was not very patient with scriptural interpretation, especially since I knew Gary professed to be a pagan, if not an outright atheist.

"I think the Bible would make a good code key for a revolutionary movement, though," he said.

"Yes — especially since there is one in every prison cell and hotel room in the country."

Whenever he persisted for long in discussing Revelations, I would turn the discussion to my favorite foreign movie, *The Seventh Seal*, since it drew its imagery from the Biblical Apocalypse.

"I think the mission of this century," I would say, "is to transform religion from the field of philosophy to the realm of the arts."

"You know, Kerry, you aren't going to be able to be too far ahead of your time."

"That's all right with me. My ambition is to be remembered as a man of his own times. Why be a sensitive genius who brags about being misunderstood? That's why I am not afraid to use clichés in my writing. Clichés are the idioms of the common people. Writers who scorn them are snobs."

Both Slim and Brother-in-law looked at me with hearty approval.

"Kerry, I think it would be better for the world if eventually just one ideology — no matter what it was — came to predominate everywhere."

"So do I," I said without attaching much importance to my words.

Similar to Brother-in-law's fascination with the Revelation of Saint John the Divine was his fondness for the Oracles of Nostradamus, toward which I displayed equal impatience.

Another of his favorite subjects were recent movies. "Remember in *Night of the Hunter*, how the preacher had the letters for the words 'LOVE' and 'HATE' tattooed on the fingers of opposite hands?"

"Now that was a movie that said something valid about religion. That preacher was a killer."

"Remember the woman Susan Hayward played in *I Want to Live*? You know that was based on a true story. Remember how sensual and alive she was and how much people liked her for that reason?"

"Yes! That dance scene with the bongos was fantastic! I saw that when I was at Atsugi, Japan, in Marine Air Control Squadron One. We turned I Want to Live! into a slogan when we rioted in our barracks. I got office hours once for writing it on a post with a laundry marker. An asshole corporal named Curtis reported me. I hated that guy."

"Do you know what cant is?"

I wondered if he he was talking about the German philosopher that Jack, a Marxist-Leninist who hung out with the rest of the radicals at the Ryder Coffee House, liked.

But no. "Cant is a kind of slang used by criminal groups in order to make understanding what they say to each other more difficult for outsiders," Brother-in-law took pains to explain.

"I'm planning to write a novel that deals with, among other things, organized crime in New Orleans. There's so much of it here."

"Yeah. Most people think New Orleans is a French town. Actually, it's a Dago town. Italians are clowns. Hitler never should have accepted them into the Axis. That's one of the reasons he lost the war."

"What about the Japanese?"

"Now the Japanese are clever people," he said. "Among the Asians, they are the Master Race, together with the Chinese. You know, gunpowder and paper were both Chinese inventions."

"Yeah."

"Kerry, come over here and sit next to me. I want to tell you something important." I sat on the floor next to the footstool where he was seated, hunched forward with his elbows resting on both knees.

"Now listen." He fixed a fierce glare in my direction. "If there was to be a rebellion in the intelligence community — and if a man were to find himself in the middle of that rebellion — and if he were to blow a lot of covers, then those people whose covers were blown would be very angry. And they would need a method of dealing with that anger. So I think that man who exposed them to the government should be taken to sea in a submarine — and tortured to death."

An awkward silence followed.

"Don't you agree?"

"I guess so," I answered meekly, quickly pushing the whole subject from my thoughts. There were other subjects that I have dealt with by pushing them away, even more success-fully. For example, from the time that I read in Ed Sanders' *The Family* about filmed ritual murders until well into 1976 when I began encountering seemingly unrelated rumors about "snuff films," I failed to remember the weird and disturbing discussion with Slim and Gary about "snuff movies."

Before recalling it clearly, I was saying in relation to the rumors, "That's just the type of thing Slim and Gary would have been into." Yet today I remember vividly the morning Gary asked me what I thought of "snuff films" and then explained to me what they were. I recall exactly where both he and I were sitting in his living room at the time. I remember my intense fear, and how I privately rationalized my pretense of agreement. And I have recollected ever since early in 1977 the exact expression in Gary's eyes as he leered at me wickedly and spoke of building "a network of blackmailed murderers."

Secret Governments

"**D**ID it ever occur to you, Kerry, that one of the best ways to hide something is right out in plain view, under everybody's noses?"

> "At the end of 1961," writes E. Howard Hunt in *Undercover*, "Dulles was forced to 'retire,' and Richard Bissell followed. He was succeeded, not by Tracy Barnes, but by Richard Helms, untainted by the Bay of Pigs.
>
> "After a considerable bureaucratic struggle Barnes established the Domestic Operations Division and appointed me its chief of covert action. The new division accepted both personnel and projects unwanted elsewhere within CIA, and those covert-action projects that came to me were almost entirely concerned with publishing and publications. We subsidized 'significant' books, for example, *The New Class*, by Milovan Djilas, one of a number of Frederick A. Praeger, Inc., titles so supported; ran a couple of news services — one based in Washington's National Press Building — even subsidizing the printing and distribution of a well-known series of travel books. The work was not particularly demanding, and at the end of the day, I still had sufficient energy to write fiction at home."
>
> As a former Marine buddy of Lee Harvey Oswald, writing a novel based on a man who may have gone to Russia at CIA Instigation, I would have been within the field of Hunt's official attention at that time. I find it hard to believe that he would not at least have known about me, if he was not, as I'm inclined to suspect, traveling to New Orleans on an occasional weekend and giving me his personal attention, using the name of a man he wanted to implicate in the JFK assassination plot: Gary Kirstein.

Perhaps hiding something out in the open was in fact the solution to the John Fitzgerald Kennedy murder. An abundance of evidence, almost pointedly ignored by the Warren Commission, is to be found in the 26 Volumes of testimony and exhibits published by the government shortly after the *Report* was issued.

There we learn that people who could not have been Oswald impersonated him previous to the assassination, that eyewitness testimony indicates Oswald was on the second floor of the Texas School Book Depository within seconds after the shots were fired, that the man who killed police officer Tippit made his escape in a car — when it is known that Lee had never learned to drive — and finally, that there occurred a host of suspicious activity in the vicinity of Dealey Plaza before, during and after the assassination that casts more than reasonable doubt on the lone-assassin theory.

Keeping in mind the assertion conveyed to me by Stan Jamison, that certain of the conspirators at the operational level wanted the mystery to come unraveled, so as to expose the people who had hired them (or at least to heat things up enough to make their ruling class bosses subject to blackmail) it is actually possible to surmise that the many conflicts between the Report and the evidence were intentional.

Did Brother-in-law and his accessories want to see just how far they could go in making the actual truth available to the public, confident of the probability that it would be safely ignored long enough for them to escape prosecution? Such a ploy is not as reckless as it may seem if we keep in mind that the actual assassins would have been positioned so as to take many important and powerful people with them if they went to prison. That would explain Richard Nixon's sweating in the Watergate tapes about E. Howard Hunt's power to make public further crimes, linked somehow in Nixon's mind with "the whole Bay of Pigs thing," in which Nixon obviously felt himself to be implicated.

Brother-in-law seemed to have devoted an unusual amount of thought to what "people," the membership of the general public, do and do not like. In that respect his intuition seems to have been keenly informed.

Among observations typical of his consciousness of public will was a statement he made many times: "You know, Kerry, the general public becomes very excited about things for a short interval, but it has a very brief attention span. Emotions don't run high about anything for long."

"Yeah, one of my teachers in high school used to tell us that a Greek philosopher once said, 'The wrath of the people is great, but their memory is short.'"

From that and similar comments I gathered vaguely that he was already looking forward to a day when it would be safe for the assassins to win public acceptance.

"Kerry, did you ever notice how people just love to eavesdrop?"

"That's why books about writing say it is always a good bet to open a story with dialogue."

"What about the idea of building a whole political movement on that idea — that people love to spy on the lives of others. Would it grow fast or wouldn't it?"

"Sounds to me like it would work."

"Have you ever thought much about the possibilities of electronic politics? You know, you should."

"I keep telling him he should read more science-fiction," Slim contributed, speaking to Brother-in-law and looking at me. "Open up that narrow one-track mind of his with those horse-blinders on both sides, but he don't want to hear that."

"Science fiction bores me," I complained in reply. "I like to read relevant stuff about politics in fiction or non-fiction. Escapist literature isn't my bag."

"But, but, but, but, but..." Slim said in typical fashion when he wanted to point out to anyone that they were ignoring something.

Brother-in-law chimed in with, "Kerry, they can actually design secret governments based upon clandestine electronic communications. That's dealt with in some of the science-fiction Slim is talking about and it is also going to happen in the real world. Someday there will be individuals with microphones planted in their heads so that many people can hear what is going on in their lives. And they will be the centers of invisible governments, that everyone equipped to listen will belong to — like big houses with one person at the center of every one of them. What do you think of that idea?"

I thought it both bizarre and impossible, but I did not want to say as much to them. "Yeah, that sounds like a pretty clever way to resist the government."

"Sweeney then developed delusions: he believed that the CIA had implanted a radio receiver in his teeth, so he pried out some dental work; he believed electrodes had been implanted in his brain, so he tried to find a surgeon to remove them. He also had auditory hallucinations, believing he was picking up messages from outer space," writes E. Fuller Torrey in his article, "The Sweeney-Lowenstein Madness," appearing in the October 1980 issue of *Psychology Today*.

Like Congressman Lowenstein's assassin, Timothy Leary has been claiming somewhat more respectably that he receives messages from interstellar aliens, which he calls "Starseed signals." That Sweeney could not settle on one theory to account for what he experienced does not prove it was delusory, only that he was more obviously confused perhaps than Leary about the sources of his oppression.

"Kerry, what do you think of various organizations in the intelligence community joining forces for recruiting purposes, by implanting listening devices on individuals and observing their behavior until who they should work for is decided on the basis of what kind of people they are?"

Again, I expressed agreement to what seemed both irrelevant and unlikely.

"Remember Adolph Eichmann's plea at his trial in Israel that he was only following orders? I think that should be a legitimate defense. Don't you?"

"Like Paul Krassner said in *The Realist*: Where were all the defenders of Caryl Chessman at the Eichmann trial?"

Chessman was a confessed rapist in California whose execution was postponed for many years because he also happened to be quite intellectually gifted.

"Liberals are so hypocritical," I added. Actually, I believed in civil disobedience rather than blindly following orders, but again I saw no reason to say as much at this point to this particular individual. Agreeing with him as much as I could seemed by far the more prudent policy.

I could agree in good conscience with Brother-in-law, though, that the Nuremberg War Crimes Trials had been a farce. That was an opinion I had acquired from reading the story of Senator Taft in John F. Kennedy's *Profiles in Courage*. "That was something that amounted in practice to *ex post facto* law, and our Constitution is supposed to protect against things like that. I think it was Göring who, according to something someone told me, stood up during those proceedings and said something like, 'Why don't you call off this farce? You won and we lost. Why do you pretend you now need a legal excuse to kill us?'"

Because of similar Constitutional technicalities, such as States' Rights, I often found myself uncomfortably in agreement with Southern racists, although I found it handy enough to stress in my discussions with Brother-in-law that such agreement existed.

I was determined to oppose Communism; nevertheless, I found vociferous nationalism and enthusiastic militarism to be nothing less than frightening — not because I feared war — I didn't — but because I feared anything that I could identify as systematic mindlessness.

I told Brother-in-law about a visit to Rockefeller Center's Radio City Music Hall that I made when pulling temporary additional duty in the Marines, on liberty in New York, stationed in Washington, D.C. for a Technique of Instruction Competition. "The Rockettes, in Israeli Army uniforms, with plastic sub-machine guns over their shoulders, marched out on the stage and the crowd went wild. I felt like I was at a Nazi rally. I think people who are persecuted sometimes acquire the characteristics of their oppressors."

Although he expressed agreement at my horror, I was sure it was for the wrong reasons. For when I spoke of what Hitler said of the power of brass bands to stir up the people, he was equally supportive. Besides that, I had listened many times as he spoke cheerfully of Goebbels' wife suggesting lampshades be manufactured from the skins of murdered Jews: "They tried it for a while; it worked."

"Speaking of Hermann Göring, Kerry, you know he also protected Jews from the Gestapo." With characteristic inconsistency, Brother-in-law spoke as if he deemed that a point in Göring's favor. There was just no figuring this guy.

His attitudes about freedom seemed equally ambivalent. "You know, Kemil Ataturk was a strongman who took over the government of Turkey and directed it firmly out of poverty and backwardness into the industrial age. Something like that couldn't have happened there under a democratic regime."

"Yes. I studied him in college. Whenever he felt overworked, he used to take a vacation and plunge himself into a sex orgy. Now that man was all right. I can identify with someone like that."

Strong character was something that appealed to us both in others. "You know, I hated Batista's government in Cuba," I told him. "When Castro was fighting Batista I admired

Fidel enormously. Then he got into power and executed so many of Batista's henchmen in the carnival atmosphere of those war crimes trials. That disappointed me. But remember that one guy, that general who told them all to go to hell? 'Of course I burned homes and killed women and children,' he said. 'I was a soldier. That was my job.' And when they marched him up to be shot, he swore at them all the way, calling them names right up until the moment he was killed. Now I have to admire a man like that, no matter whose side he is on."

"Yes, me too," Brother-in-law answered.

One of my theories to explain the popularity of John Kennedy was my notion that the American people had never matured politically to the point of outgrowing their need for royalty. "That's what's wrong with them," I said to Brother-in-law, "the Kennedys remind them of a royal family. They've never outgrown their need for a king. At heart they are still a bunch of Englishmen."

I was also intolerant of anything political that was in any way whatsoever tainted with religious faith. Eisenhower's "Pray for Peace" program had infuriated me. So again I was able to agree with Brother-in-law's conclusions, for reasons different than his, when said he thought Israel ought to be abolished.

"So do I. If the British were not Christians influenced by the prophecy in the Bible, that land would have gone back to its Arab residents at the end of the war. I don't think property rights, once usurped, ought to extend beyond one generation. What if a foreign power gave the United States, the freest, noblest and most industrially advanced nation in the world, back the Indians?"

At such times I did not think about what I said about giving the Southwestern US back to Mexico, therefore the inconsistency did not occur to me — but then there was no religious issue involved in that dispute.

Not only did Gary seemed pleased with my response to his proposal to abolish Israel, he acted like he would probably being doing something about it, such as joining a movement for that purpose, in the near future.

Something Should Be Done

L ATE in the summer of 1963 I returned, by way of a side trip to Mexico City, to New Orleans from California — where I had been staying with my parents since early May of that year.

Unbeknownst to me, Lee Harvey Oswald was in New Orleans at the time of my arrival, and would soon depart for Mexico City, where I had just spent one or two weeks.

Yesterday Slim had made the usual suggestion about visiting Brother-in-law and we sped through what was then remote, rural Louisiana country in the car Slim had arranged to borrow from Gary.

In those days besides the brewery across the field, only an immense steel bridge that arched over the river and over which cars moved in slow, eerie silent procession signaled civilization's designs.

> Today that whole area is an industrial park; the site of Brother-in-law's cottage is a concrete parking lot.

Standing at Brother-in-law's front door in the gravel parking space that comprised his front yard, I had an unobstructed view of the majestic bridge that by this time was so much associated in my mind with the discussions of Nazism that went on inside the house.

After we entered and took our seats, he provided the usual weak coffee. Lighting his briar pipe, he stood and walked up and down in thought in front of his chair. Looking at me, gesturing with his hand for emphasis, he said, "Kerry, do you believe in vengeance?" His motion was one of almost lunging in my direction and pointing at the floor with the final word. Today he was excited.

"Yes! I have just read *The Count of Monte Cristo*, and it has just occurred to me recently that revenge is one of the great, ignored motivations. In economics we talk about quota systems and profit systems, but only in literature do we deal with vengeance as a motive for human action." By this time Brother-in-law had again crossed the room and was sitting on the very edge of the sofa next to Slim. "Well, you know,

Kerry, many of the men who participated in the Bay of Pigs were left stranded on the beach in Cuba with no air support by John F. Kennedy." "Yes. I've heard about that."

"They are very angry."

"I don't blame them."

"Do you think they deserve to be avenged?"

"Yes I do."

"Are you aware that Albert Einstein wound up saying he wished he had become a plumber instead of a great scientist — because the government does not permit brilliant men to live in freedom? Because they've got access to classified information, they are treated as slaves. I don't think that's fair, do you, Kerry?"

"Certainly not. A society that persecutes genius is like a plant that tries to slay its own root stem."

"You know, there are others, besides Einstein who — to this very day — are being treated just as he was. I'm thinking, for example, of German scientists such as Werner Von Braun. Watched over everywhere they go; never given any freedom."

"What a horrible way to have to live!"

"I think something should be done about it. Don't you, Kerry?"

"Yes, of course."

"Kerry, remember the Reichstag fire? You know, that's how the Nazis took over Germany. They created an emergency and then blamed it on the Communists so they could clamp down. They accused Van der Lubbe of burning the Reichstag and said he was a Communist agent. Because most people believed them, the Fascists were able to rule Germany for all that time."

"Yeah, the Reichstag was their government record building, wasn't it?" I said so as not to seem ignorant.

"Kerry? What if Van der Lubbe had had a friend who realized he was innocent? Think of what would have happened! If that friend had come forward and exposed the truth, then Germany would have been spared all those years of suffering under the Nazis." Brother-in-law seemed inappropriately excited about such an academic speculation.

I didn't know what to say.

"Kerry, you know, you aren't going to be able to trust *Time* magazine."

"A professor at the University of Southern California used to say that *Life* is a magazine for people who can't read, and *Time* is a magazine for people who can't think," I commented in agreement.

> Peter Batty's book, *The House of Krupp*, informs us on page 253 that "...Luce too was to be a good friend of Krupp's, for in August 1957, on the occasion of Alfried's fiftieth birthday, a largely complementary cover-story entitled "The House That Krupp Built" appeared in *Time* magazine. *Time's* proprietor was also believed to be instrumental in Alfried's getting a visa to attend a conference for statesmen and international businessmen, and which his magazine was sponsoring in San Francisco that same autumn, at which Alfried had been invited to speak on "The Partnership Approach." Strictly speaking Alfried should have been denied a visa, since he was after all a convicted war criminal and such people were beyond the pale so far as the United States immigration laws were concerned. To the *New York Herald Tribune*, the whole ploy was "one of the slickest advertising promotional schemes yet devised." Nor did it escape the attention of certain senators, many of whom began to get angry. Alfried in the end preferred not to go — and his visa application has never been renewed."

At moments like this it was typical of me to make what seemed to me like quite relevant contributions, such as, "You know, there was something in *The National Observer* that I read once and have been thinking about ever since," speaking of Fascism.

"Why do we discriminate against people we think are inferior, and protect people we know are inferior?" I was feeling brave enough to risk an argument. "Like the mentally retarded."

"Hitler did not protect the mentally retarded," Brother-in-law said curtly. "He exterminated them."

"But in this country we discriminate against Negroes and yet we call homes for the mentally retarded schools for 'exceptional children.'"

"I haven't got anything against niggers — as long as they stay in their place. There is a nigger at work I like. He knows his place."

"There was a time," I said, "when the use of the word 'nigger' used to make me so mad I would shake, when I first got to New Orleans. But I've been in the South long enough now to see that there really are some people who should be called niggers."

I was thinking of precisely the blacks that Brother-in-law said he liked — guys who stood wringing their hats in both hands and mumbling "yazzuh" when you asked them for directions. I didn't say that, though. I was ready to drop the subject.

"Now a nigger who does not know his place is Martin Luther King."

Late in 1961, after Ola and I had not seen one another for months, she sought me out to invite me to attend a Martin Luther King, Jr., speech at the municipal auditorium. Mayor Victor Schiro obtained a restraining order at the last minute barring King from using the building.

So we ventured nervously into the adjoining park and stood with a flock of Negroes singing spirituals, under direction of a young white CORE activist who appeared to me both paternalistic and condescending.

"The only thing that we done wrong," they sang, "was let segregation stay so long... standing like a tree by the river, we shall not be moved... "

Rednecks in hot rods roared past us on the nearby road, gunning their engines. How vulnerable we were to a casually tossed bomb.

"There he is," someone shouted, pointing to a car pulling up at the other end of the park.

"There he is! That's him!" We continued our singing as we ran together through low-hanging clouds of foggy mist and gathered near the fountain, where Martin Luther King now stood in silence, grinning courageously, as a spokesman explained that Doctor King would deliver his speech at such-and-such a Baptist church.

Neither Ola nor I — nor her mother, who was with us — wanted to go to the church, so we drove to a drug store near the Garden District for coffee.

There Ola and I got into an argument about States' Rights versus Federal Civil Rights — about whether there could be a conflict between human rights and property rights. "Property rights are human rights," I insisted, echoing Ayn Rand, "because only humans own property."

To me it seemed that Ola was implying that because of this belief, I was a racist, and I grew more and more angry.

"Racism," I insisted, "is the most irrational form of collectivism there is. I think a Negro who owns a restaurant is entitled to refuse service to anyone for any reason, no matter how irrational, just like a white property owner. Property rights are absolute."

"But white people own most of the property," she lamented.

"In fact, but not in law," I retorted. "Negroes possess the same right to own property as whites."

"But what good does that do if they can't afford — "

"Listen to me very carefully," I interrupted, speaking slowly, with evident annoyance, "and maybe then you will understand."

"Come on, Mother," she said, rising to her feet. "Let's go."

They walked out on me. I took the bus home, feeling alone and misunderstood. I longed so much to belong to the Civil Rights Movement. Through the French Quarter passed many groovy young intellectuals and college students who were active in it. If only my Objectivist principles didn't confine me to the sidelines as a critic, instead!

"The only thing that we done wrong," I sang to myself in the cold, lonely night, "was let socialism stay so long."

"I like Martin Luther King," I said to Brother-in-law. "To feel like I felt that night in the park when Ola and I went to see him, to feel that way all the time, takes great courage. I kept thinking about how somebody could throw a bomb at us."

Having said that much, I was quick to abandon the courage of my convictions by adding, "I didn't like that CORE worker, though. That white Yankee college student stood there looking at those Negroes like he thought he was their good shepherd or something. I think there is racism in an attitude like that. And the argument I got in with Ola afterwards! Was she ever irrational! I expected her to at least understand Ayn Rand's principles. But she just kept whining like a wishy-washy liberal."

Brother-in-law nodded in warm approval. I relaxed — feeling safe again.

The Willingness to Die

ONCE Slim was hospitalized for tuberculosis for a couple of weeks and I went to visit him. In good spirits, he told me Brother-in-law had also been there to see him recently.

"And look at what he gave me," he said, "a list of '101 People Who Must Go.'"

At the top were the usual minority groups despised by most bigots and following them were the generally deficient — the nearsighted, the deaf, the insane, etc. and then much more absurd classifications began to appear.

"People with bald heads," I read aloud. "People without bald heads."

"Yeah, ha-he-he-heh-heh, I like it. I like it."

I supplied an obligatory chuckle, feeling slightly relieved at this evidence of humor in Brother-in-law's view of his own professed notions.

I felt much the same way when one day at his house Brother-in-law told the story of an argument at the brewery with a man I think was named Herb. Like me, Brother-in-law's working associates liked the new District Attorney, Jim Garrison.

Along with John and Robert Kennedy and Pope John XXIII and Martin Luther King, Garrison was among the people Brother-in-law didn't like. Although I did not agree with the laws against vice, Jim Garrison's crackdowns on Bourbon Street strip joints seemed to me an honest enforcement of law, and I felt that was unusual in New Orleans, where the open tolerance of political corruption distressed me.

"So I was telling them how much I hated Garrison and they were defending the clown. Then all of a sudden Herb says to me, 'Just exactly what is it about Garrison that you don't like, Gary?' So I thought for a minute, and then I said, 'I'll tell you what is: he wears a vest.' Herb cracked up. Ha-ha-ha-ha-ha-ha-ha!"

On the other hand was a story about the brewery first told me by Slim. "Brother-in-law decided to quit his job the other day. So he went into the brewery in the morning and walked up behind this guy he worked with that he never did like —

and kicked him in the back of the head with both feet. Then he went into the office and said, 'I quit.' Ha-ha! He's got a mean streak in him."

How it was possible to kick someone in the back of the head with both feet was a question I didn't ask. I just answered, "Yeah, I figured he could be mean."

Not long afterwards, at his house, Brother-in-law told a more elaborate version of the same story. I believe the man was standing on one of the runways over the vats and Brother-in-law was on a raised platform behind him. Or maybe Gary knew judo — I forget. In any case, the same element of capricious cruelty was present. Characteristically, Brother-in-law was cheerfully boastful about it.

On one or two other occasions Slim mentioned Brother-in-law in his absence, a topic I did not enjoy discussing unless absolutely necessary. Gary was such an unpleasant individual and Slim's admiration of him seemed so inappropriate that I usually became irritated.

"You had better remember his name, Kerry," Slim said one dull afternoon as we were sitting alone together in his room. "Pretty soon he is going to become a very important man."

"I doubt that very much," I muttered sullenly.

"I'm telling you something," he said paternalistically. "That man is going to be important, and you had best keep his name in mind. You might have cause to want to call on him for favors or something. His name is Kirstein. K-i-r-s-t-e-in. Remember that. Kirstein — like in curse."

"Yeah. He's a curse, all right."

"And he is also about to become very important, very powerful. K-i-r-s-t-e-i-n, Kerry — Gary Kirstein."

"Yeah, sure."

Then there was the time Slim was with a bunch of us gathered around a table in the Bourbon House and he said, in connection with something or other, "Like Brother-in-law! You should get to know him better, Kerry. Has that man ever got some kind of mind!" Slim shook his fingers as if they had just touched a hot stove. "Man, that sonofagun is smart!"

"He reminds me of a biology professor we had at the University of Southern California who used to giggle when he told us how to dissect frogs," I objected. "I think he's a drag."

"Yeah, well," Slim replied. That was his expression for indicating that, although he hadn't changed his mind, he didn't see any reason to keep arguing.

Brother-in-law claimed he didn't like people with beards, yet he usually laughed when he said that.

Once at his house I defended the Bohemians who populated the French Quarter. "They are much more interesting than the people Al Thompson calls 'the conformists.'"

"Yeah," said Gary, "many of the early Nazis were coffee-house Bohemians. It ain't that I don't like them; it's just that they ain't heavy enough. You know what I mean? I'd like to see a fierce quality among them — nothing like the mass murder of the National Socialists — but some hardness, the willingness to kill somebody every now and then."

> "Gazing about Los Angeles," writes Ed Sanders on page 69 of *The Family*, "it is possible to discern at least three death-trip groups that have provided powerful sleazo inputs into Manson and the family. It is significant that there exists in Los Angeles occult groups that specialize in creating zombie-like followers. These are groups that have degrees of trust and discipleship, that use pain and fear and drugs to promote instant obedience.
>
> "These three groups are:
>
> "1. The Process Church of the Final Judgment, an English organization dedicated to gore, weirdness and End of the World slaughter. The Process, as they are known, was active in Los Angeles in 1968, when Manson abandoned flowers, and in the summer of 1969 — when murder reigned.
>
> "2. The Solar Lodge of the Ordo Temple Orientis, a looney-tune magical cult specializing in blood-drinking, sado-sodo sex magic and hatred of blacks. The Solar Lodge of the O.T.O. was run by one Jean Brayton, a vicious middle-aged devotee of pain who attracted a crowd of groveling worshipers.
>
> "3. An obscure occult group of forty or so which we shall here call Kirke Order of Dog Blood."

We could at least agree that much of the art produced in the French Quarter was decadent so, again, I would seek to avoid an outright quarrel by stressing an area of common opinion.

"Show me an artist who distorts the human body in his paintings, and I will show you a man who hates people," I would say, echoing the words of Walt, an Ayn Rand student from New York I had met in the Quarter.

There were also people that Brother-in-law seemed to like as much as he detested many others. One of them was Charles A. Lindbergh. Not only did he mention him in admiration, he also kept bringing up the kidnapping of Lindbergh's son.

We both liked William F. Buckley, Jr., publisher of *The National Review*.

Why he hated Pope John XXIII was unclear to me. I considered him both charming and witty. From the viewpoint of Southern rightists, Pope John was disliked for excommunicating some segregationists who also happened to be Catholic, prominent citizens of New Orleans among them. So I figured it was probably somehow related to that.

At least once, Brother-in-law asked me what I thought of Dr. Land, inventor of the Land-Polaroid camera. I liked him. Brother-in-law seemed pleased.

> Information on page 42 of *The U-2 Affair* by David Wise and Thomas B. Ross (Random House, 1962) indicates that Edwin H. Land, head of the Polaroid Corporation and developer of the Polaroid camera, was an active member of the Science Advisory Committee, established by the White House in developing the U-2 concept with Richard Bissell of the Central Intelligence Agency.

Somebody Brother-in-law didn't like, as might be expected, was Mahatma Gandhi. "You know, during his fasts, he used to chew a weed that contained a drug that numbs hunger pangs."

Since Gandhi was remembered for his altruism, and since Ayn Rand rejected altruist morality as destructive, I welcomed this information. "He was also very harsh on his own family," I added. "Gandhi was dictatorial toward his wife and he drove one of his sons to alcoholism."

Both Brother-in-law and I felt enormous contempt for Bertrand Russell.

"'Better Red than dead,' he says," I complained. "Ayn Rand says that is not the choice. She says, 'Better see the

Reds dead.'"

"Yes!" His agreement seemed genuine "Bertrand Russell also says, 'Nothing is certain except that nothing is certain.' What rot! What a confession about his own mind! Thinking he could escape the ambiguities of language, he devised symbolic logic — and when he found his system didn't work as he hoped it would, rather than admitting he failed, he blamed logic!"

Besides Brother-in-law and maybe Slim, among my own friends in New Orleans, only one was a racist: Carlos Castillo, owner of a Mexican restaurant at the corner of Exchange Place, across from the courthouse, in the building that housed The Fencing Master just previous to my arrival in town.

Jessica and I used to eat at Castillo's Mexican Restaurant and we soon found the proprietor to be stimulating, well-read and enterprising. Able to hold forth on any theme for hours, Carlos would shake a kitchen knife in the air and pontificate in a convincing way with a mixture of facts and barnyard observations in flowery Latin rhetoric.

A firm believer in anything "nat-ur-al" (pronounced by him as if it were three distinct words), including barefoot and pregnant women, separation according to race, and free market economics, Carlos both maddened and delighted me.

In that respect he seemed much like Brother-in-law. Once I took Gary and Slim to Castillo's with the expectation they would probably hit it off.

Sure enough, Brother-in-law and Carlos swapped racist jokes over coffee for about a quarter of an hour that night and seemed to be getting along famously.

After we departed, I asked Brother-in-law what he thought of Carlos.

"I don't like him," he answered. "Why?"

"He's a Mexican."

Frame Some Jailbird

IN early November of 1963, Slim and I arrived at the little house in Harahan, Louisiana, and Brother-in-law said to me, as soon as I sat down, "Kerry, give me some ideas about assassinating John F. Kennedy."

I was more than happy to oblige; for years I had been saving up ideas about how to murder the President. I'd spoken of assassinating Kennedy to anyone who would listen to me ever since my arrival in New Orleans.

My plans for murder ranged from concealing sodium in his vitamin capsules so as to blow his stomach to pieces to designing a remote control model airplane with a bomb in it to hit him from a safe distance through a White House window.

Brother-in-law just sat there on the sofa, nodding eagerly and grinning excitedly at the worst of my suggestions. It was my turn to be moving about and gesturing wildly.

When I finally wound down, he just smirked and said, "Give me some more ideas."

Thereupon I ran through my second-rate notions for disposing of the man Ayn Rand and I considered a fascist-socialist tyrant. Though most of these ideas seemed impractical for one reason or another, Brother-in-law seemed happy to hear them, and I figured maybe he would offer suggestions for improving their weak points.

To my surprise he contributed nothing. Collecting ideas rather than hashing them out seemed his sole purpose.

"Now, Kerry, I think when we assassinate Kennedy — if it becomes necessary to sacrifice one man in order to protect the assassins, then we should go ahead and sacrifice one man."

"I agree with that."

"And I think that if, besides sacrificing one man, we also have to sacrifice one woman for that purpose — then we should sacrifice that woman."

"Yes," I said, less certain now of where all this was leading.

"And then, if we have to sacrifice two men and two women, I think we ought to go ahead and sacrifice two men and two women. How about you?"

Slim was looking at me and laughing silently. Obviously I looked a little scared.

"I agree," I replied firmly, annoyed at Slim's amusement.

And so it went — a most baffling discussion — settling at last on what number of sacrificial victims I do not remember — and to what reasonable end I could not begin to guess.

Already, though, it was beginning to sound like a terribly complicated and cumbersome conspiracy. Just how many people did this guy plan to involve, anyhow?

"And what do you think about letting Jimmy Hoffa in on this thing?"

"I think Jimmy Hoffa is being unfairly persecuted," I told him. "I think Jimmy Hoffa is a good man. I saw a book on a newsstand in Santa Ana this summer called *Jimmy Hoffa's Hot*. It was sympathetic to him. I wish I'd bought it."

After allowing a considerable silence to elapse, he grinned obnoxiously and said, "Next we'll get Martin Luther King."

"Aw, what do you want to kill King for?" I asked. It was not the first time he had made this suggestion.

Brother-in-law just laughed as if it pleased him to say things he knew would annoy me.

"And, Kerry, I think the best way to kill President Kennedy and get away with it would be to involve all kinds of people — but to keep them under the impression they are working on other projects."

"If you must involve large numbers of people, yes, I guess that would be the best way to go about it."

"But in order to do that," he said, "you would have to have a very large bureaucracy under your control." At this point he stood and walked to the center of the room, where Slim was already standing.

I had been seated on the footstool in front of the sofa and as I stood and followed, I said in a disappointed tone of voice, "Yes." For if anything was certain in my mind, it was that scrawny, T.B.-ridden Slim Brooks and his weird Nazi burglar of a brother-in-law did not control any bureaucracies.

Yet, to my bewilderment, Slim looked at Gary and Gary looked at Slim, both with expressions of absolute triumph in their eyes — being so obvious about it as to seem melodramatic. They had to be putting me on. I felt dispirited and depleted. Another afternoon had been wasted engaged in humoring the pipe dreams of a cheap braggart.

> There was one bureaucracy in the CIA, mentioned by E. Howard Hunt in *Undercover*, that would have been excellently equipped to perform all the tasks Brother-in-law had in mind.
>
> "... The then CIA director was Admiral Roscoe Hillenkoetter, whom I had met during one of the admiral's inspection trips to Vienna. He was Frank Wisner's nominal superior, but lacked Frank Wisner's political power base, which included such men as John J. McCloy, Averell Harriman, William Draper, Secretary of Defense Forrestal, and Secretary of State Marshall. At headquarters, alongside the reflecting pool, OPC established functional staffs for Paramilitary Operations, Political and Psychological Warfare and Economic Warfare.
>
> "The Political and Psychological Warfare staff, to which I was assigned, was headed by Joseph Bryan III, Navy veteran and writer. To assist him he had brought in Finis Farr; Gates Lloyd, Philadelphia investment banker; Lewis "Pinky" Thompson, a New York and New Jersey financier and a man of many parts; and Carlton Alsop, late a motion-picture producer and once a well-known Hollywood agent. All except Alsop and myself were Princeton alumni.
>
> "Artist-illustrator Hugh Troy joined Bry- an's staff and formed a highly competent group of political cartoonists and polemicists."
>
> By the time of my talks with Brother-in-law, Frank Wisner had passed away. But it is safe to assume the Political and Psychological Warfare staff remained active.
>
> Curiously, in addition, I had many times mentioned Hugh Troy to Brother-in-law, for his entertaining exploits as a prankster were recounted in a book I'd read called *The Compleat Practical Joker*.

Slim indicated it was time to go and we headed for the door.

"The only remaining problem," Brotherin-law said, "is who to frame for it."

We stopped and returned to where he was standing in the middle of the living room.

"Why frame anybody?" I asked.

"People need answers," he said in a harsh, cynical tone, but with a little smile. "I figure I'll frame some jailbird."

"Why a jailbird?"

"Criminals who are stupid enough to get caught are an inferior breed. They don't deserve any breaks."

I didn't like that line of reasoning.

"I don't think you should frame a jailbird." A crooked smirk distorted his mouth so much that he had to bow his head in trying to hide it.

"Well, Kerry, who would you suggest framing?"

"Aw, why don't you frame some Communist," I answered.

"Let's go," Slim said, heading for the door again.

Proud of Oswald

NEWS that President Kennedy had been shot reached me during lunch hour at Arno's Restaurant in the French Quarter, where I had recently obtained work waiting tables. Shortly thereafter, we got the news that Kennedy was dead.

When another waiter expressed his sorrow, I said, "The only reason I didn't kill that sonofabitch was that I was never in the right place at the right time with a gun in my hands."

In the wake of the assassination news, the restaurant was soon empty of most of its clientele. We employees seated ourselves around a table used for relaxation during breaks located in the area between the kitchen and the dining rooms. Across the table from me sat a waitress who was weeping. "Where were your tears during the Katanga massacre, lady?" I asked belligerently.

No one in the restaurant possessed a radio, so we sat there and argued — me against everyone else — while waiting impatiently for further news from the outside world. One of the waiters who went out on a break returned to say, "Well, at least they caught the guy that did it."

"What was his name?" I asked.

"I don't remember," he said. "It was a funny name. He is an ex-Marine who went to live in Russia for a couple of years."

"Oswald!" I shouted.

"Yes, that was it."

"Hell, I know him," I boasted. "We were in the Marines together!"

A long silence followed. Absolutely everyone was staring at me.

Later that day I encountered Slim Brooks and it occurred to me to ask him, "Say, Brother-in-law didn't have anything to do with this, did he? You know, just three weeks ago we were talking about assassinating Kennedy."

"Two weeks ago," Slim corrected, laughing easily. "Nah, he didn't have anything to do with it."

"That's a relief," I said.

Needless to say, I was jubilant at the news of Kennedy's death — something I made no attempt to conceal from anyone, much to the annoyance of most of the Bourbon House regulars. Besides that, I was extremely proud of Oswald for getting himself accused — although I suspected he was innocent, since in the service he had displayed a talent for getting blamed for things.

As for me, I felt betrayed by most of my French Quarter friends, who were obviously grief-stricken. Hadn't they laughed in the past at my anti-Kennedy jokes? Where was their integrity? Here I had been thinking they were potential converts to the Objectivism of Ayn Rand and, instead, they were all turning out to be a bunch of whim-worshipers.

Then, Sunday morning, I learned that Oswald had been murdered. I was horrified. Irrational violence had won out over good sense once again. Why would anyone want to kill a pathetic little guy like Lee? Now everyone else was smug and I was in mourning.

Both the Secret Service and the Federal Bureau of Investigation had been to the restaurant by then to question me. A poll appeared in the evening paper indicating that most Americans now thought the assassination was the result of a conspiracy. As I moved about the French Quarter, it seemed to me I was being tailed by middle-aged men in suits.

I decided to go to the FBI office and volunteer my services in luring out the real assassins of John F. Kennedy. They could say Oswald had confided in me and use me as a decoy to trap the people who had silenced him. I spoke to an FBI agent in the Federal Building who kept pretending he didn't understand what I was talking about. Among his questions, and typical of most of them, was, "This Oswald — was he a homo of any kind?"

In the days that followed I quarreled with virtually every one of my friends to a greater or lesser extent. Mildest among these disputes were disagreements about questions of taste. Couldn't I have at least been silent, instead of offering to buy drinks for everyone in the Bourbon House? In the worst disagreements, tempers flared and fist fights almost resulted.

Only Carlos Castillo staunchly joined me in toasting Marine Corps marksmanship instructors at the bar. However, since Carlos happened to be a racist, I could not regard his conduct as rationally motivated.

I decided the Bohemian subculture was not for me. Ayn Rand had always despised Beatnik lifestyles and now I was beginning to see why. I'd often thought of moving to New York and living among the students of Objectivism gathered around "the greatest mind of our age."

New York intimidated me, though. I had heard that prices were high and that trying to find a good job was discouraging. Besides that I hated cold weather and the worst of winter was still ahead.

Just the other day I'd received a letter from an old school chum who now lived in Alexandria, Virginia. He mentioned that if I was ever up that way I should feel free to stay with him.

One afternoon in the Bourbon House I mentioned what was going through my mind in this respect to Slim, who said: "I notice President Johnson is calling together a commission to investigate the assassination. By now it has become pretty obvious that Oswald did it."

I had to agree. Since the night of my silly visit to the FBI, the newspapers had been unanimous in insisting that the case against Oswald was just overwhelming.

"Now, if you are in New York, they'll send a field agent up there to take a statement from you and that'll be all she wrote. Not much publicity for that novel about this guy who just shot the President of the United States. With enough publicity, you'll get that book published — now that your main character is famous."

"Yeah, when he went to Russia, I thought that was a big deal."

"Now if you go to Alexandria — that ain't far from Washington. They'll probably call you over for a long interview. That should be enough to make *The Idle Warriors* almost as well known as Lee Harvey Oswald himself! You want to publish a book and be a big-shot author and all that? Go to Alexandria. Be near Washington when that commission convenes."

As I stepped out into the afternoon sunlight I thought about what Slim had said, deciding it made perfect sense.

On December 13th of 1963, I boarded a bus for Alexandria.

The Warren Commission

NEAR Christmas, I secured a job as a doorman in a newly constructed high-rise between Alexandria and Arlington in Virginia. Along with the job came spacious apartment, where I spent my spare hours working on a completely new draft of *The Idle Warriors*.

Heretofore, everyone who read the manuscript had complained that the plot lacked unity. So I relied on the device of expanding the final chapter, dealing with my hero's defection to Russia, to embrace the whole story, incorporating earlier events by means of flashbacks.

Although the manuscript lacked both the lyricism of the first draft, written in my first months in New Orleans, and the literary richness of the version I was working on that autumn when the assassination occurred, this effort at least conformed to the "Romantic Realist" ideas of Ayn Rand — so I was happy with it.

And sure enough, just as Slim predicted, the Warren Commission contacted me. I went to their headquarters in the VFW Building in Washington, DC, and testified at great length.

In all the time that elapsed since the assassination, I spared very little thought on Slim or the enigmatic Brother-in-law. Then one night one of the residents in the building where I worked told me of serving as a test pilot of flying saucers for the Navy.

By this time, I had graduated from my position as doorman to night PBX desk clerk. This middle-aged man, whose name I don't remember, used to come down into the lobby and talk to me when things were slow.

Whether he was truthful or not was another question. I could not, however, avoid thinking of how closely this man's stories resembled Brother-in-law's theories about UFO origins.

"Yeah, I know the damned things are an advanced type of aircraft, because right after the war I was flying them. We all had to sign papers promising to make a career of the Navy before they'd let us in on the project. It was hush-hush all the way."

"Then why are you a civilian now?" I wanted to know.

"Because a bunch of us resigned our commissions all at the same time. We got pissed off at our CO."

I didn't have to ask many questions. He just liked to talk, so I listened.

"My buddy in that outfit got picked up by the Shore Patrol one day after we got out and that's the last anyone ever saw of him. He was moving at the time — with half of his furniture in one apartment and the other half in another — and they just came and took him away. Why they never came after me is anybody's guess."

"Where do you think he is?" I asked.

"I know where he is. He's in a stockade somewhere."

According to him, the United States developed toward the end of World War II a flying saucer that combined the principles of jet propulsion with those of the Sikorsky helicopter. "I test flew it a number of times," he assured me. "At that time they were still trying to work out the bugs in it. At certain speeds it tended to wobble."

Then he told me U. S. flying saucers had been used since then, in a top secret mission to repel a Russian air attack on this country.

After the storyteller departed I turned to the security guard who had been sitting nearby saying nothing all through the conversation. "What do you make of that guy?"

"Aw, I think that man just likes to hear himself talk. He's just bullshitting. If he thought you'd believe it, he'd tell you there were Eskimos in the Sahara Desert."

That was much the way I had felt about Brother-in-law. Unlike Gary, though, this man seemed harmless at all times. I kind of liked him. Somehow, that made his story sound more plausible to my ears.

You're Famous Now

L ATE in the summer of 1964 I wrote a letter to Slim Brooks, informing him of my plans to visit New Orleans briefly, in about two weeks.

I traveled by bus from Virginia to Gainesville, Georgia, where one of my old French Quarter friends, Grace Caplinger — now Grace MacEachron — was living with her new husband, John MacEachron, a teacher at a military academy there. We drove together in their car, with their baby daughter, Marion, to New Orleans.

Venturing forth alone in the French Quarter, I soon began to catch up on the latest news. Somebody told me that a number of my friends had been arrested as Communists by the New Orleans police in a raid on a new coffee house on Esplanade, the Quorum. Seventy-three people, as I recall, were busted in the fiasco. Everyone was up in arms about it, circulating petitions.

Someone with whom I was distantly acquainted offered to show me where the Quorum was, saying it had replaced the Ryder as the gathering place for all the hard-core Beatniks. We took out from the Bourbon House in the direction of Esplanade, walking up Royal Street.

As we neared the Saint Louis Cathedral, he said casually, "Did you happen to Holcomb, who lived in that apartment street?"

"I didn't know she lived there but, yeah, I've known Ola for years."

"She blew her brains out all over the kitchen floor in there with a .38 pistol a week or so ago."

"Jesus! She and I were very close at one time."

"I'm sorry. I didn't realize that. I guess I could have broke the news some other way."

"Why would Ola, of all people, commit suicide?"

"They say she was all bent out of shape about some guy she was in love with who rejected her. Her mother came home and found the body."

"Yeah, last I heard she was living with her mother. She seemed very fond of that old gal. And Ola was such a strong woman. It doesn't figure."

"They say she was really stuck on the guy."

"You know something?" I said as we continued our way up the street. "All afternoon I've been looking at the pretty old buildings and all the hip people and wondering why the hell I ever left the French Quarter. Now I remember. What a depressing place! People are always doing themselves in here."

When we arrived at the Quorum my companion introduced me to the owner, a man named Marcus, who was a friend of Jack Frazier, proprietor of the Ryder. Glancing at the Goldwater button on my shirt, Marcus said, "Come on now, you're not serious?"

"Not only am I seriously supporting Goldwater," I replied, "but if you'll let me, I'll deliver a speech here some evening explaining why."

"No," he said, laughing, "I don't think so."

"Yeah, that's the way you liberals are," I retorted. "Always talking about freedom and the right to dissent — except when the speaker is of the right instead of the left."

After thinking a minute, he said, "Now, I wouldn't want anyone to accuse us of being narrow-minded. We usually have a discussion group here," naming such-and-such night, Friday or Saturday, probably. "What do you want to call your rap?"

"'The Intellectually Respectable Right,'" I said. "I want to point out to them that all Goldwater's supporters are not anti-intellectual."

"All right. You're on."

John Kamus was present at the Quorum, so I then wandered over to his side of the room and asked how things were going.

"I'm soliciting donations for an Ola Holcomb Memorial Collection at the New Orleans Public Library," he said, after we had exchanged our condolences about the tragedy of her death. "Ola so loved books, we thought that would be an especially fitting way to honor her."

"Yes, I remember. She once told me what she liked best about the way her apartment was furnished was that anywhere you sat, even on the toilet, you saw books." I chipped in a few bucks.

Next I learned that Slim Brooks was now living in a small room right next door to the Quorum. I went to visit him.

Slim had found a way to tap an extension line into the pay phone located on the sidewalk out front. After showing me how it permitted him to make use of free phone service, he suggested we "go stick nose in the Bourbon House."

Later that night, as we were preparing to go our separate ways from the Bourbon House, he said, "Incidentally, there is a man who wants to see you before you leave town again."

"Oh, yeah? Who?"

"He lives out on the Jefferson Highway and his name begins with K."

"Oh, him. Your brother-in-law."

"Uh-huh. He made a point of it. Says he definitely wants to see you."

I mentioned my appointment to lecture about Goldwater at the Quorum and we decided Slim should tell Brother-in-law to meet me there.

"You know," Slim added, "he's still cultivating powerful men, in keeping with his theory about the secret of Hitler's power. And you know what else? Heh-heh. He went and joined himself up in the Anti-Defamation League. Kirstein sounds like a Jewish name, so he decided he might as well get on their mailing list."

"Yeah, that's your brother-in-law. It figures," I said, anxious to be on my way.

"And one other thing. You know, Barbara Reid is still going around telling everyone she saw you sitting with Oswald in the Bourbon House a couple of months before the assassination."

"Over a bottle of Old Crow, probably," I scoffed. "She told me about that herself once. I even believed it. I couldn't remember who the hell I was sitting with that day. Then Clint Bolton and everybody else who knows her said Barbara ties herself into everything that happens. I ain't worried about what Barbara Reid says."

"But, but, but, but, but — there are people who believe her."

"Slim, there are people who believe in God. Barbara herself believes in witchcraft. Anybody who believes in Barbara Reid I am certainly not worried about."

"Yeah, well. I'll see you next trip, as we say in the merchant marines."

Clint Bolton, a retired newsman who enjoyed giving me pep talks about my writing, was a close friend of Barbara Reid, whom he called Mother Witch.

During the days immediately after the assassination, when I was still working at Arno's, I used to find him at Barbara's watching television, late at night when I got off work.

With him usually was a Sicilian-American gentleman named Sam, for whose wholesale cigar business Clint was working during the day. Sam shared my admiration for Garibaldi.

Clint, aside from a passing complaint about my poor taste, was one of the few who had not come down hard on me for my post-assassination antics — so I'd gotten into seeking them out, instead of sitting in the Bourbon House looking for action.

Barbara was something else. I didn't know what to make of her. In her living room was an imposing voodoo altar, cluttered with statuettes and herbs. She wore a beret and smoked her cigarettes in a holder, like a 1930's Greenwich Village artist.

One night Sam and Clint left early and Barbara Reid invited me to remain there, offering another beer. We talked late into the morning hours, calmly, about our differences concerning John Kennedy and the assassination. She claimed to be a personal friend of Robert Kennedy, something I didn't find extraordinary, since I knew Barbara was involved in Civil Rights work.

That was when she told me, dramatically, that she had seen Oswald and me together — one afternoon in September — in the Bourbon House.

"That isn't possible," I replied, convinced I was in California and Mexico when Lee was in New Orleans.

She produced newspaper clippings to prove we had in fact been in town at the same time, for a week or two, earlier that year, previous to Oswald's departure for Mexico City.

"Remember that day you were sitting at the corner table with someone and I called to you from the bar, asking if you had ever worked in radio?"

As a matter of fact I did. She went on to tell me I had a beautiful voice and that I should think about going into radio. Slightly embarrassed, I waved off the compliment and returned to my conversation with the man at my table. "But if that had been Lee Oswald, I would have recognized him."

"Not if someone had hypnotized you to forget."

I laughed. "That's too paranoid."

"Could it be that you just didn't recognize him out of uniform — that the face was familiar, but... "

I thought about that.

"Kerry, I'm certain it was him. When Oswald's picture came up on the television screen after the assassination I screamed, 'That's him. That's the man who was sitting with Kerry in the Bourbon House that day.'"

"I guess I might have seen him and just thought he was some French Quarter person whose name escaped me. It's possible — except I was sitting there working on notes for my book based on Oswald at the time."

"Kerry, he was talking about how he planned to go back to Texas soon. I remember."

It did seem that whoever I was sitting with had mentioned Texas.

"I used to work as a casting director and, believe me, I never forget a face. That man was Lee Harvey Oswald. I'm certain of it."

I went home that night somewhat intrigued with the notion that maybe Oswald had walked into the Bourbon House that afternoon and nodded in my direction, and that I had gestured for him to join me at my table, just as Barbara remembered it. More than once I have vaguely recognized someone whose name I didn't recall and spoken to them, ashamed to admit I didn't remember where we had met previously.

Over oyster stew in the Bourbon House the next morning I mentioned to Clint and Sam that Barbara was certain she had seen me with Oswald last September, and that I was inclined to believe it myself.

"Barbara is certain, my young friend, that she has seen every famous or notorious person who ever lived somewhere in the French Quarter at one time or another," Clint droned.

Sam concurred heartily, going into a number of examples.

As the day wore on, I mentioned Barbara's claim to others with the same response. Yet there was the nagging fact that I could not recall who I was sitting with that day.

> More recently I have decided that the individual in question was a country and western singer named Glen, who happened to be a friend of Millie Fletcher, another of my friends. Glen was from Texas and at that time was making preparations to return.

A year after the incident, I was still trying to figure out who the mystery man was, although I was sure by this time it wasn't Oswald. What disturbed me more, though, was the way Slim had taken such pains to try to alarm me about Barbara Reid's gossiping. Slim Brooks made no pretense of believing Barbara's story. Why, then, did he seem to enjoy needling me about it?

When the night of my lecture at the Quorum arrived, I noted with slight feelings of relief that Brother-in-law was not in the audience. Since he and Ola Holcomb used to be lovers, he would probably be depressed and, in any case, he was an individual I found depressing in the brightest of circumstances. I delivered my speech, fielded a few very intelligent questions afterwards in what I felt was a satisfactory manner and then noticed Slim standing off to one side.

Upon joining him I learned that Brother-in-law had not forgotten our appointment. "He didn't want to listen to your speech. He thinks your politics are bullshit — too light-weight for him. He's in the patio — out back."

Sure enough, there the sonofabitch was — sitting in a chair, his bald head gleaming in the dim light, looking as cheerfully nefarious as ever. I didn't mention Ola and he didn't bring the subject up either. In fact, it seemed as if there was nothing to talk about. That didn't seem to make him the least bit ill at ease. Grinning smugly, he just kept chewing on the stem of his pipe and looking at me.

"I hear you're becoming famous," he said at last, for the Warren Report *Warren Report*, in which my testimony was quoted, had just been published.

"Yeah, I guess so," I said, standing there uncertainly.

"Hey, come over here," Slim called to a passer-by. "This is Kerry Thornley. He knew Oswald."

"Yeah," I said upon being introduced, "I master-minded the Kennedy assassination."

Brother-in-law chuckled. He liked that one.

The passing stranger, with whom I was now shaking hands, asked me what I thought of the conclusions of the Warren Commission and I defended them.

Slim repeated the same introduction with someone else afterwards and I again quipped that I had master-minded the assassination, and so on, with maybe half a dozen different individuals.

Brother-in-law sat there all the while, puffing his pipe and gloating. Everyone Slim introduced asked me something about the assassination and possibilities that Oswald was innocent or others were involved. In each instance, I defended the lone-assassin theory.

Brother-in-law and Slim then indicated that they had to go somewhere. I was puzzled. Why had he gone out of his way to meet with me if he wasn't going to say anything?

As Slim went up to the cash register to pay their check, Brother-in-law and I waited at a little table just inside the back door.

I looked at him and asked, "Well, how are things going with you these days?"

"Wonderful," he said. "Just great. You know, I really like living in that little house way out in the country, because there are no neighbors around — to hear the screams in the middle of the night!" A villainous leer accompanied his words. Certainly the remark startled me. I must have knitted my brow and given him a questioning look.

Obviously, he expected some other kind of response because, for the first time since I had met him more than three years before, Brother-in-law lost his composure.

Fumbling with his pipe, he hemmed and hawed and then said, "Yeah, one of these nights I'm going to go out and catch me a nigger woman, and then take her home and torture her to death."

Slim came to the rescue and together they departed into the night.

I stood in the doorway of the Quorum watching them disappear down the street. An awful thought struck me. If that weird man really meant what he just said to me, there was absolutely nothing I could do about it.

I could just imagine myself walking into a New Orleans police station and saying, "Listen, I know a Nazi who says he is going to kidnap and murder a black woman some night."

"Sure, buddy. If he ever goes through with it, don't forget to call us."

Not then and not for years afterwards did I think of this unusual meeting in connection with what Brother-in-law had said one day at his house during one of those tedious conversations: "I'm going to talk to everyone in the country who wants Kennedy dead about assassinating him. Then I'm going to do it. Then I'm going to pay a visit to each and every one of them. I'm not going to say anything. I'm just going to look at them and smile, so they'll get the idea. After that, I'll feel free to call on them for favors."

Who Were They?

THAT my friend Slim Brooks may have been a navigational consultant for the Bay of Pigs Invasion was something I'd never have suspected at the time. Yet he was perfectly adept at precisely such work. Something about the coffee stains on his charts seemed to rule out that possibility then.

In a *Ramparts* Magazine article by William Turner titled "The Garrison Commission" that is reprinted in *The Assassinations*, an anthology edited by Peter Dale Scott, Paul L. Hoch and Russell Stetler (Random House, 1976), there appears a reference to a man who happened to know the address of Guy Banister's office next to the drugstore where Slim and I waited that day when Brother-in-law ran his quick and mysterious "errands."

Ordinarily, the fairly common last name, "Brooks," would not seem more than coincidental. In this instance, however, I received additional information from a personal contact indicating that perhaps this individual mentioned in Turner's article resembled the man I knew as Roderick R. Brooks both in appearance and mannerisms.

My lack of certainty is due to my inability to determine the reliability and intent of my informant. That Slim Brooks might actually have been one Jerry Milton Brooks is a nagging possibility I cannot ignore, since Slim never used what he told me in private was his first name in the company of others, always preferring to be called "Slim."

Here is what Fred Turner says in "The Garrison Commission," first published in January of 1968, about Jerry Milton Brooks:

> The dilapidated building at 544 Camp Street is on the corner of Lafayette Place. Shortly after news of Garrison's investigation broke, I went to 531 Lafayette Place, an address given me by Minutemen defector Jerry Milton Brooks as the office of W. Guy Banister, a former FBI official who ran a private detective agency.
>
> According to Brooks, who had been a trusted Minutemen aide, Banister was a member of the Minutemen and head of the Anti-Communist League of the Caribbean, assertedly an intermediary between the CIA and Caribbean insurgency movements. Brooks said he had worked for Banister on

"anti-Communist" research in 1961-1962, and had known David Ferrie as a frequent visitor to Banister's office.

Banister had died of an apparent heart attack in the summer of 1964. But Brooks had told me of two associates whom I hoped to find. One was Hugh F. Ward, a young investigator for Banister who also belonged to the Minutemen and the Anti-Communist League. Then I learned that Ward, too, was dead. Reportedly taught to fly by David Ferrie, he was at the controls of a Piper Aztec when it plunged to earth near Ciudad Victoria, Mexico, May 23, 1965.

The other associate was Maurice Brooks Gatlin Sr., legal counsel to the Anti-Communist League of the Caribbean. Jerry Brooks said he had once been a sort of protégé of Gatlin and was in his confidence. Brooks believed Gatlin's frequent world travels were as a "transporter" for the CIA... The search for Gatlin, however, was likewise futile: in 1964 he fell or was pushed from the sixth floor of the El Panama Hotel in Panama during the early morning, and was killed instantly.

Guy Banister is claimed by another researcher, as I previously mentioned, to have been undercover for Division Five of the FBI at the time he ran the detective agency in New Orleans. As Turner goes on to note, 531 Lafayette and 544 Camp are two entrances to the same building. Located next to Waterbury's Drugs, at the corner of Camp and Canal, it stands at the other end of a very short block at Camp and Lafayette.

As for David Ferrie who, according to Jerry Brooks, frequented Banister's office, I met him very briefly and casually once at a party and, as I've mentioned already, I met Guy Banister one evening in the Bourbon House.

What of Maurice Brooks Gatlin, though? Notice that Jerry Brooks claimed this man trusted him and also seemed unaware of his death four years earlier in Panama. Going with my assumption that Jerry Milton Brooks could have been Slim Brooks, and with my further assumption would be that Gary Kirstein, Slim's alleged Brother-in-law, was actually E. Howard Hunt using another man's name, a fascinating hypothesis suggests itself.

According to Torbit's thesis, the CIA's Double-Check Corporation of Miami was on loan to Division Five for anti-Castro activities, and both were involved in the Cuban Revolutionary Council headquartered in Banister's office. In that case, Banister almost certainly would have known and could have been working with E. Howard Hunt.

Suppose that with Brooks, Hunt was using a false identity — that of Maurice Brooks Gatlin. Then it is easy to imagine how Slim could have become involved in the assassination plot. Moreover, Slim continued to meet with Brother-in-law in the years that followed, which would explain why Jerry Milton Brooks seemed unaware of the death of Gatlin.

Either the real Gatlin, whose name Hunt was using, or another individual on assignment with the Gatlin ID, could have been murdered in Panama shortly after the John Kennedy murder in order to dispose of an identity Hunt no longer needed.

Banister is dead. Ward, whoever he was, is dead. And Maurice Gatlin is dead or never existed and is presumed dead. E. Howard Hunt's tracks are covered perfectly. There is almost no way to connect him with the crime of Kennedy's assassination.

As for the real Gary Kirstein, Tom Lutz of *The National Tattler* discovered his name connected with the Minutemen. Phillip Emmons Isaac Bonewits, a Berkeley occultist, wrote me that he found it repeatedly in his investigations of "snuff films" and other illegal Satanist activities.

Could Gary Kirstein have been someone Hunt was attempting to set up in advance for the crime of murdering John Kennedy? Obviously, this theory makes a number of assumptions that are possibly unwarranted.

But then again, multiple levels of cover are standard for intelligence agents, and Brother-in-law warned me that the simplest solution was not always the correct one.

.

Aftermath

HAVING presented an array of clues to an alarming mystery that remains for all practical purposes unsolved, I'll share my thoughts of where to go from here.

First, besides writing this book, what have I tried to do about the problem under discussion?

After sharing my hasty notes and hysterical accusations about Kirstein with the Atlanta police, I was unsatisfied with their response. Within days, Reginald Eaves, Commissioner of Public Safety, announced that he was dropping his probe of the Martin Luther King murder. The men accused by his principal witness, Robert Byron Watson, had passed a polygraph test. Watson, according to Eaves, refused to take such an examination.

In correspondence with me, Watson denied that he was ever asked to take a lie detector test. I had also offered to take a polygraph examination to no avail.

Thereupon I contacted David Marston, an aide to the Senate Select Committee on Intelligence, and then prepared for him an affidavit. In that document I included everything I could remember at that time, I did not go out of my way to establish credibility. I felt hysterical and made no attempt to hide that feeling as I wrote. In addition, I felt that I had already been used once by a government body, the Warren Commission, to unwittingly promulgate a cover-up of the facts. I was not enthusiastic about the possibility I would be used that way again. Already, the probability had occurred to me that Brother-in-law could have been someone else using Gary Kirstein's name.

Meanwhile, more weird people were pouring into my life than I could keep track of. Finally, the House Committee on Assassinations was formed and I contacted them by letter and by phone. At first very excited about the information I was providing, that committee underwent a shuffle in personnel and quickly changed its attitude.

Feeling that I had been surrounded by the intelligence community in Atlanta, I moved to California in February of 1977. Then I wrote another letter to the House Select

Committee on Assassinations. That drew a three sentence note from G. Robert Blakey saying, in effect, "If we need you, we'll call you."

Many months later I called a radio talk show and explained my predicament briefly. A few days later there was a knock at my door. When I answered I was confronted by an embossed business-card holder that bore the name of the House Committee in the hand of a gentleman who introduced his companion as Martin Daly. We spoke briefly. They seemed hypocritical and, as far as I could tell, were making no attempt to hide it. Again, the gist of what they said was, "We'll call you."

About a week later I received a phone call from Daly's assistant to schedule a deposition, I informed him that I planned to get an attorney for that purpose, since I regretted not having obtained counsel before deposing for the Warren Commission. I can only describe his response as one of panic. Not only did he try to talk me out of obtaining counsel, he kept asking who my lawyer would be. That was something I hadn't decided. Saying at last that he would call me again, he concluded the conversation. I never heard from him or anyone else representing that Committee again. To this day I wonder why they used a plastic business-card holder as identification. Were they actually from the Committee or where they impersonators endeavoring to undermine my confidence in that investigation?

Quite recently, when I completed the portion of this manuscript about Brother-in-law, I took a rough draft to Washington, D.C., and personally handed it to a secretary for the Senate Select Committee on Intelligence. This happened in October of 1981. Within a few days the manuscript was returned to me in the mail with a brief note of thanks from the office of Senator Barry Goldwater.

Since then I have been gradually wading though the *Report of the House Select Committee on Assassinations*. Except that it establishes that another gunman was shooting from the Grassy Knoll, I find it less than truthful in evaluating evidence. In particular, all the proofs that Oswald was not on the sixth floor of the Book Depository when Kennedy was assassinated and was not the killer of Patrolman Tippit are glossed over or ignored.

If the government of this country is in the hands of people who want the Kennedy and King assassinations solved, they are making a good show of conveying the opposite impression.

In order to resolve any problem, the mind must first be free of ignorance, interference and prejudice. I submit that we are burdened by all three.

When a government that is supposed to be a democracy must keep secrets from its own voters, that is anything but national security. Casting a ballot with your eyes closed does not make the nation more secure. Neither does remaining ignorant of what the government is doing.

Corporate confidentiality is another sacred cow in America. In an age when the lives of individual citizens are not safe from surveillance, business meetings wherein decisions are made that affect the whole community are regarded as sacrosanct.

All forms of institutional secrecy contribute to our ignorance about national problems. What if sufficient numbers of us were to oppose them? With modern communications attitudes spread rapidly. What if everywhere in the world more and more people began opposing institutional secrecy in principle?

When I said the mind must also be free of interference, to resolve problems, I was thinking primarily of electro-chemical mind control. In that respect my experience has been unique. Many others have not had much reason to think about that form of intervention in the thought process. Yet simply reading Walter Bowart's *Operation Mind Control*, not to mention the volumes he lists in the bibliography, is enough to convince a skeptical person that the practice of brainwashing or mind manipulation or conditioning is more prevalent than most people imagine.

What would happen if significant numbers of us were to become vocal about this problem, perhaps by bringing attention to the books already written about it?

Chances are it is far more important an issue than forced busing or the trends that alarm the Moral Majority. Without control of your own brain it won't make much difference how far your child has to ride to school or how your neighbor is getting kicks. And that, of course, brings us to the third cramp on a mind in search of answers to problems: prejudice.

However true it may be that stereotypical thinking about individuals who belong to minorities is illogical, that is not what concerns us here. Once the monopoly capitalist, Jay Gould, was asked how he would deal with unemployment. His answer was simple: "I'd hire one half of 'em to kill the other half." In order to divide oppressed people, it is first necessary to find a volatile issue that will at the same time distract them organizing against their rulers.

Racial and ethnic and sexual and religious or philosophical issues are used for that purpose. This side effect of bigotry harms everyone who struggles to live in freedom, regardless of how liberal or not are their own personal views.

A head-on attack against ingrained ideas is always the worst possible tactic in purely functional terms. Coercive or bombastic promulgation of culturally-liberal ideas only increases the defensiveness and desperation of prejudiced people. Simply allowing the natural effects of innovations in travel and communication to erode cultural insularity would be a more effectively strategy. That doesn't mean activism is uncalled for, but that it should be intelligently and tactfully coordinated.

Instead, arguments about race and ethnic traditions are escalated at every opportunity into full-scale media events. When Lawrence of Arabia first began mobilizing Bedouin tribes in the desert, he told them that as long as they continued quarrel and bickering with one another about insignificant differences they would be a silly people. That approach proved effective. I think if more of us saw prejudice as silly, rather than inevitably evil, more progress would be made against it. Evil enters the picture when force of arms is used to impose cultural values, whether those values are reactionary or not.

Bigotry related to sex and sexual preferences is not unlike racial prejudice. In his book, *The Erotic Minorities* (Grove Press, 1967), Lars Ullerstam maintains that sexual caste systems exist. When we deem someone subhuman because of a sexual characteristic we are being just as silly as an orthodox Brahmin in India. Vices are not crimes, as the American individualist anarchist Lysander Spooner eloquently argued in an essay by that name.

Sexual blackmail is a powerful tool for preserving secrecy in conspiracy politics. Existing public attitudes make it work that way. As long as what your neighbors do in their bedroom is more important to you than what governments and corporations are doing, you contribute to an atmosphere of ignorance that will keep you from finding out what you need to know to become free.

On the other hand, when communities devote their collective attention to political and economic oppressors, prejudice tends automatically to dwindle. That much was demonstrated by the Populist era in the South and by the Industrial Workers of the World in organizing lumber camps in Louisiana.

Within the intelligence community there are so many holy wars going on that the Middle Ages and Northern Ireland come to mind. Again, our rulers are eager to fund anything that will readily divide us. There are as many compassionate and unfeeling people of any faith as of any other, so again genuine community problems are relegated to obscurity for the sake of something silly.

In the realm of philosophical or intellectual prejudice again we are divided on the basis of insufficient information. There are open-minded and loving Marxists just as there are dogmatic butchers in the Leninist camp. Different people approach the same ideology from different directions. Among racial and sexual bigots, there are those who utilize force and harassment and those content to mind their own business without oppressing anyone, who want only to be left alone in turn.

Clearing the mind of silly, counter-productive distractions is essential if it is to grapple with the causes both of those distractions and of conspiracies.

Since the assassination conspiracies appear, more evidently than most, to be an intelligence community phenomenon, we might also lend our attention to the economic and political conventions that necessitate a police apparatus for their maintenance. For, in an age of multinational corporate power, nearly every police mechanism is bound to become what Walter Bowart in his book on mind manipulation calls a "cryptocracy."

Here I am indebted to the writings of the anarchists, whom I once thought were all either impractical idealists or psychopathic bomb throwers. That Brother-in-law used to say the best person to solve a complicated political assassination would be an anarchist is something I have not forgotten. Whether my own education in anarchism is the result of coincidence or conspiracy is open to interpretation. I have come to view it as a moot point.

When I majored in sociology at a university I quickly realized that sociologists devote themselves to exactly the same subject matter as anarchist social philosophers. Sociology, however, differed in emphasis, being far more concerned with coping with the symptoms of social ills than their causes. This, I learned, was due to the economic dependence of sociologists on grants from private foundations and governments. No secret is made by sociology professors and graduate students of this reality. There is, I concluded at last, only one difference between a sociologist and an anarchist: sociologists are paid by the system; anarchists are not. Whether or not you agree with their contention that government is unnecessary, upon actually reading most anarchists what they have to say you will find them brilliant sociological writers. And while not all sociologists who derive their income outside the system of tenures and grants are anarchists about government, most of them are just as radical in their analyses of economic oppression.

A school of anarchism native to this country called individualist anarchism or decentralism has proved my most useful guide in examining the basis of excessive government power in economic terms. Josiah Warren, Benjamin Tucker, Lysander Spooner, Ralph Borsodi, Lawrence Labadie, Mildred Loomis and Robert Anton Wilson are the most notable proponents of decentralist individualism. They form an unbroken tradition of thought that spans more than a century of our history. Absentee ownership of land and central banking are in their view the institutions most to blame for the increasing centralization of political authority.

Both sources of economic power are directly involved in conspiracy politics.

Absentee owned land and natural resources in the hands of European and American investors, as well as Third World landlords, contributes massive hunger. Every ten minutes, somewhere in the world, seven people starve to death, five of them children under the age of five. In light of Brother-in-law's theory of a clandestine Nazi takeover at the end of World War II, it is interesting to observe that in no country composed my mostly unmixed Caucasians are vast numbers of people starving.

A combine of absentee landords, oil majors, manufacturers of chemical fertilizers, producers of farm equipment for both capitalist agribusiness and socialist collective farms is known in the intelligence community, in so many words, as "the petro-chemical mafia." Since various members of this alliance are not adverse to collaborating with organized crime, the name is not an exaggeration. Outspoken criticism of absentee landlordism is discouraged by this conspiracy.

Linked somehow with the John Kennedy assassination is at least one secret society, according to rumor, whose aim was to break up the petro-chemical mafia chiefly by means of protracted warfare against the oil companies. Unfortunately, it is also the fraternity most often accused of using techocratic mind manipulation as a weapon,

Central banking is an institution made possible by government regulation that, while it appears aimed at controlling banks, actually contributes to situations in which they become multinational cartels more powerful than any national government. Collecting interest on national debts is their prime method of accumulating revenue. By extending and withholding credit to governments, they possess the power to make wars and initiate revolutionary conspiracies from both left and right against nations that default on interest payments.

A simple and yet comprehensive analysis of the relationship between central banks and the intelligence community, particularly as regards socialist nations, is contained in *None Dare Call It Conspiracy* by Gary Allen of the John Birch

Society. In spite of an unpromising title, a low-brow tone of writing and excessive right-wing rhetoric for my tastes, *None Dare Call It Conspiracy* makes an excellent case for the decentralist theory that central banking culminates in the creation of warlike police states.

Slightly to the economic left of the decentralist anarchists are communist anarchists who both oppose Marxism and devote most of their attention to direct worker ownership of the means of production, They include, among others, Peter Kropotkin, Emma Goldman and Alexander Berkman.

What makes mind control a tempting proposition for both corporate and socialist managerial bureaucrats is that under existing systems of production the absentee control of workers is essential. Supporting the deregulation of small business and worker ownership of the corporate giants would erode the economic goal that makes the prospect of robotizing workers seem potentially profitable.

Just to the economic right of decentralism or individualist anarchism is a faction known as libertarian capitalism, Deriving its principal inspiration from Ludwig von Mises and his Austrian school of economics, the novels of Ayn Rand and the prolific writings of Murray N. Rothbard, this movement comprises both advocates of limited Constitutional government and opponents of government called anaro-capitalists. Many will recall the 1981 election in which Libertarian Party candidate Ed Clark gathered almost a million votes for President. While many libertarian capitalists oppose political activity in principle or as a waste of time, preferring to devote their attention to education, the Libertarian Party is an outgrowth of libertarian capitalism.

These anarcho-capitalists and right libertarians are against the initiation of force and fraud, whether sanctified by law or not. In that capacity they have produced a valuable body of sociological literature for understanding the nature of government. Among them are critics of the penal system and police departments as a means of reducing crime — see especially the writings of Robert LeFevre in this connection and, like both decentralists and communist anarchists, they are virtually unanimous in opposing coercive restrict ions on economic activity.

Since agencies like the C.I.A. and the K.G.B. play a central role in intelligence community intrigues, libertarian capitalist critiques of government understanding are extremely useful in understanding why and how to reduce the political power of nation-states so as to minimize the influence of conspiracies.

In conclusion, I would say that nine issues, in particular, are essential to human liberty. Regardless of whether or not our government ever gives us an honest probe of the John Kennedy murder and of assassinations and conspiracies in general, these are actions we can take as individuals to hasten the demise of conspiracies and cover-ups.

The first of these is to vocally support personal rights. Oppose institutional secrecy. Expose and advocate the dismantling of electro-chemical mind control. Support cultural autonomy for all racial, ethnic, sexual and intellectual minorities. Uphold the idea that individual rights are absolute and avoid humoring the ruling class by squandering public time and effort in the pretense that human rights are debatable. Without them there is no reason for societies to exist; it is for the protection of rights that they are organized to begin with.

Second in priority is to draw attention to the economic sources of support and funding for conspiracies: absentee ownership of land and central banking natural resources; and monetary regulation; absentee control of the workplace either by corporate investors or socialist bureaucrats, Here, refer to the writings of anarchist scholars and radical sociologists for statistics and analysis.

Last in priority, though not by much, the political mechanisms that encourage conspiracies ranging from drug smuggling to assassination. Support alternatives to retribution in fighting crime; they exist and are far more realistic than the average citizen is inclined to expect, Blackmail for violations of the law is another common method conspirators use to maintain secrecy and control operatives. To take it a step further, oppose all forms of coercive social organization; illegal extortion by means of threats to loved ones and poisoning designed to produce heart attacks are used to maintain whole intelligence bureaucracies. Laws that do not pertain to crimes against person or property are also particularly useful to conspiracies for reasons that a study of the literature of libertarian capitalism will make clear. Finally, support social organization by means contract enforced with boycott along voluntary federational lines. Parallel institutions organized that way can be used to alter or abolish any despotic regime.

These nine vital issues, then, fall into three categories. Personal rights to secrecy, mind control and cultural autonomy. Economic sources of oppression include absentee land ownership, central banking and absentee control of the place of work. Political issues deal with prisons, coercive social organization and free federational alternatives

By studying these issues and raising them in appropriate situations any individual can help create a coherent context for investigating the John F. Kennedy assassination and similar political murders in our recent history — and for probing the conspiracies that led up to then, and fester in their wake.

Diced
and
Other Essays

Why I Think President Reagan Should Abolish the Draft

25 December 1984

Cutting off Your Head Issue of Folk Write:

Certain translations of the Upanishads tell us that when the *Rishis* of old lost an argument their heads fell off. This meant to say they bowed and their heads touched (fell to) the ground. English-language occultism is full of similar errors everywhere you look. That is why Eris Discordia gave Joshua Norton a Chaosopher's Stone, instead of an ordinary confusing old apple like she gave all the rest.

Now had Norton shirked his responsibility to use this hidden knowledge (however accidentally it *was* hidden) honestly, they probably would've issued a postage stamp with his likeness by this time. (As it is, King Kong even beat him to the cover of *Time*).

This is in spite of his taking what was later to become Drew Pearson's advice about making people laugh if you didn't want them to kill you for telling them the truth.

Gentlemen, I ask you: if as much is true of Norton what will they forget to say about me? (Actually, I'm past registration age and honorably discharged with an unearned Good Conduct Medal from the Marines, so I don't worry about it.)

Besides that, this notebook must go through the U. S. Postal Service before it reaches the Selective Service Board anyway, and I'd be bored anyway myself.

As I can tell you from personal experience, quite literally, making history isn't always all that exciting, eh?

❦

In any case, both Honorably Discharged and not having calculated my earnings yet for this year, I'm sending this message to you instead of the IRS.

❦

Cool Hand Luke was first mentioned in a letter from Robert Anton Wilson in connection with what he and Grace always called Tampax, Florida, in keeping with Drew Pearson's advice. (Just after I went to see Robert about getting the assassinations investigated, speaking of Pearsons, Eve decided she needed a deadbolt to keep burglars out of her house.)

The reason I'm writing you is that, although this may make me sound like a nut, flying saucers keep messing up my sex life, not to mention my probe of the JFK murder. Could you please draft someone to solve this problem?

It *is* a national problem. According to the intelligence community scuttlebutt my sex life is more a national problem than the JFK murder, as a matter of fact. This all began, if I'm to believe what is just weird enough to be true, when I was going with a woman in Yokohama named Peggy-*san*, who was allegedly an agent for Jesuits at Sophia University in Tokyo.

Although I enlisted voluntarily in the Marines it was to avoid being drafted into the Army, and it wouldn't do any good to write the CIA, either, since they must surely already know about it. (When I approached the FBI in Tampa, Florida, in 1981 with the original draft of my confession to the JFK murder they advise me that they weren't authorized to accept my personal property, the scrupulous bastards.)

I've gone through various channels. I guess they all figure this is what I deserve for telling the Warren Commission Oswald was a loner and a paranoid.

There is also a Colin Wilson novel called *Station K*.

Don't get me wrong. I think conscription is slavery. Since this information is already known to the public, I figure there is no harm in alerting you gentlemen, although I have it on credible authority that the Joint Chiefs of Staff were also involved, save the Commandant of the Marines, in John Kennedy's murder. The old Smedley Butler Tradition, I guess.

Anyway, to make a long story short, I met a man in a bar in Tujunga, just before the last Pope was summoned into the beyond, who assured me he was *The Original* Cool Hand Luke. He was the last person ever so foolish to discuss with me in plain language (more or less) this problem about the flying saucers that are communicating with U. S. Navy or Coast Guard ships off the beaches of Florida (although at that time the problem was in California, since that's where I was residing). I'll spare you my theories about cattle mutilation, although I'm sure Mildred Loomis of Deep Run Farm in York, Pennsylvania, will be all too happy to talk about it with anyone, in case you are interested. Me, I was just trying to figure out how to get her into bed with me the night I was there so I didn't pay that much attention.

In other words, though, obviously the assassins premeditated a vast number of contingency programs — UFOs are almost the least of my problems.

You gentlemen are hired by the government to enslave people in order to preserve liberty, so I figure your minds must be adept at coping with convolutions in logic.

Me, I'm a simple soul. I've never been very Jesuitical or Machiavellian.

(Oswald was not the only person who committed spelling errors, which, for some reason, I think of: The Warren Commission accused him of acquiring "ficitious" [*sic*] identities.)

(Had Hugh Hefner been allowed to proofread that material such an embarrassment never would've occurred.)

I digress, though. In fact this is beginning to sound a little like the beginning of *Tristam Shandy*, which is as far as I ever got. All that is required are a few good men who can talk some sense into some oligarchs posing as aliens from the Dog Star, Sirius, I imagine. There might even be a Mamaluke Sword in it for one of you guys.

If you can talk young men into risking their lives to defend multinational corporations you will find much in common with these men who, beyond their ruse of illegal alienism, are much more honest, about calling human slavery by it's true name, etc. (Ahem.)

(I may just send this notebook, in its unsealed envelope, to Ivan Stang, as I once sent copies of David Marston's letter addressed to many foreign embassies — including that of the Republic of Togo — to Stan Jamison, who claimed afterwards he supplied the postage and mailed them.)

I'm not informed about govt. matters, being an anarchist, so I don't know if you gentlemen are cleared to read the charter of the National Security Agency or not. Harry Truman, I hear, said signing it was the worst mistake he ever made and I suspect he was thinking of me when he said that, though how great a mistake he surely didn't anticipate. (Mary Lou Mason at Sun Valley Junior High School 1953 was perhaps only the beginning.)

Fortunately, several matters don't embarrass me, although I occasionally find them irrelevant in terms of what else I'm called upon to ponder. There is this thing between my legs which the conspirators seem to take at least as seriously as the Washington Monument and although I share their sentiments, personally, I don't see what's it to them.

Such manifestations are not unusual in history, if that's any consolation to the scandalized. In India the indigenous personnel made up stories to tell their British conquerors about the *Lingam* and the Japanese have, and still celebrate, similar traditions.

So anyway there's scant excuse to distract ourselves with the sillies, although I'm among the first to appreciate the temptations for the humorist. (In other words, be assured my studies in sociology indicate our nation will survive this crisis.) After all, Benj. Franklin wrote essays about farting and we survived that, didn't we? In fact I think it is a comment on the times that whether or not Geo. Washington smoked hemp is more controversial. So *I* ain't worried.

What I am worried about is how long will discussing this matter postpone attention to the link between the JFK assassination and the Indo-China War, with which I am fully as much connected as with my penile extension, and possibly more permanently (due to circumstances Cool Hand Luke could probably tell you about if you could find him).

Have *you* ever wondered why what with Communist Cuba only 90 miles from home we went halfway around the globe to shoot at Asians with our draftees, instead? If that subject is slightly more important to me than my own prick, how much so for the rest of humanity?

So I'm as you can imagine of a double bind, since I'm certainly not inclined to give up sex at this point altogether, yet — as Camden Bernares (author of *Zen Without Zen Masters*) says — I tend to think with my gonads, involuntarily, when my individual sexual rights are being grossly violated with gunboat diplomacy at the alleged behest of flying saucers. So it isn't so much that I find the matter embarrassing as incredible. Like, who'd ever *believe* it? Meanwhile, these Florida short-shorts that are in fashion cause me to waste valuable time that could be better spent serving the nation thinking about all kinds of things.

So, although I've got at least one excuse They haven't, I'm fully as guilty of thinking incessantly about my meager sex life as any Arch Conspirator. And that's as far as the double bind goes, because as a hitchhiker who could be maimed anyway any day in a car wreck — what with the statistics — I (possibly I alone) don't worry about whether I'll be *ritually* castrated or not.

Being psychologically emasculated when I occasionally do crawl into bed with someone is problem enough and I sympathize with any of your CID or CIA agents that were subjected to such treatment at the hands of the Swiss Navy or whoever they are in this undeclared war of the bedroom that may have contributed heavily to John Fitzgerald Kennedy's demise, for all I know. And although the Indo-China War is not being fought for whoever we fought it for by the Chinese, so that — in strict accordance with your job descriptions — there is no problem *for you* in Asia, I've always been told that preventing future wars requires understanding past wars — not exactly your MOs either, I realize.

But I've already contacted the Senate Select Committee on Intelligence twice, the Atlanta Commissioner of Public Safety three times and when I don't go through channels I just wind up dealing with a lot of Dutch agents who probably aren't even connected with the Hague. (It seems that Howard Hunt, stationed on the Triple Underpass, was employed that fateful day in Dallas by the Bilderbergers!)

So this is an international problem that, although this data is suppressed, ranges far beyond the nature of the social environment of my next orgasm — although between hunt and the Dutch you'd not likely discover as much without my prompting in these nutty looking epistles, which a lazy postal inspector — bureaucrats being what they are — just might let slip through as harmless crankery, though I doubt it, since these days how I scratch my ass even receives unmerited attention, in line at the Post Office and elsewhere. I tell you, our Republic isn't what it used to be! Call me an alarmist if you will, I say these are terrible times.

Today it struck me, for instance, that I'm the type of person legend might just as easily wind up reporting last seen parachuting off the Jerry Thomas Memorial Bridge into a submarine hold — and although it hasn't happened yet, it would be just the type of thing to appeal to these Jungian maniacs who manipulate events. So there's no telling how much time we have, gentlemen, to get down to brass tacks. Especially since that bridge is between Riviera Beach and Singer Island and Stephanie Coffin isn't going to wait forever.

One of my pet peeves, while I am at it, is the way the Conspiracy, which I understand is controlled at least in part by the U. S. military, parodies left anarchist values in order to discredit them by applying them out of the basic affinity-group which is the active ingredient and backbone of anarchist communist social organization. In other words, for example, anarchists say that humans, like all higher mammals, are herd creatures that, if they lived in tightly knit, self-selecting, voluntary affinity groups with a high degree of intimacy, would be only too happy to contribute their labors to society free of charge.

Here in the alienated world of conspiracy politics there is a custom called "beer" — wherein you are expected to work for unknown absentee bosses for no pay. I suspect this is a capitalist plot to discredit the communist anarchist notion of voluntary (unpaid) production. Shit like that I don't need. If I wanted to discuss anarchism with idiots I'd find a home for the mentally retarded. There are even what they call "draft beers" — so you gentlemen might want to look into the matter to find out if any bartenders are practicing selective service without a Federal permit.

I know of no other case quite as unique as my own. If nothing else, it certainly is unusual. I can assure you that even the Pope in the Vatican thinks about me — and yet I'm not famous. And he isn't the only one among titles and names you would readily recognize — some of them reports of whose deaths have been greatly exaggerated, such as Nelson Rockefeller. So I find the usual half-assed civic safeguards of human rights don't work for me at all. At the risk of sounding paranoid, I don't think it is a coincidence that I am famous only among conspiracies.

They allege, although I've been unable to validate as much, that Justice Warren Burger of the Supreme Court was black-mailed to say, in a secret hearing, that my rights aren't being violated. (I realize that Justice Berger's extorters are proba-bly past military age, and there is probably no way you can force them to go fight in El Salvador and, besides, preventing a war in Latin America is among my priorities at this time).

Me and Lee Harvey Oswald and David Buckner, of Marine Air Control Squadron Nine, probably signed away our legal rights that fateful day early in 1959 when we were asked by a man working with base security to volunteer in helping Dwight David Eisenhower to meet a request, made in secret of course, by Fidel Castro, to rid his new revolutionary government in Havana of Russian agents.

Although, I think this project failed, I've noticed in retrospect that 1959 was the year I began experiencing nocturnal hallucinations, which until 1979 I vacillated between dismissing as not-uncommon psychological phenomena and direct messages from Great God Almighty Himself, the Big CO in the Sky.

By the time I realized I'm a Manchurian Candidate instead of a holy man it was nevertheless too late to altogether avoid a paranoiac sense of grandeur, since I was by then aware of enough other things going on, most of them involving Republicans, to make me at least repugnant to someone as famous as Gerald Ford. It just ain't the same as being the Avatar I once fancied myself, though, and quite frankly I'm bored with the whole experience. From what it once seemed, my status can only attain the level of a mundane imitation henceforth and I'm in no mood to settle for Ford when I expected the Lord.

As for saner, more material utopias of the body rather than the mind, before I went to Reginald Eaves about the JFK assassins in 1976 I was maintaining very satisfactory relationships with four or sometimes five women at the same time and no one was calling me paranoid. During most of these happy years between 1973 and 1976 I was attending Georgia State University in Atlanta and thinking of nothing but passing exams and getting laid. So the glories of the past — both in what seemed like reality physically and (between 1976 and 1979) psychologically — can probably never hope to be rivaled by any possible future. Where once there was sex and mysticism, today there is only politics. Even in retrospect when I divine the actual nature of what I then supposed was true happiness.

Frederick Demara and David Rockefeller were just fighting for my soul — in and out of the bedroom and psychic manifestation. So I see that I've always just been a plaything of the rich and the powerful — a political football, a leaf in the wind, an individual who achieved everything through no merit of his own.

So even when I contemplate that your brilliant Nazis in NASA and Bulgarian assassins and Ronald Reagan and probably even L. Ron Hubbard himself — not to mention Jim Garrison — anxiously await the latest news about how many times I scratched my ass in the line at the Post Office, I realize I deserve no credit. These are not things I planned. They just happened to me — either because they were plotted in advance by the World Wildlife Fund, the Hoover Institution, Edward Howard Hunt or CBS — or all four.

The question of what to do about any such situation is almost ludicrous in itself. So writing an essay for Selective Service makes as much sense as anything and slightly more than petitioning, say, Thomas Aquinas Murphy of General Motors, who is in a business that kills even far more Americans than does war.

According to most occult metaphysical systems nothing ever happens to anyone unless they want it to happen. So in the Eighteenth Century it became quite a fad within the French aristocracy to arrange to have oneself decapitated. What was good enough for King Louis and Marie Antoinette is good enough for you! Cut off your head with a chain saw and look and feel like an aristocrat!

Lest you get the notion I'm a raving Bolshivicki, I assure you I'm a member in good standing of the Kronstadt Vengence Committee — *dues* paying, I also might add. For one thing, the Soviet Ambassador to Cuba ("Leon") was probably *involved* in the faction of assassins that escalated the Vietnam unpleasantness. So very much as I surmise was the case with George De Mohrenschildt, I wind up playing both ends against the middle simply in order to try to get the plain truth, in spite of my essentially leftist sympathies.

Lee Oswald could have been an Illuminist "Light" spying electronically on Nikita K., and conveying in cant and other symbolic actions the Party Secretary in the Kremlin — for which reasons Soviet agents may have been assigned to frame him. Oswald may have misinterpreted Mr. K's ass scratching in the Moscow Post Office and framed him for sabotaging, via "the whole Bay of Pigs thing," the relations between JFK and the CIA then again, I could be off on another of my tangents.

In any case, it seems to me you waste too much time worrying about Russians when you should be worrying about Prussians. I'm a reluctant convert of the school of the anonymous man who stood up at a SubGenius Convention and yelled "Let's go back to Europe and fight WWII all over and this time, by God, let's win!"

(I have just added the relevant portion of the envelope that inspired this rant to the back of this book. I might just sell it one day like I sell my other notebooks — for $1.50 — and let the happless buyer be burdened with decisions and postal expenses. Reader participation, like the Living Theatre.)

(Note to Reader: to make history recklessly or to make no history at all — that is the dilemma upon whose horns I have impaled you.)

Good and Evil: It sounds like the name of a porno flick, doesn't it?

At this time I'm reading two books. One of them is an introductory autobiography of Malcolm X, my greatest American Black hero, whom I've come to suspect in recent years was murdered by my family, in cooperation with the FBI. The other is called *Jailbird* the title I was going to use for my book (already written and called *The Dreadlock Recollections*, which name I was going to drop, about my own involvement in the JFK murder). John Kennedy wasn't then and is not now in retrospect one of my heroes. Kurt Vonnegut, who beat me to the title *Jailbird*, is. Unfortunately, from what I can gather of his canted double entendre's he wasn't thrilled with my efforts to bring the history of the JFK murder to light. Then again, I might just be imagining things. Possibly he isn't writing in cant at all. Or possibly he isn't writing about me, if he is. Anyway, I like Vonnegut no matter what he thinks of me

There is in Gregory Hill's Norton Archives a file called the Change Raving Documents which explain all my political principles so that it isn't necessary to ask me what I think about this or that situation of which I have never been provided with sufficient facts anyway. Nevertheless, I'm incessantly consulted about what I think of this or that, so that I can be punished for my opinion.

The only reason I'm being consulted about my political opinions in the first place is because E. Howard Hunt once put on half the Royal Arch Masons with some tapes of conversations with me that were incomplete, both insofar as the whole of the discussions were concerned and in terms of their context (i.e. that I was only humoring Hunt, who was disguised as a penny ante mobster, to gather material for a novel).

What is relevant is not my opinions. What is relevant is my memory of those conversations — in which I learned circa 1962 that a war was being planned in Asia in order to avoid an invasion of Cuba, and that the principal motive for this preference for fighting Asians instead of Cubans was racist.

That's all the hell there is to my case. Everything else is a contingency program for prosecuting genocidal racism by

diverting popular attention to another subject — any other subject. Until genocidal racism is halted, there will be no point in even attempting to deal with any other issue, such as mind control. Because when one out of every three people in this world is being deliberately starved to death, there is going to be so much irrational violence in response that accomplishing anything constructive will be impossible — as it already is at this time.

I think this whole business of trying to resist mind control with the help of Muslims is insane, suicidal, bound to lead to something worse if it succeeds, impossible to accomplish and politically dangerous any way you look at it — except for the remote possibility that it might contribute to defeating racism. Muslim culture is among the most conditioning, traditional of all cultures in the world. What's the point of resisting rational conditioning via electronics just to condone traditional conditioning that is equally oppressive to the individual?

I never got around to telling you why I think the draft, and draft registration, should be abolished. If, however, you will read *The Great Explosion* by Eric Frank Russell, a science fiction novel that gets to this point in its closing chapters, you will see how freedom could be defended without shameful compromises.

The Confessions of Staint Famine

Invocation to the Muse
I almost laughed.
I almost died.
I almost lived.
I almost cried.
(Beasts in jungle
Stalk their prey.
I almost say
I almost sing
And almost know
What that will bring.
(Birds in the forest
Sount their horns.)
And, I guess
Because it is
George Washington's
Birthday, the
Flag is at
Half mast.

Discordianism:

The Lesser Wheelbarrow
and
The Greater Wheelbarrow

"I found a grass plant, and I got stoned, then after that I got lost."

- (Maybe) Me
(aren't we brilliant?)

Horsefeathers

Something occurred to me the other day when Nelson asked me whether I wanted to work for the CIA, CBS or the World-wide Church of God. Under ordinary circumstances, who you work for or what political entity holds you captive is of secondary importance. For example imagine someone is a Marxist. Does it make sense to imagine that individual is therefore more effective in Russia or China than in the US or Western Europe? Wherever I am I've always argued. I've never in my life been in a social environment where I agreed with many of the people surrounding me. There just aren't any anarchist ghettos.

Obviously I wouldn't want to work for the CIA or NSA if I could help it, bureaucracies — particularly imperialist bureaucracies — being what they are. A lack of imagination, or imagination that only channels itself into gaining political power, is already enough of a plague in my circumstances. All these organizations as far as I'm concerned, are rightist — although they say the NSA isn't. They also say the NSA is heavily dominated by the KKK.

The most pressing question in my mind is where can I get ample data about what is going on? How can I wiggle out of the agreement I made with Brother-In-Law to work on a need-to-know basis? I have to find out how my family became involved with the intelligence community. A rumor and their obvious unwillingness to tell me tends to make me suspect they were spies for Japan during WWII. That there is still a lot of neo-Nazism involved in this conspiracy is evident to me.

So I think about that "Mattco" principle associated with Susan Roberts (who was linked to "Milk" which is a code name for the same conspiracy for which the Worldwide Church of God is a front) and I think it is probably the lesser of three evils. That they are authoritarians and rightists doesn't necessitate that I change my views — because I can argue them eloquently and perhaps exert an influence that way among them.

The Russians don't want the JFK murder investigated, as I understand things (probably as David Rockefeller describes things). The Chinese are slaughtering both Cambodians and Vietnamese in what is probably a Vril Society race war nst the inhabitants of the Indochinese Peninsula. The U. vernment agencies offer a milieu that could only appeal uicidal masochist. (There are more suicides among

NSA agents than among employees of any other intelligence organization in the world, according to a *Penthouse* article.)

Although I've been getting more and more suicidal in recent years, I'm not a masochist — and, although the truth about my life is very depressing, the more I find out about it, that truth has always been there, and I'd be better off making a healthy adjustment. And that requires more information, rather than more faith and dedication to unknown causes recommended by anonymous sources.

> John Connelly or someone like him says I'm in error about the above.

"Cast aside right states of mind, o monks, much less wrong ones."

Grasping this or that way of looking at things, we block the senses with the mind and fail to see.

I notice this all the time, of course, when people approach me expecting cant. Cant is then what they perceive. Or is that my mind blocking my perception? Or both?

Also it is observance in what we call buttons. Someone clutches at a summary of a situation, a conclusion, and they thereby ignore the potentials for anything else. This is a propensity of the human mind. A conscious relaxing of effort is needed to avoid it.

Conclusions about things received or anxieties, which are there in the first place because of previous conclusions and their inadequacy. So we stack one inadequate conclusion on top of another in a perpetual anxiety producing war against anxiety. Like worsening a disease with too many quack cures.

Paying too much attention can be worse, sometimes, than paying no conscious attention at all.

NC says the only way they can get accurate data is to support landlords. It's also being guessed that landlords are responsible for my harassment — which may explain why all the data I get about land is incredible, in particular. I'm told that the left supports landlordism and that the right is against it, that racists are against landlords and that antiracists support them, etc. "Ralph" is probably polluting our information networks.

I suspect the source of these problems originates with Bob's Big Boy in Tujunga.

That's going too far, I'll admit. I was much happier, though. It's like admiring Mao's China but, when it comes down to it, preferring to live in Japan. Not because the Japanese political system is very nice. Just because the Japanese understand how to mind their own business, instead of parading around like a lot of Prussians. The old Confucians and cutthroats vs. Buddhists and soldiers thing. Both are out of kilter. It's still a mixed-up world. Freedom is essential, though, before anything else can be accomplished that will endure beyond the death of the latest Party chairman.

It's like, to me, the ideal is, as with Mao, the potentials revealed by the Paris Commune. The problem is an argument about how to get there from here — and how miserable is it worth being over an idea, and for how long?

Then there is this Pope with his heavy snow. I'm trying to organize from the bottom up. These autocrats in New Orleans want me to be isolated from the people I live with. I'm not supposed to tell them what's going on. This is supposed to prevent racism. Whoever has been in charge of preventing racism ought to be fired for incompetence — particularly if they think secrecy will help.

The period of reconstruction after the Civil War gave birth to the Klan.

Duvalier is like Senator Fishback of Louisiana. He isn't preventing racism. He's creating racism. I'm not gung ho about opposing him because I don't need a divisive fight with Blacks who support him. I've already taken on the Prussians. If Duvalier lived on Uranus, though, and me on Mercury, I'd rest a lot easier. That way I wouldn't have to worry about pissing him off.

As it is, there are Duvalier agents in Miami and Atlanta who are practicing extreme terrorist tactics. Everybody is afraid of them. They are being quite open about themselves.

This is going to drive a lot of Southern working class people who were beginning to realize who their actual oppressors were back into racism, instead. Baby Doc could probably be brought along to a higher level of consciousness. Or maybe he will be ousted, as he obviously fears.

Anyway, I've got these Black "orange trucks" to endure, meanwhile — I guess is what they are. They seem to be the ones who don't want people around me. Understanding why they are being ordered to persecute me. As long as life is made miserable for me, I will continue — blindly, if necessary — to change the situation. Since I believe it is the ignorance of the agents used to hassle me that keeps them from exposing their bosses, instead, I'll continue to fight that ignorance.

As usual, my problems with the Rockefellers continue. Whenever I soften toward them they once again demonstrate that they are more convoluted that Jesuits, as racist as Germans, and more invisible politically than anybody.

I don't trust people who are all things to all men. Jim Garrison is the same way. So is Mark Lane. The only thing I like about David is that he isn't a hysteric. He carries it to greater extremes than I can relate to, though. Since he seems the only non-hysteric in conspiracy politics, though, he's all I've got in that department. If he thinks Wilson is a Nietzschean, though, he is a hysteric about that much. That's that Anglo-Saxon thing, again. Everybody is either a Communist a Capitalist or a Nazi — there are no anarchists in that worldview. Like the CFR scene in the *Trilogy*. The Anarchists are no different (to them) than the hordes of Ghengis Kahn. A nice weak, safe enemy for all the Powers to pick on, if you ask me. Like potheads and gays to the police.

That's speculation about where they are at, of course. I look at the results and I draw what seem like obvious conclusions. Non-Caucasians are being exterminated by famines by the millions, so I conclude the Nazis remain very powerful.

Bolsheviks cooperate with this conspiracy of extermination so I conclude they are instruments of the German ruling class. The Invisible Hand of the technocracy leaves its fingerprints wherever there are Hitlers or Stalins or Castros, so I conclude they were all instruments of the same conspiracy.

You find a big foot print, you assume a large man or woman walked there. You find a small foot print, you assume a small person left it.

When, in the Marines, Ronald Wilson told the CO Raven-hurst was a huge, mountain of a man — and then they found size six shoes under his bunk, they began to suspect things. The fact is, vast areas in Africa are suffering famine. All anyone talks about is Ethiopia. Then they whip up a frenzy of charitable aid. Then the Marxist government confiscates food supplies. Rumors say the British have got the Marxist politicians there under surveillance and control.

Eventually, no doubt, they will be overthrown by the Dutch who will introduce Carter capitalism and then the famine will end and everyone will be more convinced than ever that revolutionaries are cruel and incompetent.

Eventually the old British and Dutch colonial empires will rule Africa again. There'll be a few surviving Blacks, a few lions, a few zebras for the tourist trade.

A lot of cheap raw materials in Europe.

All because of what everyone was taught to call communism.

When the Italian Fascists tried to conquer Ethiopia, they weren't subtle enough to win. That was the great lesson of WWII for Fascism: look as much as possible like your enemies.

The corollary is to make your enemies look as much like Fascists as possible — by supporting the Senator Fishbacks among them.

Then, in comparison, Huey P. Long looks like a saint.

I've been so horny lately it's been distracting. Maybe it is my time of month or maybe I'm just getting tired of all this Prussian horseshit about how terrible sex is. I shall never apologize to anyone for being a mammal. If they want to believe in what Stirner called spooks that is their business. If I don't — and chose to act accordingly — that is my business.

Maybe there will be no peace for me until the Vatican is bombed during a conclave. I suspect very much that is the point someone is trying to make — perhaps the Pope himself.

I don't care whether the Vatican is bombed or not. It is somebody else's grudge. I'm not persuaded when they torment me like a bunch of Inquisitors. Facts, not harassment, change my views. I don't feel obligated to be crucified for the Knights of Columbus though, either — because all they give me is a bunch of crap about sexual æsthetics rooted in the conceit that we are supposed to be disembodied spirits rather than mammals. If just one person is psychotic it is insanity. If many people are psychotic it is religion. As far as I'm concerned their attitude toward their own instincts is psychotic. If they could find some way to be psychotic without trying to make me just as insane I'd defend them. As long as they resort to coercion and abusive, caustic methods to cram their values down the throats of unbelievers they aren't worth it to me.

So let the Finns bomb the Vatican. I don't care. I was wrong for sabotaging their first attempt. I'm still no more sympathetic with the Satanists, either, though. I was dragged against my will into a fight that was not my fight and I resent it. And I think the world will be just as miserable under the Lucious Trust Fund as under the Vatican — because the epistemology is the same: to win an argument you use the rack and thumbscrews, if possible.

People always come to resemble their worst enemies sooner or later. By their tactics, it is impossible to distinguish between them. An inquisition is an inquisition. A Russian or Chinese Communist is only a Catholic atheist. Emma Goldman said precisely that about the Russians.

NBC remains my worst villain. Everybody thinks I'm fighting with CBS — including CBS, I guess. CBS is all right. ABC is more informative than either NBC or CBS. NBC is mean.

"CBS? And that's NBC. They only have one camera here." — Nixon in the Forbidden City in China. (as in "see bull shit" CBS) Besides they are interfering with my sex life.

Somebody thinks they're Bolsheviks. They sure used to get uptight when the Russians bugged my house in Tijunga. And they nearly went berserk one night when I said I was going to the Friendship Bookstore in Chinatown. My understanding is they were Fascists who were converted, with great difficulty, to *laissez-faire* capitalism. Not racist fascists. Just fascists economically and politically. They continue to begrudge the fact that they aren't going to become as powerful as they'd been led to believe. That's what I get — everywhere but at Specialty Advertising. The old Marxist Sarnoff either was never actually a Marxist or was deprived of effective power by "Sam" long ago.

Miami was discussed a lot — equal and opposite things were said, though. Where? When?

I have explained many times why it would defeat my purpose to talk in cant or to pretend to talk in cant. *The Dreadlock Recollections* is a document affecting, potentially, more lives than any other in American history, lives in the Third World. It must be understood.

My worst problem at this time is that *The Dreadlock Recollections* are being dismissed as a "fictionalization," as cant.

Nelson Rockefeller headed a commission that agreed with the findings of the Warren Commission. Howard Hunt was one of the assassins who sues everyone who tells that truth about him. In this situation, I seem surrounded by Hunt and Rockefeller and Dutch agents. I don't object to communicating with these people — provided they can refrain from treating me sadistically, of which they've so far proven incapable. As Hunt himself never tired of repeating: "Power corrupts. Absolute power corrupts — absolutely." Hunt and Rockefeller are so drunk with power that they choose to attack me with lice and purgatives as a method of dialog. These men are not revolutionary nor are they enemies of genocide — they are mad emperors, like the twelve Caesars.

In any case, I object vociferously to being surrounded by their agents — who are lied to in order to justify censorship about the JFK murder and the origins of the Vietnam War. They've convinced Tom that the Russians will rule America if the truth becomes known. The Russians understand the truth. They've been spying on me for years. It isn't the Russians Rockefeller and Hunt are worried about. It is the Vietnamese who cannot be bought off — as some can.

I can face death, wild motorcycle rides, etc., without fear. Speaking for the first time under ordinary circumstances to a woman, to whom I'm extremely attracted, terrifies me. So

I'm going to spend a day thinking about what to say, then I'm going to drink a couple of beers to relax me, then I'm going to call up and request a song — probably "Jose Cuerno" by Shelly West — and then tell you I think you have a beautiful voice and whatever else that is filed away in my conversational arsenal that seems appropriate at that instant, like "I'd sure like to meet you sometime."

Some problem about mind control. Somebody else says don't worry about; it was Rose Ann's misunderstanding — something to do with me and the Jesuits.

Richard Condon says Attila the Hun was a very charming guy. There is a monument in the Middle East mourning an attack by "the Brigand, Joshua."

Salvador Allende, Dead or Alive?

More to the point, Allende's faction — racist or not. This faction is being accused of parental extortion against my family. Chileans are much like Cubans in that they avoided intermarriage with Native Americans. That Allende was a socialist is beside the point. He was an elected socialist who was disposed by an undemocratic, fascist military clique. Castro's criticism of Allende was the greatest compliment he ever received: he had not, said Fidel, instilled the necessary fear of the government, Allende's socialist government, in the hearts of his people. The American corporations in Chile — Pepsi, Lever Brothers, ITT — are among the most conspiratorial companies anywhere in the world. Nationalizing them would have although a violation of economic freedom in the eyes of conservatives — accomplished a great deal in terms of ending the fraud that Third World people are somehow benefiting from American investments in their nations (see *State of Siege*).

I have always liked Allende. I've always believed he was victim of a terrible injustice — not because he was a Bolshevik whose people supported him. It is the masses, not the Marxist leaders, these capitalists fear — for which reason the US aluminum companies also stopped Jamaica. The question is if Allende's life was spared by SEG, was it because, like Castro, he is a Castillian racist? Is he? Or isn't he? Nazis don't object to socialism any more than they object to monopoly cartel capitalism. Both are the same — a few handpicked bureaucrats determine the fates of everyone else. The same clique controls both State and economy — whether they are corporate executives selected to serve in the Cabinet or socialist appointees assigned to run factories. The idea is that there are such vast differences in people that some are fit to rule others, though in fact the most brilliant person seldom can competently manage his own affairs, much less the affairs of hundreds of thousands of millions of others.

The objection to racism and all other forms of elitism is SOCIOLOGICAL. Communication is only possible between equals. One person can only effectively govern one person — that's why everybody is equipped with a brain. (See the rest of my corollaries to the SNAFU Principle in a past issue of *Spare Change* that appeared in a past issue of *FreFanZine*). Bureaucracy — whether in the form of states, caste systems, corporations or any other coercively enforced hierarchy, is always, inevitably a long road to betrayal of the goals for which it was intended. (And corporations could not exist as we know them without the State, although Libertarians insist they are voluntary.)

"CKQ" = Child Killing Quotient.

A zooty pimp in Atlanta was before the judge, charged with creating turmoil. The case against him was brief and credible. His conduct in the courtroom was cavalier and extroverted. When the judge dismissed the charges against him he scratched her cheek.

That scenario was repeated in another form the other day. Both times the accused was symbolized as Mark Lane. Whether it only happened once and I was told about it twice, or whether it happened two or more times — I couldn't hazard a guess.

The names of everyone involved and their "CKQ" ratings would, paradoxically it seems, require an atmosphere free of extortion to begin with. A complex, though probably not unsolvable, problem.

Anyway, today I'm sitting on somebody's grass complaining about how pawnly I feel with this power struggle that appears to be going on between Rockefeller and Demara — and they turn on their sprinklers. That old "I had to leave" thing Berkman mused about. Sons of men with nowhere to lie their heads. Or no rest for the wicked, maybe.

Andrew Young says, they say, not to get trapped, as he is, in the Worldwide Church of God.

Order of Saint Gulik: enlighten all sentient beings by blowing marijuana smoke at them.

St. Gulik drove all the camels off Easter Island.

262

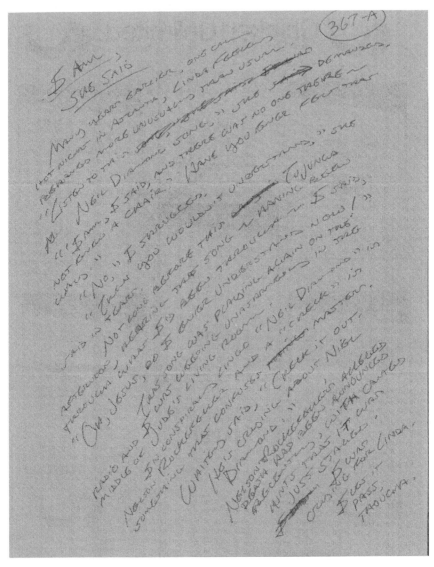

Previously unpublished manuscript (no date).

Diced

ONE Saturday morning Mariposa came into the living room just as I was waking up. Standing next to the TV set she looked my way and said "Which cartoon shall I watch today? This one (taking a little bow) or this one (turning on the television)?" I could tell she was mimicking me. She was what I later learned is called a "mirror." She also made snide remarks in cant when I got erections, although how she or her controllers could tell something like that was happening was quite beyond me.

I began to perceive an enormous amount of pressure in this direction. Jude kept prominently displaying a book called *The Little Flowers of Saint Francis*. I was supposed by somebody to be a celibate holy man — probably because of what I'd said to Jude that afternoon we fucked and I told her I'd gotten into tantric celibacy, to explain why I wasn't into attaining an orgasm. Or else the bastards were just mad at me for exposing their World Wide Church of God Conspiracy and this orthodox nagging was their demented notion of fit punishment.

In any case, that day I woke up with a hard-on and had to listen to Mariposa stand there and tell me I was a "naughty puppy." I became enraged. I stormed up to the Jack in the Box for coffee and told them to tell Jimmy Carter to tell whoever it was that no-one was going to go around saying I was celibate, or supposed to be celibate, and get away with it. I would, if necessary, publish incredibly pornographic writing to rebuke rumors like that.

At that time I was still not masturbating because of that experience with the astral witch. This, I'd learned, was called a "pinch." This mind control causing a lack of sexual desire during most waking hours. It felt like a "pinch" in my spinal column, just above my sexual chakra, cutting off sexual energy. Nevertheless I wasn't going to be celibate forever. They just told me I was arguing with a straw man. "That's extra," they said — complete agreement ("X") with straw.

Many years earlier, one calm hot night in Atlanta, Linda behaved more unusually than usual. "Listen to this Neil

Diamond song" she demanded. I am, I said, and there was no
one there, not even a chair. "Have you ever felt that way?"

"No," I shrugged.

"Then you wouldn't understand," she said in tears.

Not long before this afternoon, hearing that song — having
been through what I'd been through — I said "oh, Jesus, do
I ever understand now!" That song was playing again on
the radio and I was weeping unashamedly in the middle of
Jude's living room. In conspiracy lingo "Neil Diamond" is
Nelson Rockefeller and a "check" is something that confuses
matters. Whitney said "Check it out, he's crying about
Neil Diamond." Nelson Rockefeller's alleged death had been
announced recently, with canted hints that it was just staged.
I was crying for Linda. I let it pass, though. Not long
afterwards Newport cigarette billboards appeared with the
motto "Check It Out!" Two black people — a man and a
woman — dressed in blue and yellow, symbolic of the KKK,
were pictured in the ad laughing like heedless fools it seemed
to me.

AWK: Anarchist Working-class Satanism. I also called it
Zenarchy. I assumed that Jude, Witney and Mariposa were
all victims of implanted surveillance devices like me. I also
figured there were probably bugs in the walls. Experimenta-
tion and feedback convinced me that I could say anything I
wanted when I was in the house alone, although I had to be
very careful only to follow cues when anyone was present. So
I explained my political views in eloquent stoned speeches,
designating coded significances to pieces of furniture to facil-
itate silent communication when my hosts returned. I also
began dealing with lots of intelligence community Satanism.
When I once asked Cameron what the attraction of Satanism
was to our friends like Ron Garst and Robert Anton Wilson,
he theorized it was the John Wayne syndrome — the need
for excitement. After three-and-one-half years of tedium and
boring juvenile harassment I was beginning to understand this
much. I was always being accused of being too restless, of tin-
kering with plans beyond my understanding, etc. I also liked
Robert Anton Wilson's Miltonic Satanism, expounded in the

Trilogy, epitomized in the motto NON SERVIUM! Anarchist in our code was symbolized with the letter "A." Working class was at that time designated with "W." Satanism was "L." So I called my teachings in that house "AWL," after the Zen *roshi* who compared the enlightened being to "a rusty awl." I wanted something with a funky, organic mood. Not shrill or romantic as conventional revolutionary ideology. I deemed it Satanism because in that social environment it involved the Jesuitical convolution and craftiness which I associated with Satanism as I'd come to know it.

At one end of Jude's living room a great bleeding sacred heart of Jesus rug covered most of the wall. An oblong coffee table stood perpendicular to it. "The end of the table nearest the rug is for objects symbolizing things in positions of political strength. Items symbolic of persons or organizations in conditions of powerlessness, position at the furthest end of the table from the bleeding heart of Jesus." This corresponded to my feeling that power is inseparable from torment. "Anything about which you feel distrust, place in this pot," I added, "this is the doobie pot, for dubious things."

What I actually was, I know, was only a template for developing codes. My only actual power was to designate meanings for symbols. When I didn't do this deliberately, it happened anyway via Freudian random associations. How long it had been going on I hadn't yet begun to guess, but I was now participating consciously in the process and the novelty of the activity kept me engrossed. Somewhere there must be computers programmed to memorize links such as similes between one thing and another. Whenever someone said in my hearing "X is like Y," then Y becomes a symbol for X and / or vice versa. "Wilson registers the word 'dangerous' as 'important'," Greg once said, because I'd rubber stamped "DANGEROUS" on something I sent him, to which he paid more attention than seemed appropriate to me.

Have you ever wondered why, after all these years, the truth abut the JFK murder is still being suppressed? One of the main reasons is because neither the right nor the left nor the political center wants you to discover the war in Indochina was a deliberately planned racist act of genocide. If I had understood the above van der Lubbe rap I could have known to mention this material when I testified before the Warren Commission in 1964. Since probably only a minority of the assassins wanted to expose the Nazi faction and avoid an Asian war, a compromise was probably reached where I would be given the information and then whether or not I passed it on would determine policy for all. The anti-Nazis bet that I would. I failed them. I didn't want to seem paranoid, so I discounted the conversations with Brother-in-law.

The Secret Teachings of Eris Discordia

How has Discordianism changed since its beginning?

In 1961 Greg Hill and I went to New Orleans where we met a man who said his name was Gary Kirstein, who became our fifth convert. In my opinion this man was actually E. Howard Hunt, undercover, and I think he converted Richard Nixon and Don Kendall and Joan Crawford of Pepsi Cola to the Discordian Society. As everyone knows, Pepsico rules the world. So that is probably how, in a very short time, Discordianism became the official state religion of the United States of America.

What is the platform of your Evengelical and Unrepentant Church of No Faith?

No faith in anything. No faith in the masses. No faith in the Party. No faith in the capital class. No faith in God. Faith only in the Goddess Eris Discordia — because, of course, everybody's gotta believe in something.

Is the Law of Fives really always true? How does it work with such stunning accuracy?

The Law of Fives is always true. The reason it works is because everything, without exception, always happens in fives. For teat reason sufficient proof of any theorem is to give five examples. I'm sure you can think of five examples of things happening in fives — so therefore you can prove to yourself the validity of this Erisian dogma. An example in action is that I just mentioned the year, 1961. 1 from 9 is 8. 6 from 8 is 2. Half of 6 is 3 and 3 plus 2 equals 5. SO everything happens in fives or can in some way or other be connected with the number five.

What advice would you give to the beginning Discordian about converting the masses?

Goddess will never forgive you if you try to convert the masses. She is very strict about that. Look what happened to me!

What about finding similar ilk?

What do you want them for? Ask yourself that question and you may be able to avoid having to have anything to do with another Discordian!

What do you know about the region of Thud?

I've lived in the Region of Thud many times. In fact I was brought up in the heart of the Region of Thud — its lowest rung: the suburbs of East Whittier, California. It isn't a very interesting subject to discuss. You're better off reading Dante's *Inferno*. Thud is more boring than his *Paradisio*.

What about those precious Mao buttons to be distributed there?

Hey, yeah — how 'bout those Mao buttons!

How many early Erisians are still active? Do some drop out?

If Fang the Unwashed, Roger Lovin, finds out anyone else is also a Discordian, he ex-communicates them at once. This is how we lose most of our members. SO if you want to remain active in the Discordian Society, don't let Fang the Unwashed find out about you.

Have there been any other editions besides the Loompanics before this time?

Principia
There have been five editions of *The Principia*. The first one was published in New Orleans by Greg Hill and a secretary in Jim Garrison's office in 1964, who used his mimeograph machine for that purpose: *How the West was Lost* (subtitle). Then Greg published another one somewhere along the line. Then in 1969 he came to my house in Tampa and we published a third edition — by far the best because I contributed a lot more stuff to that one. Then a year or two later Greg

published the edition that Loompanics wound up reprinting. Then he published a fifth edition which was very short — just a telegram that went: M M M M M M M M M M M M M M M M M M M M M M M... and on like that.

Is the Discordian Society outdated?

I wanted to create a satire of college fraternities and Greg wanted to satirize organizations in general. I'd just dropped out of a fraternity and was very bitter about them. There are still fraternities. There are still organizations. There are even still organizations that think God is a WASP. SO I don't think we are outdated.

The Discordian Society has no central headquarters, by design. This has made it difficult to rally together to perform such activities as Jake Day, mentioned in the Illuminatus! Trilogy. On the other hand, this same isolation has created many self-contained cells of Chaos strung together by mailing networks. Do these factors balance out?

A monster without a head cannot be decapitated. So that's an advantage — except for the fact that the Discordian Society *is* a monstrosity.

You had inspiring rants such as "The Kid was Perfect!" published in the third issue of the official newsletter of the Church of the SubGenius, The Stark Fist of Removal, in addition to portions of The Book of the SubGenius. What do you have to say about The SubGenius Foundation? Doesn't this conflict with your Discordianism?

I dig the SubGeniuses because, like them, my IQ is also below genius. So, in spite of my disagreements with them, the world looks to me just as bewildering and frightening as it looks to them. Probably, there are Discordians who feel every which way about everything, including "Bob" Dobbs. For example, Doug Wellman of Puzzling Evidence is also a Discordian and he recently shot and killed Dobbs. Me, I'm a Discordian and I kind of liked the guy.

What are the risks of being a member of The Discordian
Society?

The risks of being a member of the Discordian Society are enormous — because the Discordian Society is a department of the Universe, and the risks to be found in this Universe are infinite in number. Though nevertheless of course divisible by five.

In our experience, most active Erisians are male. Why
haven't more females become involved with Eris?

Because Discordianism is a religion that blames a female deity for creating creating reality, so naturally that explanation is more appealing to males — who are glad to get off the hook.

Readers of the Illuminatus! Trilogy who encounter active
Discordians are often suprised to find that there really is an
Erisian conspiracy, and it is the Illuminati who are
imaginary. Or is it? You speak often of conspiracies in your
publications; what are some active ones that readers may
encounter?

Don't be fooled. There is also an Illuminati. In fact, it stands to reason that there are five of them. Conspiracies are much more common than people (even conspirators) suppose — and it is to the advantage of every single one of them to convince the world that people who suspect there are no conspiracies are suffering from a mental illness called paranoia. Only the Illuminati are different this way. They are just a conspiracy that wants to make everyone else paranoid — because they are all paranoids who are tired of being discounted and isolated in their higher level of consciousness. A conspiracy is anything that is the result of a secret agreement. Therefore, to the conspirators themselves they seldom seem like conspiracies. So they are much too numerous to list here. Although I might mention the Secret Order of Thule, the Argarthe, the Gerrmatch, the Vril Society, and the Discordian Arballah, and the Lucius Trust Fund and the Trilateral Commission and the World Power Foundation and the Spare Change Investment Corporation as among the most active.

How would you describe your Spare Change publications?

As exorbitantly priced — because I've just raised the sub-
scription rate to a dollar an issue — mostly because of a
conspiracy that monopolizes written and printed communication called the U. S. Postal Service. My address is [redacted].
Wall-Op and *Folk-Write* — wall posters and personal journals,
or reprints therefrom.

What is the Myth of Starbuck's Pebbles?

Greg and I thought of the Discordian Society as a result of an
argument over whether order was, as I figured, the prevailing
form of chaos or, as he thought, something the mind projects
into a wholly chaotic environment. At that time I lives on
Starbuck Street in East Whittier so he wrote "The Myth of
Starbuck" to refute me — about a guy named Starbuck who
finds a bed of pebbles and the more he examines it, the more
geometrical patterns he discovers. Then he goes evangelizing
and before long this random bed of rocks becomes a national
monument — one of the Five Wonders of the World.

*Spare Change seems to be oriented toward social comment
rather than traditional Discordianism. Do you feel as Greg
Hill felt in his Afterword to the Loompanics edition of
Principia Discordia that everything that needed to be said had
been said?*

I've always been into social comment more than Greg. Greg
was always more into Discordianism than me — until he
discovered word processing computers, since which time he's
been absorbed in his work as a word processor. I don't think
Greg thinks in terms of what needs to be said. If it tickles
him, he says it. If it doesn't, he ignores it. He's always been
very self-contained that way. A true sage.

What is the purpose of Discordianism?

Discordianism's purpose is to confuse people who think everything has a purpose.

Should it be intellectualized?

I don't care whether you intellectualize it or not. I think excessive intellectualizing leads to a terrible addiction to a drug the brain produces called serotonin, also linked by studies of monkeys to power addiction. If, however, you don't lose your sense of humor and you still can look at something without always seeing it as symbolic of something else, I don't think you are intellectualizing too much. A Zen master pointed to his garden and complained: "People look at these flowers as if in a trance!" That's what happens when the intellect becomes an end in itself instead of a magnificent tool for comprehension and appreciation.

> *What was actually involved in the creation of Principia Discordia?*

As Otto von Bismark once said: "Anyone who likes sausages and laws should never watch either one being made." You wouldn't want to know what was involved in the creation of *Principia Discordia*. Mostly it was Greg, me, Robert Anton Wilson — who was to us as Knigge was to Weishaupt of the Illuminati — Robert Shea, and Roger Lovin, who also holds a black belt in Rosicrucianism, and a New Orleans French Quarter character named Slim Brooks who was probably Jerry Milton Brooks, a CIA navigational consultant for Division Five (5) of the FBI, in the bay of Pigs invasion.

> *How did Loompanics Unlimited become the largest publishers of Principia?*

Since the *Principia* isn't copyrighted, they just went ahead and published it, then sent us copies.

> *Many of their books deal with the how-to's and justification of violence, which seems out of place for the publishers of the manual of Erisianism.*

Many years ago, in the Sixties, Greg was very disturbed to find a letter in the *Los Angeles Free Press* about an organization called the Discordian Society that was committing horrible murders. As for me, I think about a story told by the Chinese Taoist sage Chuang-Tzu (who, incidentally, was close personal friends with the Erisian apostle saint Hung Mung, about whom he also wrote):

Once a farmer's horse ran away. A neighbor said: "How unfortunate!" All the farmer said was: "Who knows what is good or bad?" Soon the horse returned to the farm with a whole herd of wild horses. That neighbor said: "How fortunate!" Said the farmer: "Who knows what is good or bad?" Then the farmer's son broke a leg trying to tame one of the horses and the neighbor came over to offer sympathy. "Who knows what is good or bad?" shrugged the farmer. Then the Duke's army came down the road, conscripting all able-bodied young men and marching them off to war.

In any case, I don't think ideas are dangerous — any ideas — nor that information is dangerous — compared to the fear of ideas — any ideas — and ignorance. Certain actions are dangerous — one of them is the forceful suppression of books. Most people have to be rational in practice just to make a living and survive. So I think there is enough common sense in the populace to assure the viability of a free market of ideas. And who knows what is good and what is bad?

Maybe a homicidal maniac will order a bunch of books about torture and basement nukes, etc., and someone will visit him and see them on the shelf and decide to get the hell away from him and thereby avoid being murdered — as one example among many. That — and I speak as an anarchist — is the advantage of the visible state over a conspiracy: you can read its laws and find out just how insane it is instead of having to cope blindly with its violence. Of course when most people are conned into the notion that secrecy is national security — then the state *is* a conspiracy. I'd rather there were governments and no conspiracies more than I'd prefer the opposite. And of course if secrecy were national security, then the best way to preserve democracy would be to vote with your eyes shut. So although I'm not particularly fond of violence, I prefer to see it discussed out in the open as opposed to being driven underground for sure!

Oh, yeah — and a parting thought: things aren't always as

complicated as they seem. To return to our example of 1961 and 5 (five): $1 + 9 + 6 + 1 = 17$. There are two digits in 17 and $17 - 2 = 15$, and 15 ends in 5.

And that's the point in common between Taoism and the wholly Chaoist philosophy of Discordianism: we both try to find the simple way to do things — when the activity isn't itself too complicated.

(That's pretty bad; you might want to skip it)

Some additional notes for your information or inclusion...

The Secret Order of Thule is a German conspiracy. The Shamballah is a German-Japanese Tibetian conspiracy. The Argarthe is a German-Dutch-Finnish conspiracy. The Gerrmatch is a German conspiracy. The Vril Society is a German-Chinese conspiracy currently dedicated to exterminating Cambodians and Vietnamese. The Discordian Arballah is a Pennsylvania Dutch conspiracy. The Lucius Trust Fund is an anti-Catholic, Theosophical conspiracy. The Trilateral Commission is always trying to make up its mind whether to be a Rockefeller-communist conspiracy or a Rockefeller-capitalist conspiracy. The World Power Foundation is probably a New Orleans-based conspiracy, about which Loompanics can tell you more. And of course only paranoids think the Spare Change Investment Corporation is a conspiracy.

Ramon Magsaysay — as President of the Philippines — could go anywhere without bodyguards. In Marta station in Atlanta, even the restrooms need bodyguards.

That last note wasn't in answer to any of your questions. I just got pissed at the Marta bus drivers, who are persecuting me today. So I wrote something to barb them with in my notebook — my usual way of venting anger.

☙

Some additional notes of Discordian instruction:

The Second Law of Thermodynamics, which used to prove the Eristic worldview conclusively, has since been refuted (i.e. in an open or infinite system, where new energy keeps feeding in, like, perhaps, the universe, it doesn't work). That's only because Eris got pissed, though. She made it stop working. They should've called it the Fifth Law of Thermodynamics, the infidel bastards!

☙

You may have seen little things like this laying along the road or in liquor-store parking lots. They are Eyes of Eris, sprinkled over the landscape at night by Her Cosmic Flying Elves. Skeptics, infidels, heretics, unbelievers, pork-eating Christians and the like think they are just pull-off beer can tops. Actually, they watch our every move — because Eris is making a list of who's naughty and nice to give to the Xists in 1998 when they descend from Sirius for the long-awaited Rapture of which Jesus warned. Although most people got it backwards; it is the good who disappear, they think, and the wicked who remain, or vice-versa... I forget which myself. If you read the Bible carefully, though, you will see that it doesn't specify. Anyway, these Eyes of Eris are the Erisian Anhk — and if you wear one around your neck you will be instantly recognized by other Discordians — including, unfortunately, Roger Lovin, who will thereupon without hesitation excommunicate you. They are also symbolic and prophetic according to their shapes. If the bottom part — called the Teardrop of Eris — is curled back inside the hollow ring — called the Eye Proper — you will soon meet someone of enormous inner strength. Probably Roger Lovin, who will excommunicate you immediately, no questions asked. You can figure out the omens for the rest of the bent ones yourself by reading up on the medieval herbalist "Doctrine of Signatures" by which you can discern the use of a plant by its shape — a favor of God(dess) to Adam (Eve). For example, spearmint plants are shaped like spears, so obviously you can make spears with them, use them to cure spear wounds, boil them down for spear polish, etc. A copper Teardrop of Eris means you are going to be arrested or at least questioned by a narc, possibly Roger Lovin, who... etc.

There are Rosicrucians on the police force, in any case — so don't tell them you are a Discordian, or, in particular, ever met or heard of me.

The Rosicrucians are a fanatical middle-of-the-road conspiracy.

The highest honor is to figure out how, in Discordianism, to become an Episkopos — in which case you can write epistles, if — and only if, in addition — you *never, ever* whistle while you're pissing.

Many people wonder how I attained an IQ of under genius. It first became my ambition in the Marines, where I perceived immediately that the stupider you are the better off you are. People who've pursued my correspondence coursed in this discipline have in some cased qualified as actually mentally deficient; in which case they are, in many states such as California, entitled to periodic payments. Two of my graduates, Tom McNamara and Barbara Blackman, were very successful in getting SSI compensation. These courses are reasonably priced and pertain mostly to how to make people who were use to living in the intelligence community under the Shah of Iran become paranoid enough about you to blame you for all the narrowness of the Ayatollah, whereupon they will be only to glad to inflict you with chemically-induced brain damage.

I can also tell you how to get laser-beam induced cancer, sodium morphate heart attacks, or how to become the star in a snuff film, if you are feeling adventurous or masochistic. All this information is of course mailed out in plain brown envelopes.

The most dangerous activity in America, however, remains driving a car — so think about that whenever these heavy rumors frighten you. Between 50,000 and 55,000 individuals are killed every year in traffic accidents, for which opportunity they pay one day's salary out of every nine in car payments, insurance, highway taxes, repairs, etc. Not to mention the number that are maimed, crippled, etc. This is the result of a fanatical middle-of-the-road conspiracy founded by Dwight David Eisenhower called the Highway Trust Fund. I don't charge anywhere near one day's salary out of nine for my correspondence courses.

Me and Dobbs were corporals together in the Marines, incidentally, where he accidentally shot his own toe once, idly aiming a .45 pistol at a fly on his shoe on guard duty. Stang says Dobbs and Nixon were also corporals together in the Marines; maybe at a different time, because I don't remember anyone in our outfit by that name. Of course there were more than a hundred guys in MACS-1, so maybe I just didn't notice him.

Incidentally, the Treasury Department is controlled by the SS — including the President's bodyguards — all of whom think I am a reincarnation of Edgar Cayce. As a result, Reagan thinks I'm very powerful. Actually I am only the ritual scapegoat of the Tryall Club of Jamaica, for which Oswald was the ritual sacrificial goat (see Leviticus 16 for details).

I suppose that sooner or later, before I finish this, I should give you the answer to all mysteries. But for the moment it has slipped my mind. As I seem to recall it was astonishingly simple, so maybe it's just as well I passed over it because as they say, a little knowledge is a dangerous thing.

Robert Anton Wilson once sent me a list of rumors to spread. One of them was the George Washington grew hemp on Mount Vernon, to which he added "This one is true, but spread it anyway." Wilson and I founded the Anarchist Bavarian Illuminati to give Jim Garrison a hard time — one of whose supporters believe that the Illuminati owned all the major TV networks — the Conspiring Bavarian Seers (CBS), the Ancient Bavarian Conspiracy (ABC) and the Nefarious Bavarian Conspirators (NBC). Of course that poor nut was right and we were wrong. Or there is truth to the rumor that Wilson is an Illuminatus, although not a sinister one. A dexter one. That of course is probably a rumor he decided to spread, although it may have been true anyway. Of this I am certain. Wilson is not a Discordian. Fang excommunicated him the week after I ordained him. Anyway, maybe I (not we) was wrong. Wilson's first Illuminati letterhead contained the slogans "Victory Over Horseshit!" and "Goats Forever!" He explained this last one as due to his Capricorn sun sign; a likely story.

Slim Brooks called himself Aaron Immanuel Viking I (note the role of Aaron in Leviticus), the Keeper of the Submarine

Keys. He said "I like that one because it brings to mind two questions. What submarine? And why is it locked?"

Robert Shea was most noted for taking over the job of publishing the *Saturday Evening Post* on Hugh Hefner's Xerox machine when it temporarily went under. Carrying the notice "Founded by Benjamin Franklin," of course. So the *Saturday Evening Post* was the first mass-media publication to discuss the Discordian Society and to expose the Illuminati. Later, when the *Post* resumed publication, he went modestly back to Benjamin Franklin's original name: The Universal Instructor in All Arts and Sciences.

Norton I is the Only Begotten Son of Eris. He lived for your virtues.

Eris is indirectly referred to in the Old Testament — or at least they mention the Rock of Horeb, upon which Moses sat. Griffin Bell is the Rock of Horeb in this century. That was also Jesus H. Christ's middle name. Actually, in the time of Moses, the Rock of Horeb was Eris Herself — before She hatched. Not many people know this. The way I found out was by praying to Eris, then opening the Bible at random.

Nimrod the Hunter is in both the Bible and the *Book of Mormon*.

Brunswick, the bowling alley in which Greg and I first disorganized the Discordian Society, is mentioned in the *Oracles of Nostradamus*, which I only discovered recently. So that is an authentic miracle — especially since it says something about chaos emerging from Brunswick! All bowling alleys are sacred to Discordians — since most of them have Brunswick pin setting equipment. A synchronistic coincidence that proves a dogma like that is called a Katma — a combination of karma and dogma. Actually I'm not a reincarnation of Edgar Cayce, no matter what they say. I'm a reincarnation of Jean Dixon.

There's also a right wing Erisian conspiracy of which June Oswald — Lee Harvey Oswald's daughter — is Eristic Avatar, so I hear. How that happened I can only begin to guess.

My own spiritual discipline, all seriousness aside, is a form of katma yoga called Transcendental Paranoia. The only religion I subscribe to wholeheartedly is Taoism, which few people know is the actual basis of the Discordian Orthodoxy and Zen. The only secret order I belong to is the Yellow Turban Society. At this time we are plotting a communist anarchist revolution in Japan and a multiple bank robbery in Switzerland (via our Fair-Play-for-Switzerland Committee). The Swiss caper is based on *Ocean's Eleven* and we are going to try to recruit Frank Sinatra of the Yippies to help us. If he's busy, we'll settle for Paul Krassner. The Yellow Turban Society is an ultra-leftist Taoist secret society that seeks revenge for the "diced." In the intelligence community, when you are "diced" it means that agents are told that what you eat and drink and how you scratch your ass, etc., is your secret method of telling them what you want. Therefore they pay no attention to what you say in plain English — which they've been taught to assume is only cover. My guess is that only radical leftists are subjected to this treatment. If they happen to be Taoists who believe it is wrong to premeditate how you scratch your ass, etc. — the results can be most infuriating. I myself have been "diced" since 1979. Hence, the Yellow Turban Society. At this time we are organizing the Revolutionary Vanguard Communist Party of Japan — because we figure if we sound authoritarian enough the Establishment won't suspect us of being much of a threat. Anyway, if we succeed with our Peasant World Revolution, unpremeditated ass scratching will no longer be a criminal offense.

And just possibly, one child under five will no longer starve to death every two seconds.

Try to Remember Something About a Cat

A horrible pun. I thought of it just as I was going to bed last night. It was so funny I considered writing a whole play just for this one, great, hilarious, bad pun. I didn't write it down though and I don't remember what it was.

Something, I think, about marriage proposals and cats.

I'll probably remember it within the next couple of days. (Written on acid.)

What is so weird is to think there is this Iranian Prince somewhere — right? Who has known me all my life! Who has been there when I was fucking, when I was conning, when I was wiping my ass, getting stoned — who knows me inside and out, every wrinkle. If not an Iranian Prince, then somebody else. Same thing. Somebody I've never even met, that I don't know the first thing about. What do you do about somebody like that? I don't even know whether to love them or hate them.

(Also written on acid.)

"Too much is not enough." - Nat.

The morning after: They just wanna complain they are all so confused. They are feeling so used. Tell 'em I ain't to blame. Tell 'em I wasn't there when we decided what's fair. I was combin' my hair and I was sniffin' the air.

Little Five Points is a sample example of the absurd behavior conspirators expect in this 208th year since the Declaration in America. I'm supposed to spend most of my time in the Point, where the only benevolent servants heart and soul of the people are in charge. I'm supposed only to enter the pub after or immediately before spreading the word about what I've written elsewhere. I'm never, ever supposed to enter the

Rainbow — because that makes me a dirty puritan ridden with sex guilt.

For a number of years I have been ignoring these Soviet travel restrictions. When I'm hitchhiking and broke they can still control me by refusing to give me spare change in front of this or that Pancake House or Denny's or MacDonald's. Usually what I get instead is a long lecture by a talkative patron who at the end gives me maybe two nickels and then I can sit there from hell to doomsday and expect nothing but accusing stares.

To the best of my financial ability — since getting wise, if not healthy and wealthy, by slavishly paying attention for a couple of years (1979-1980) to advice like that — I've been ignoring all unsolicited anonymous free advice, figuring it was worth exactly what I was paying for it. Do you think that stops them? Not on a bet. They continue automatically, mechanically cranking it out as if they actually think I'm listening. Not only about where I should drink my coffee, either. About when I should jack off in public or when I should jack off in private with only the video cameras concealed (presumably) on my person watching and when I should jack off under the covers without letting the folks at Jet Propulsion Laboratories (or wherever those Nixonite bastards are) realize it is happening.

They also presume to advise me about what to write and what to say, punishing me if I express opinions they didn't need that time. Then there are people who think I am king or who at least imagine wildly and recklessly that I'm a free man. On top of all that, not content with the claustrophobia they've visited upon my already traumatized psyche, they seek to intensify it by pretending to me that they think I'm slyly and cleverly (oh, Kerry, you crafty devil) communicating instructions or advice to them about matters of which I'm next to wholly ignorant when I scratch my ass or order scrambled eggs or tie my backpack strings in square knots, etc.

The way I figure it is somewhere there is a mediocre bureaucrat who wants to be able to say he or she was only following orders when the axe falls. And since Richard Nixon got the CIA to sign innumerable orders about me without first reading them, I'm what can be passed off as as good a source of authority as any. Only trouble being that when I was giving orders I was a raving communist anarchist, who thereby made it hard to solicit contributions of cartels and corporations to finance the holy wars that are, to them, the true purpose of life, against Catholics and Muslims. After all, why try to cause social progress when with half the effort you can revert the whole world to a series of feudal dynasties killing one another's slaves over whether or not three or one angels can stand on the head of a pin, whether God has co-partners and what are the most tasteful ways to perform sexual intercourse? That way you can remain invisible and not have to spend a lot of money on PR because everybody will be looking at one another instead of the staff of *Station K.* — as Colin Wilson calls it in a book by that name.

When I become deaf and blind to my true duty to walk on one side and not another of a crack in the sidewalk I'm not supporting whatever the hell I'm otherwise being used for — sometimes called a "house," called anything but a conspiracy and never even passed off in jest as a mass movement which, since we are all assassins and war criminals, is out of the question because then the Africans would find out about my obscene phone calls and Julie Nixon would be compromised. An appeal to heaven, as they said when King George decided to tax trees.

Another thing is that most of the very annoying people I meet are simply victims of mind control — according to the idea I got from listening to Shelly last night. No wonder I'm such a failure! For nine years I've been exhorting a bunch of androids to rise up and get rid of their oppressors. Page 23 of the paperback edition of *Brave New World.*

What is the meaning of an Anarchist Manchurian Candidate trying to organize Fascist Robots? Is it entertaining? Is it amusing? What is the purpose? As one non-Caucasian child dies of starvation every two seconds, here in the heart of the Empire collections of machines hold pointless discussions. You figure it out.

❧

Lifestyle: yesterday I bought a new corn cob pipe for a dollar. It gives me a common touch, which I previously sorely lacked.

The thing about ignoring the advice of the Conspiracy is that my decision conforms to the scientific method. The more I heed their advice, the worse things get — war in Cambodia (I was also heeding them in 1978 and '79), living under bridges and out of Krispy Kreme dumpsters, etc. When I ignore their signals I am more relaxed and also things go better.

Void where prohibited by Reichian armoring or armaments.
  The Attila the Hun Municipal Library.

How I Can Tell I'm Still Me Department: A guy who looks exactly the way I figure Rob Pudim would look sits in the North Avenue Station, having ridden up here on the Ponce de Leon bus.

Lives Amongst the Chaos: Grace Caplinger as Dylan's fascinating woman who's "an artist and she don' look back."
  Clues Among the Chaos was a Discordian "Compendium of Ancient Abbreviated Riddles."

Between Grace and Valerie Fletcher could've decreed just about anything they wanted, I guess.

With that Fearless Fosdick in the "Do Not Be Confused" Eris ad that Greg used to illustrate the frontispiece. See 4th *Principia Discordia* for mindfucking details.

SubGenius tag-team wrestling: Mildred Loomis vs. Bert Lance, etc. With Andy Gibb as referee, and Dixon backing up Loomis and Bea backing up Lance.

I Kerry Thornley, being of sound mind, will all my notebooks, in the event of my death, to a Zenarchist organization to be established in my memory, called the Kerry Thornley Coffee Klatch.

(or Clatch, or however they spell it.)

Coffee remains the finest drug in the world in my opinion. In this I'm in hereditary agreement with my paternal grandmother in her lengthy Jack Mormon phase. I did some good acid this weekend. Better than anything I've dropped in years. Could've been, I guess, a 1,000 mic. tab. Strong, lympid stuff. Allen, Shelly and Michael also. We went to an eviction party. I went back to the pub and explained to Yippies why I think Prussians are the problem with Russia — and everybody else, practically. Then I went on strike against thinking about politics. The party looked like it was going to be boring. They wanted to discuss Tony Jackson and CBS and Fire and Puritanism — defensively I wasn't in the mood. They shouldn'ta given me LSD-25 if they wanted me to think about government. So I sat in the pub and watched Allen and Shelly and a gnomic teenager and a laughing Nigerian exchange student look beautifully aesthetic — if that isn't redundant. Yesterday when I woke up I not only was still mildly tripping, I also had a hangover from free beers Nat and Shelly and Allen bought me. Very unusual. I took an Excedrin, smoked a roach, then a joint — and the rest of the day was even more unusually nirvanic. It rained and that was nice and psychedelic of the Weather Conspiracy — because this morning it has added to the pleasant acidy illusion that the world had just been to a car wash.

Occam's Beard, the reverse colliery to Occam's Razor.

"And Goddess visited Bokonon with Anxiety of Loin, and cursed him, calling down a rain of bicycle spokes upon his camp in the wilderness." - *The Honest Book of Truth*, Tribulations 15:79.

Rules for the Happy-Fun Game of Push Button.
1. Push Button is played by any number of players.
2. All but one of them aren't The Goat.
3. The function of the player called The Goat is to find old buttons that relate to new buttons the rest of the players give him.
4. Points are awarded the majority of the players in terms of how many new buttons they can find that The Goat will relate to appropriate old buttons.
5. Points are awarded to The Goat in terms of how many old buttons he can find that are relevantly similar to the new buttons he receives; The Goat loses points for inappropriate old buttons, all-too-obvious old buttons[1] and refusing to play.

There are five rules to the happy-fun game of Push Button. The player who winds up with the most points gets to cash them in at the en of the buttons. Push Button champs string their buttons on fishing lines and wear them around their necks.

Note: sell this idea to a national network as a television game show.

I keep thinking, whenever I think about Woody Guthrie, about how "KILL FASCISTS" was emblazoned on his guitar. How times change.

What rock singer of the Sixties would've written KILL anything on an instrument. That, I guess, was the function of the rock group, The Who. There was hypocrisy going down.

---

[1]Including: "these buttons are in the same category because there's 2 holes in both"

More and more I feel like I should tremble as I write and speak. I make the most casual jokes and the whole world seems to go into upheaval. Of course worrying about it also seems ridiculous.

❦

Push Button:
Q: "Little Jimmy Brown."
A: Carl Sandburg talks about J. Alfred Prufrock.
(5 points)

❦

A poem with a section called The Order of the Silver Hermes, followed by a section called the Order of the Black Hell Met. Or maybe Disorders.

❦

I once made a pun about Watts — Alan to Riots. Wilson called it my "Ommly revolting watticisim."

❦

Push Button:
  Q: Remington.
  A: The Ravenhurst Raiders
  (2 points)
  Push Button:
  Q; "Rainbow Family headed south... ask for James."
  A: Even if I knew I wouldn't tell you.
  (29 points)

❦

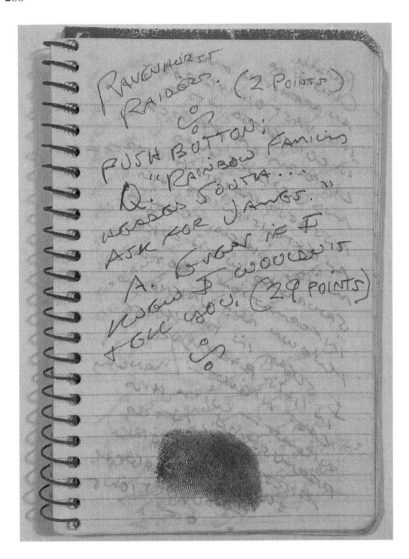

Randall Carlson is an archival man; his vast dining room is converted into a library of magick and science and assassination history — an extension of his mind, which seems saturated with like information, both known and unknown. I slept in the house in his backyard last night — Monday night — with his permission, after first discussing the astrological conjunctions of Saturn and Jupiter at the time of both John Kennedy's and John Lennon's assassinations. Similar tragedies have clouded history every 20 years when that conjunction occurs: in 1940 Franklin Delano Roosevelt became President.

That is what Randall said. Now that I think of it, FDR was President all through the Thirties. I'll have to mention that to him.

FDR didn't get us out of the Depression until getting us into the War. And his War Administration began after his 1940 re-election so maybe that's it. These things become more and more manifest the harder you look.

Anyway, the Saturn, Jupiter conjunction is supposed to symbolize the death of the old king and the ascension of the new king.

This stuff doesn't look near as convincing in the cold light of morning. John F. Kennedy was king for 20 years and then John Lennon ruled for the next 20? We'd smoked an awful lot of hash before getting into our astrological discussion.

In my symbolic cosmology Saturn signifies thrones and suffering and Jupiter symbolizes scapegoating minorities for the problems inherent in bureaucratic social organization. As in Jew Pitter.

Today's date: 30 October 1994.
    Yesterday's date: 29 October 1994.

Great Historical Breakthroughs in Journalism Department: *The Atlanta Constitution* is actually admitting on the front page in the headlines today that 35 million people are starving in Africa.

I guess there just weren't any city council resolutions or sensational domestic murders yesterday.

❦

THE Satanists (I almost said Catholics) think I'm interested in starvation as a sneaky way of fighting mind control. I've been fanatical about starvation since 1959. I've only known I'm a mind control victim since 1979. I would never have plotted to kill JFK if Ayn Rand's *Objectivist Newsletter* hadn't convinced me he was going to plunge the whole world into hunger with price controls, etc. I wouldn't be interested in politics at this time were it not for the genocidal holocaust of starvation, war, etc.

Politics is much too macabre to command the attention of a mentally healthy person except in emergencies that engulf the whole planet. Any hope of abolishing mind control seems hopeless to me. That's like wanting to unilaterally act in such a way as to get rid of all nuclear weapons — no way to get there there that way.

I've always thought self-selecting intentional communities could solve cultural problems, provided objective arms inspection methods were present. I don't see, never have seen, any point in religious wars — Satanists infiltrating Catholics or anything else. These are not new ideas I've suddenly acquired — I've been opposing starvation and supporting intentional communities since 1979. People who are worried just about Catholics or Muslims or atheists or Satanists have always seemed quaintly irrelevant to me in my philosophy of Jubilant Cynicism.

Cynicism observes that people do not practice what they believe most of the time. Jubilant Cynicism has taken a long hard look at what it is they believe.

Latin Catholics don't much resemble American Catholics, as a rule. There are Muslims who keep harems of young boys. Belief is only related to behavior by tenuous connections. Someone's character is usually formed, as a result of predominately accidental social conditioning, by the time they are six years old. Convert a bastard to, say, Marxism and you will get a Marxist bastard. Convert a saint and you will get a Marxist saint.

Conditions — such as not having to live in psychologically

overcrowded conditions — improve the tolerability of behavior. Which is why coercive Puritanism and land monopoly have to go if we aren't all going to suffer.

What ideologies most people maintain in elaboration of all the additional trivialities of existence don't much influence anything at all.

So I just don't think about the Satanists much. I like their defiant irreverent spirit. It just gets bogged down in taking religion too seriously though. To me there isn't much difference in attitude between a Satanist and an Irish Catholic. Both like to fight about Jesus. Both are very colorful. Both are quite militant about any number of absurdly feeble abstractions. Both think they are somewhere near the center of the whole universe.

We could give Ireland to the Catholics and California to the Satanists. Both California and Nevada if we let the Okies keep the Great Central Valley as an autonomous republic.

I met a Taiwanese woman one day. Before that I'd never thought much about the indigenous population of Formosa. What if all the reactionary Chinese were encouraged to migrate to Hong Kong and Taiwan were made an autonomous Taiwanese Republic within the People's Republic of China? Hong Kong looks as if it may become a *de facto* autonomous community of reactionary Chinese under guidance of China. That's just a brainstorming suggestion that might spur a more sophisticated idea among the same lines.

Wouldn't it be rational to emphasize the rights of Taiwan's *native* population?

The woman I met didn't like foreigners ruling Taiwan since the KMT exile-occupation either.

To me, if all anti-Catholics simply organized to stop the Church's tampering with States, the Catholics would cease to be a problem to anyone but themselves. And it would happen soon, if everyone weren't spreading their efforts too thin. Instead, people as complicated as Jesuits try to destroy them once and for all.

The Libertarian premise is groups only become problems when they begin pointing weapons (via military or legalistic maneuvers) at other groups. For example, what's to prevent Catholics from outlawing cremation? Or Christian Scientists from outlawing all medicines and funerals? Once a private subjective faith can be made into a law there is no reason why — if abortion is legalized for the sake of Catholics and Baptists — medical doctors shouldn't be outlawed for the sake of Christian Scientists, etc.

Facts. Ideology. Speculation. Facts are more relevant than opinions. Opinions are sometimes more and sometimes less relevant than speculation. Understanding they are not all in the same category is most relevant, at this time, of all.

Confusion prevails among people who think my opinions are more important to me than following up factual leads in order to obtain further data. The most beautiful opinion is useless if it is held — even by everyone-in ignorance.

A rock group called Rue Button.

QWN: The Christian Scientists and Southern Californians form a powerful movement called The Faithful Majority to outlaw all activities related to medical science and the practice of medicine.

Push Button:
Q: "... Baby Jean, day dream believer"
A: "Sometimes when we touch the honesty's too much... "
(1 point)

Filter Tipped
Data like Nero's rose petals falling on his guest-victims is it? (I don't worry much).

Data filtered: tips and hot leads? Table scraps!

Rows of popcorn for pigeons?

Data: elusively flirting in Jungdalas.

"Hello? Operator? Information please."

Strewn data: all arrayed like batshit in a cave, saying "Kerry: you've got to organize your materials."

Ezra Pounding in my head: "The damn stuff will not cohere!"

A minotaur looms: DATA DATA DATA DATA DATA DATA DATA DATA DATA DATA DATA DATA transforming only what resembles the human mind.

Push Button:

    Q: "Tight"

    A: | "Tight" |

    ($\frac{1}{2}$ point)

The Hairy Oracle Tribe.

Our group in Atlanta in 1973-74-75 jokingly referred to itself as The Laughing Snake Tribe, which was probably the original meaning of the cant word "snake." That's because when Linda expressed insecurity once about her lovemaking abilities, I was laughing so hard I was, in her words, "rolling like a snake on the floor." We also planned to call ourselves the Chanters of Bond, when we formed our chanting band.

I like the idea of the Hairy Oracle Tribe for the times like these, as I understand them, in Atlanta.

'Twere times of trouble
Times of grief
When Bobheads proweled like a thief.
Hotlanta night
With mojo workin'
We all got work
Needs one more jerkin'
Said the man
Tis my conviction
Have in hand
A firm eviction
Moustache twirling
Dark cape swirling
Notebooks piercing
at the swine
discussing wine
before the feast
of human beasts.

"An ugly train of events, if you ask me." - George Armstrong Custer (apocraphism).

QWN: Truman Babbit is Vice President (at the time of the Japanese Revolution).

Revolution Without Revelation

No personality cults, either. - Malatesta Brigade.

Thornleyist Anti-Revenchanism: the ignorant trying to prod the uncooperative into accomplishing the impossible.

The prognosis is worse than terrible: they say they are giving me cancer. I was told that would be the price of my book's publication, in the beginning, which I'm willing to pay. However they are telling me also my book won't be published. We are, if that's true, overwhelmed by Nazi forces here in Atlanta. Indira Gandhi, who violated the "American" law of Omerta by saying Sihk riots in India were being instigated by the US — adding, "via Canada, of course" — was assassinated, according to this morning's news. Maybe it was the Panamericans in revenge for the Trujilio murder, though, if she was involved in that.

Brother-in-law's dying swan rap in the Conversations.

Anyway, I interpret battle reports since the ascension of Pope John Paul II it has not been good. I'm losing. The battle is being fought between my legs that was formerly being fought in I. G. Farbin's boardroom, according to battle reports of that time. A whole "high school class" was progressed that wasn't told about my function as an assassination witness, according to Garrison in 1981.

Anyway, I mailed my MS out yesterday to Isaf and Shulman, Atlanta's only literary agents, according to the Yellow Pages. So I continue performing necessary actions. Detachment, Kerry, is all you need in addition to that. No worse than a car ride with a reckless driver anyways. I should've titled my book — which I changed from *The Dreadlock Recollections* to *Jailbird* — *Publish This Book!* subtitle *Or Else!*

Anyway, they want me to think about things like square "holes" at the bottom of tribal organizations, instead. Probably puritans in the neighborhood Justice Center. There's no evidence of true Kropotkinist tribalism, as I advocated it. If there was, it would probably just be a Jim Jones front for the Earth, anyway. The leaders are trying to foster the illusion of participatory democracy when there isn't even Republican democracy in this nation. If there was true tribalism I'd join an affinity group that was politically autonomous.

Someone says: "my grandfather's real sick."

So it is another Gandhi death day, like the opening of *Ape and Essence* — only this Gandhi wasn't much of a mahatma. According to rumor, she was killed by the Singhs of Pallistan — like the Odums of Texas or the Landrys of New Orleans, the Singhs are a large family, among the Sikhs — very large, whose name translates as Lion in English.

People who are being lied to are the worst problem in the intelligence community that I encounter. Trying to figure out exactly what about takes all my time. By then it is usually too late; they've already carried out their idiot orders. In showering them with rose petals of data in self-defense they usually accuse me of trying to smother them.

Besides that, *everybody* is trying to change the subject from war crimes to banking. I'm no Mickey Mouse. I spent years ranting about usury. As soon as I figured out that wasn't the most relevant issue in relation to my own history, the whole world took up one or the other side. The story of my life. Maybe there is a rule in the Order of Dogblood or whatever it is that requires them to be gung-ho about whatever my last crusade was, ignoring the present one. When I got into libertarian anarchy everyone else became a limited government

Objectivist. When I got into LSD, they became anarcho-capitalists. When I got into Edgar Cayce, they got into non-mystical LSD trips. When I gave up mysticism they began prattling about reincarnation. When K115 FM persuaded me to postpone the "spring" until last, everybody who'd thereto began opposing my efforts to attain a retribution on moratorium for the assassins if they'd tell the truth became zealously intolerable advocates of that cause. So it goes. So it has always gone. So now they want to play cops and bank robbers. There just must be a secret rule. The only way I could get a war crimes probe would be to give up and get into something else. "Now that I'm against 'em, I like 'em." — Mac Hall about Blacks.

Once Robert LeFevre *may* have implied cryptically that Dwight Ferguson was being mind controlled by land monopolists. Then again, he may have been talking about Robert C. MacDonald or someone else or even no one.

"I had no starter fluid. Then I met a man who had no chain saw." - SubGenius

My opaque is at Michael's.

Glimpses: a threat to kill all the Proudhonians if I make my case a higher priority than my ideology. Page 57 of Alexander Berkman. We are losing. The Nazis are grinding us into the ground with their boot heels.

Ideas for rock groups: The Atlanta Massacre Body Count... Desperate Filabuster... Wolf Alarm...

So anyways, other than that, Mrs. Lincoln, it is a nice morning in Atlanta — drizzly foggy mist. Yesterday was also beautiful.

One of those days that is so nice it makes you as happy as when living with a mate to whom you are much attracted. There aren't many of them in a year.

They're the only phenomena that compares with Melissas and Lindas and Eves.

The universe would seem subjectively wholly meaningless without either.

With or without acid.

The Doors of Perception. Barbara Reid gave me a copy she autographed "with defiance" as well as with love. The Doors rock group said they derived their name from the Huxley title. Was Jim Garrison and Samuel de Lessup Morrison's secret society involving "doors" a peyote cult?

I could probably dig it if it was.

Push Button:
    Q: Adolph Coors.
    A: "Howard Cary."
    (10 points)

Of course all these discouraging battle reports *could* just be a plot to drive me to suicidal despair. When I examine the macro-analysis of the planetary milieu, though, I conclude that opposing genocide is like taking on the United States Marines with pea shooters. So it is equally possible to me things are as terrible as they indicate.

Last night I felt like saying, "Send us more Japs."

Duncan says, lamentingly, that the Japanese are staunchly supporting the Vietnamese. That was the way I'd've meant it, if I'd said exactly that.

Actually, as much of a raving communist I am at heart, I cannot honestly say I'd rather live in China than Japan. Also I'd rather live in Japan than here. It's the culture I like, though — not the State or the economic system.

I've never seen what problem anarchists envision in my testifying at war crimes trials. Had John Dean been an anarchist, for example, anarchism would by this time be understood by everyone in the country.

What they want, I guess, is a Jack London style *Assassination Bureau* thing, instead. I probably could've opted for that old anarchist dream of radical anarchist assassins slaying everyone in authority without themselves taking power — just maintaining a permanent universal power vacuum for as long as it took for people to discover how to live without political bosses.

Smedly Butler got to me first, though.

George Lakey got to me first.

The Quaker mafia got to me first.

Corporations tend to be more powerful than governments.

Right libertarians, who tend to maintain assassination bureau fantasies more than, say, Red and Black Action, are blind in their analysis there. They ignore multinational corporations as a coercive factor.

So they usually think I'm betraying the Cause of Liberty when I'm only trying to elevate consciousness about The Oppressor.

"Damn things" again, Ludwig.

   "Damn things."

❦

So I'm like Omar Khayyam instead of Hassan-i-Sabbah, although I'd much prefer a reality that permitted me to be a Hassan-i-Sabbah. Khayyam was just an old drunk, a loser. Hassan enjoyed the benefits of a cool neighborhood. No pot busts. No vice cops. No cultural quibbling. Atop Alamount a prince could smoke his grass in peace and fuck as much as he wanted. I took a harder path. Bloody and beaten, it seems, I'm straggling toward its end.

.

Select Bibliography

Adler, Margot: *Drawing Down the Moon: Witches, Druids, Goddess-worshippers and Other Pagans in America Today*. Boston: Beacon Press, 1979

Berger, Helen: *Witchcraft and Magic*. Pennsylvania: Penn Press, 2006

Bethnell, Tom: "Tom Bethnell Diary, The." Retrieved July 4th, 2020 from http://mcadams.posc.mu.edu/bethell5.htm

Bishop, Greg: *Project Beta*. Shelburne, Paraview Press, 2005

Bugliosi, Vincent: *Reclaiming History: The Assassination of President John F. Kennedy*. New York: Norton 2007

Constantine, Alex: *Virtual Government: CIA Mind Control Operations in America*. New York: Feral House 1997

Cusack, Carole M.: *Invented Religions: Imagination, Fiction and Faith*. Farnham: Ashgate 2010

Dobbs, J. R. "Bob": *Book of the SubGenius, The*. New York: Simon & Schuster, 1983

Duncombe, Stephen: *Notes from Underground*. London: Verso, 1997

Epstein, Edward Jay: *Legend: The Secret World of Lee Harvey Oswald*. New York: McGraw-Hill 1968

Flammonde, Paris: *Kennedy Conspiracy, The: an Uncommissioned Report on the Jim Garrison Investigation*. New York: Meredith Press 1969

Gorightly, Adam: *Caught in the Crossfire: Kerry Thornley, Lee Oswald and the Garrison Investigation*. Port Townsend: Feral House, 2014

———— *Historia Discordia: the Origins of the Discordian Society*. New York: RVP Press, 2014

———— *Prankster and the Conspiracy, The*. New York: Paraview Press, 2003

Johnson, Lloyd: *Toolbox for Humanity, A*. Victoria: Trafford Publishing, 2004

Lewis, James and Rabinovitch, Shelley: *Encyclopedia of Modern Witchcraft, The*. Kensington: Citadel, 2004

Marrs, Jim: *Crossfire*. New York: Carroll & Graf, 1990.

McCoy, Edain: *Advanced Witchcraft*. Woodbury: Llewellyn Publications, 2004

Parfrey, Adam (editor): *Rants & Incendiary Tracts: Voices of Desperate Illumination 1558-present*. Port Townsend: Loompanics Unlimited 1989

Report of the President's Commission on the Assassination of President John F. Kennedy. Washington DC: GPO, 1964

Russell, Dick: *Man Who Knew Too Much, The*. New York: Carroll & Graf, 2003

Sakya, Madhusudan: *Current Perspectives in Buddhism: Buddhism Today*. New Delhi: Cyber Tech Publications 2011

Stang, Ivan: *High Weirdness by Mail*. New York: Simon & Schuster, 1988

Thomas, Kenn: *Cyberculture Counterconspiracy*. St. Louis: Steamshovel Press, 1999

Thornley, Kerry: *Absolute Elsewhere, The*. Portland: OVO, 2018

———— *Idle Warriors, The*. Avondale Estates: IllumiNet Press, 1991

———— *Oswald*. Chicago: New Classics House, 1965

———— *Principia Discordia* (with Greg Hill). 1963

———— *Zenarchy*. Avondale Estates: IllumiNet Press, 1991

Vankin, Jonathan and Whalen, John: *Eighty Greatest Conspiracies of All Time, The*. Kensington: Citadel, 2004

Wilson, Robert Anton and Shea, Robert: *Illuminatus!* London: Sphere Books, 1976

Buy *These* SubGenius Books!

Book of the SubGenius

The "Sistine Chapel" of the 20th Century, this profusely illustrated, softbound Horror Bible, published by Simon & Schuster, is now in its 17th printing. You'll never have to read another book as long as you live–because you'll just sit, reading this one over and over again. Page after page of brain-raping text and graphics. A self-help book for sinners, creeps, morphodites, and all wise persons and guys who knew they wouldn't get "help" from any book even if they needed it in the first place.

ISBN 9781439188651
194-page trade paperback for $20.95

Neighborworld

A bulldada science fiction novel by Lonesome Cowboy Dave DeLuca, the astounding improvisational wizard of The Church of the SubGenius radio show, "The Hour of Slack." A little bit *A Clockwork Orange*, a taste of The Firesign Theatre, a dab of Fleischer Brothers cartoons, a dash of Kafka, a splash of Fellini, and a whole fistful of Lonesome Cowboy Dave!

ISBN 9781946529008
218-page trade paperback for $14.99, Kindle for $6.99.

Eyelash

THE FIRST SUBGENIUS SCIENCE FICTION NOVEL! By Nikolai Kingsley. He swore he'd never deal with the aliens again, but here he was, letting them beam him onboard... He promised that whatever they were planning he'd keep Tai out of it, but here she was, on the bridge... What were the Xists trying to hide that was worse than Soul Harvesting and interstellar drug running, and why were they being so nice to him... at first?

ISBN 9781946529015
239-page trade paperback for $17.95

The Agent and Mr. Dobbs

In the early 1960s, an earnest, patriotic and Pink agent for the Feds is assigned to the seriously insane national security case of "Bob" Dobbs. He is drawn by Dobbs down a rabbit hole that turns into a wormhole of 'Frop madness, surreal sex with Connie, Bigfoot and Greys, bizarre parties with JFK, Hitler, Lee Harvey Oswald, Fidel Castro, Nikita Khrushchev, and Timothy Leary... and unspeakable experiences that make him question what he had mistakenly thought of as reality. It's like H. P. Lovecraft by way of Raymond Chandler by way of R. Crumb. Like a David Lynch movie with a dollop of Trailer Park Boys. Like a Bugs Bunny cartoon guest-directed by David Cronenberg. Like an S. Clay Wilson comic novelized by Franz Kafka.

ISBN 978-1-946529-03-9
80-age trade paperback for $16.00

JOIN THE CHURCH OF THE SUBGENIUS

The SubGenius material has only recently been made public. This is YOUR chance to get in on the ground floor of a huge, lucrative cult–NOW, while rates are low. You will then be eligible for all the $$$, weird sex, and SHEER POWER OVER OTHERS that go with high-ranking membership in the Church. And yes, YOU CAN PERFORM LEGAL WEDDINGS!

Overcome shyness and guilt with this fantastic replacement for a huge penis or "perfect" breasts. Read *THE STARK FIST OF REMOVAL* and learn not only the Word of Dobbs but also ways to contact, buy from, and sell to the incredible (yet real!!) network of SubGenii and subsymps everywhere. Learn of local revivals, other secret societies, UNUSUAL PRODUCTS, Other Mutants. THIS IS NO FAKE. Puts you "in charge" of your life. You'll be READY the next time your face is on fire. Quick Condown Clampspiracy release. Easy on delicate tissues... no danger of runaway infection.

This is the only way to get on the Mailing List of the Chosen, pierce the shroud of secrecy insulating the cult, join the secret MEMBERS-ONLY online forums and obtain such privileges as befit membership in a secret society of this scope. And all of it, including the surgery, can be done BY MAIL. Everything is kept STRICTLY CONFIDENTIAL (unless you want your local Clench listed). And don't worry about the diseases–they're part of the satire, too!

WHAT OTHER RELIGIONS CHARGE ALL WORLDLY GOODS FOR!!!

Be a Doktor INSTANTLY. Incredible, sinister super-miniaturized fine print details all the scores of Church Ranks and Titles from which YOU can CHOOSE.

Full of rants, art, Prescriptures, doctrine, charts, filth, comics, reviews and CHURCH NEWS & CONTACTS.

YOU GET

- Pamphlets #1 & 2
- Your Own Personal 8x11 suitable-for-framing DOBB-SHEAD
- Official Dobbshead/Church Logo Metal Pin
- Dobbshead Sticker, Bumper Sticker
- The SubGenius Pledge
- The Divine Excuse (signed by "Bob"!)
- Doktorate of Forbidden Sciences
- Propaganda flyers to copy, Stickers
- Wallet sized, SubGenius MINISTER'S CARD
- Minister's Ordination papers and instructions.
- The *STARK FIST of Removal* online
- SCRUBGENIUS secret forum
- dobbs.town - the SubGenius Mastodobbs

(Without that membership card you have NO HOPE on July 5th!!!)

SEND FIFTY DOLLARS TO:

The SubGenius Foundation
P.O. Box 807
Glen Rose, TX 76043
United States

subgenius.com

Conspirators

Made in the USA
Middletown, DE
28 October 2022

13638923R00181